Evolutionary Computer Music

UNIVERSITIES AT MEDWAY
DRILL HALL LIBRARY

UNIVERSITIES
at MEDWAY

Eduardo Reck Miranda and John Al Biles (Eds)

Evolutionary Computer Music

 Springer

Eduardo Reck Miranda, Msc, PhD
Interdisciplinary Centre for Computer
  Music Research (ICCMR)
University of Plymouth
UK

John Al Biles, BA, MS, PhD
Information Technology Department
Rochester Institute of Technology
Rochester, NY 14623
USA

British Library Cataloguing in Publication Data
A catalogue record for this book is available from the British Library

Library of Congress Control Number: 2006933300

ISBN 10: 1-84628-599-2   e-ISBN-10: 1-84628-600-X
ISBN 13: 978-1-84628-599-8 e-ISBN-13: 978-1-84628-600-1

Printed on acid-free paper

9 8 7 6 5 4 3 2 1

Springer Science+Business Media
springer.com

Foreword

From Glorified Adding Machines
to Evolutionary Computer Music

I was very pleased when Al Biles and Eduardo Miranda asked me to write a foreword for this delightful volume on *Evolutionary Computer Music* (ECM). I have been a fan of the field from my first passing involvement as a co-author on an ECM paper in 1991. Like many others, I have enjoyed listening to Al Biles jam with *GenJam* at various conferences, and I have watched the state of the art advance with each passing year. Evolutionary music is particularly pleasing to its practitioners and observers alike, I believe, because it simultaneously asks deep questions about what computers can do and what it means to be human.

Genetic algorithms (GAs) and evolutionary computation (EC) are devilish fun partly because they permit us to tweak the noses of those who share the conventional wisdom that 'computers only do what you program them to do.' This cold war view of computer as glorified adding machine is still with us, but it seems to me generally that the accomplishments of EC must be giving those who still hold such views some pause, as field after field is changed by the computational innovation and creativity embodied in GAs and EC.

Perhaps nowhere is the challenge to conventional wisdom greater than in the area of ECM. Philosophers have held that the ability to compose and perform music is a uniquely human talent, and the current success of EC with creating music either contradicts that proposition or suggests that the innovative–creative mechanisms embodied in EC are powerful in ways that bear at least functional similarity to those of human composers. Either way, the evolutionary computer generation of digital sounds and music that please human beings challenges stereotypes about what computers can do and what constitutes the unique province of our species.

This volume is a special contribution to the literature. It runs the topical gamut from using EC to create pleasing digital sounds and compose or improvise musical compositions to thinking about the philosophical implications of a community of musically inclined robots. The volume demonstrates methodological diversity using different types of evolutionary algorithms, including those kissing cousins of EC, particle swarms and cellular automata; as might be expected in such a volume, emphasis is placed on exploring interactive EC techniques for using human judgments about musical aesthetics efficiently and well. In short, if you are a practitioner or aficionado of ECM or perhaps you are one of those cold war fuddy-duddies who still thinks computers are merely glorified adding machines, I strongly urge you to buy this book, read it and listen to the pleasing products of ECM creation.

October 2006   David E. Goldberg
University of Illinois at Urbana-Champaign
Urbana, IL 61801 USA

Preface

Musicians, perhaps more than any other class of artists, have always been acutely aware of the scientific developments of their time. From the discovery almost 3000 years ago of the direct relationship between the pitch of a note and the length of a string or pipe, to the latest computer models of human musical cognition and intelligence, musicians have always looked to science to provide new and challenging paradigms to study and compose music.

With the great technical and scientific advances being made at the crossroads of computing, biology, and natural history, a new approach to music has recently emerged: *Evolutionary Computer Music*.

Evolutionary computing, also referred to as evolutionary computation or EC, can be broadly defined as a field of computer science that focuses on the use of computational models of Darwinian-like evolutionary processes as the key elements in design and implementation of computer systems. Because EC normally deals with complex phenomena, its development has fostered the creation of a pool of research tools for modelling and studying complex natural phenomena such as nervous systems, cells and living beings. It is interesting, though, that these tools are also proving to be useful in areas as diverse as economics, social sciences, linguistics and music. Indeed, a number of new fields of investigation have emerged within the last 20 years or so, as a result of these developments in a way or another. A notable example is the flourishing new field of Artificial Life.

Evolutionary computer music is an exciting new development for composers and musicologists alike. For composers, it provides an innovative and natural means for generating musical ideas from a specifiable set of primitive components and processes, reflecting the compositional process of generating a variety of ideas by brainstorming followed by selecting the most promising ones for further iterated refinement. For musicologists, EC techniques are used to model the cultural transmission and change of a population's body of musical ideas over time; e.g. to model the development and maintenance of musical styles within particular cultural contexts and their reorganization and adaptation in response to cultural exchange. In both cases, the musical evolution can be influenced by a variety of constraints and tendencies built into the system, such as realistic psychological factors that influence the way that music is experienced, learned, stored, modified, and passed on between individuals.

This book discusses not only the applications of the EC to music, but also the tools needed to create and study such systems. These tools are drawn in part from research into the origins and evolution of biological organisms, ecologies, and cultural systems on the one hand, and in part from computer simulation methodologies on the other.

The opening chapter introduces the topic of EC, outlining the main technical details and raising issues pertinent to musical applications. This chapter is intended to furnish readers with the necessary background needed to understand the remaining chapters, as well as open up a number of important themes relevant to this collection. The second chapter complements the first by introducing music as a problem domain for EC. The author conducts an informal task analysis of music to identify the tasks musicians perform and surveys how EC has been used to support these tasks.

Historically, many digital audio applications have required some form of optimization, particularly replication of musical instruments in music synthesis. Recent work has used evolutionary algorithms, such as genetic algorithms, to evolve parameters for these applications. Chapter 3 presents a survey of the use of EC in music synthesis, music processing, and other digital audio applications such as music recognition. Chapter 4 follows by focusing on the use of EC in creative sound design. The author introduces two systems of his own design, *MutaSynth* and *Path Mutator*.

Chapter 5 introduces an innovative application of EC, which is the design of systems for musical performance. Here the authors present a prototype system that uses a genetic algorithm (GA) to evolve *performance profiles* to perform pieces of music.

Chapter 6 describes the compositional uses of the author's own GA-based program called *GenDash*. The program has been employed to compose a wide range of pieces from short vocal works to pieces for string quartet and operas. The development of *GenDash* is chronicled, the ideas behind the program are documented, and the chapter details the pieces composed using the program. Chapter 7 follows by focusing on the application of EC to musical improvisation. After briefly discussing the notion of improvisation and defining some musical dimensions for improvisation, attention turns to *GenJam*, a pioneering EC-based real-time interactive improvisation system.

Chapter 8 introduces the use of cellular automata (CA) for sound synthesis and composition. After a general introduction to CA and its potential for music, the author introduces the development of his own CA-based systems, namely *Chaosynth* (for sound synthesis) and *CAMUS* (for composition). Complementing the use of CA, Chapter 8 introduces the use of swarms for modelling compositional processes with focus on the author's *Swarm Music* system for real-time composition of music with swarms.

Following the development of fields such as Artificial Life and memetics, Chapter 10 proposes a computational modelling approach to Evolutionary

Musicology: *Computational Evolutionary Musicology*. This involves the use of computer modelling and simulations to study the circumstances and mechanisms whereby music systems might originate and evolve in artificially created worlds inhabited by communities of interacting autonomous agents. The authors describe their own model for studying the role of mating-selective pressure in the evolution of musical expectation. Next, they introduce a mimetic model for studying the evolution of musical lexicons in a community of autonomous robots furnished with a vocal synthesizer, a hearing apparatus and a memory device. The application of neural networks to evolve generative sequencing rules in a community of rhythm players and imitators is also discussed.

The accompanying music CD features pieces composed by, or with the aid of, EC. The diversity of musical styles and compositional approaches illustrated on this CD are clear evidence of the capabilities and scope of Evolutionary Computer Music, which go beyond the realm of academic theory. Here are examples of tangible practical benefits for the music industry.

We would like to express our gratitude to all contributors who kindly produced new original chapters for this edition and provided the pieces for the accompanying music CD. We are thankful to Springer's editorial and production team for their support, especially our commissioning editor, Helen Callaghan, for her encouragement to edit this book.

The editors would like to dedicate this volume to the memory of the late Drew Garlant-Jones, whose enthusiasm and contribution to the development of Evolutionary Computer Music shall never be forgotten.

January 2007   Eduardo Reck Miranda
                                                         John Al Biles

Contents

List of Contributors

Prof David E Goldberg
Dobrovolny Distinguished Professor
Illinois Genetic Algorithms Laboratory
(IlliGAL) Department of Industrial and
  Enterprise Systems Engineering
University of Illinois at
  Urbana-Champaign
117 Transportation Building
104 S. Mathews Avenue
Urbana, IL 61801
USA
Email: deg@uiuc.edu

Prof Phil Husbands
Professor of Artificial Intelligence
Cognitive and Computing Sciences
University of Sussex
Brighton, BN1 9QH
United Kingdom
Email: philh@cogs.susx.ac.uk

Dr Peter Copley
The Music Department
The Open University
Walton Hall
Milton Keynes, MK7 6AA
United Kingdom
Email: arts-music-enquiries@
  open.ac.uk

Ms Alice Eldridge
Creative Systems Lab
Evolutionary and Adaptive Systems
  Group
Department of Informatics
University of Sussex
Brighton, BN1 9QH
United Kingdom
Email: alicee@sussex.ac.uk

Mr James Mandelis
Creative Systems Lab
Evolutionary and Adaptive Systems
  Group
Department of Informatics
University of Sussex
Brighton, BN1 9QH
United Kingdom
Email: jamesm@cogs.susx.ac.uk

Prof John Al Biles
Professor and Undergraduate Program
Coordinator Information
Technology Department
Rochester Institute of Technology
102 Lomb Memorial Drive
Rochester, NY 14623-5608
USA
Email: jab@it.rit.edu

Prof Andrew Horner
Department of Computer Science
The Hong Kong University of
Science & Technology, Clear
Water Bay Kowloon Hong Kong
Email: horner@cse.ust.hk

Dr Palle Dahlstedt
IT University, Chalmers University
of Technology Innovative Design /
Art & Technology Program
SE-412 96 Goteborg
Sweden
Email: palle@ituniv.se

Ms Qijun Zhang
Interdisciplinary Centre for Computer
Music Research (ICCMR)
Faculty of Technology
University of Plymouth
Smeaton Building 206
Drake Circus
Plymouth, PL4 8AA
United Kingdom
Email: qijun.zhang@plymouth.ac.uk

Prof Eduardo R. Miranda
Professor of Computer Music
Interdisciplinary Centre for Computer
Music Research (ICCMR)
Faculty of Technology
University of Plymouth
Portland Square B326
Drake Circus

Plymouth, PL4 8AA
United Kingdom
Email: eduardo.miranda@
plymouth.ac.uk

Dr Rodney Waschka II
The Music Department
North Carolina State University
Price Music Center
2620 Cates Ave.
Campus Box 7311
Raleigh, NC 27695
USA
Email: waschka@ncsu.edu

Dr Tim Blackwell
Department of Computing
Goldsmiths College
University of London
New Cross
London, SE14 6NW
United Kingdom
Email: t.blackwell@gold.ac.uk

Prof Peter Todd
Professor of Informatics, Cognitive
Science and Psychology
School of Informatics
Indiana University
Informatics Building
901 E. 10th St.
Bloomington, IN 47408-3912
USA
Email: pmtodd@indiana.edu

1
An Introduction to Evolutionary Computing for Musicians[1]

PHIL HUSBANDS, PETER COPLEY, ALICE ELDRIDGE AND
JAMES MANDELIS

1.1. Introduction

The aim of this chapter is twofold: to provide a succinct introduction to evolutionary computing, outlining the main technical details, and to raise issues pertinent to musical applications of the methodology. Thus this chapter should furnish readers with the necessary background needed to understand the remaining chapters in this volume as well as open up a number of important themes relevant to this collection.

The field of evolutionary computing encompasses a variety of techniques and methods inspired by natural evolution. At its heart are Darwinian search algorithms based on highly abstract biological models. Such algorithms hunt through vast spaces of data structures that represent solutions to the problem at hand, which might be the design of an efficient aero engine, the production of a beautiful image, timetabling a set of exams or composing a piece of music. The search is powered by processes analogous to natural selection, mutation and reproduction. The basic idea is to maintain a population of candidate solutions that evolve under a selective pressure favouring the better solutions. Parent solutions are combined in various ways to produce offspring solutions, which then enter the population, are evaluated and may themselves produce offspring. As the cycle continues better and better solutions are found. This class of techniques has attracted a great deal of attention because of its success in a wide range of applications.

Once the Neo-Darwinian framework, which unified Darwin's theory of natural selection with genetics, had been established in the 1930s and 1940s and emerged as a powerful theoretical underpinning for biology (Fisher 1930; Haldane 1932; Huxley 1942), it is perhaps not surprising that computer pioneers wondered if it was possible to abstract general problem-solving methods from the logic of natural evolution. During the 1950s a number of prominent thinkers, such as Alan Turing, suggested the use of artificial evolution as a possible methodology for developing adaptive machines. He envisioned its use in developing learning

[1] This paper is dedicated to the memory of our late friend and colleague Drew Gartland-Jones, who was crucial to the development of much of the thinking presented here.

machines. Such machines would have hereditary material (artificial genes) encoding their structure, mutated copies of which would form offspring machines. A selection mechanism would be used to favour better-adapted machines – in this case those that were best at learning (Turing 1950). Such ideas were relatively common at that time – the golden age of mid-century Cybernetics when biological inspiration was rife and adventurous researchers were mapping out a visionary landscape, but it was not until the 1960s, when computer hardware became more powerful and easily available, that concrete instantiations began to appear. Three different variants independently emerged. Ingo Rechenberg and Paul Schwefel developed evolution strategies (Rechenberg 1965) to tackle engineering design optimisation problems. Fogle et al. (1966) describe a the technique of Evolutionary Programming, primarily concerned with evolving finite state automata for machine learning tasks. John Holland and his group at the University of Michigan developed the more general genetic algorithm, which became the best known of the methods (Holland 1975). Holland's early work in this area was concerned with building a powerful general formalism for adaptive systems (Holland 1962), and this lead to his notion of a general reproductive plan (Holland 1966) which, slightly modified, was christened a genetic algorithm by Bagley (1967). It was during the 1980s that the field really took off, when it was at first dominated by work in genetic algorithms. In the 1990s general frameworks were developed, which unified the various strands under the now widely used term of evolutionary computing (Back and Schwefel 1993). It is beyond the scope of this chapter to look in detail at all the historical flavours of evolutionary algorithms (EAs) that emerged during the development of the field (see Eiben and Smith 2003; Mitchell 1996 for good introductions), and rather the main properties of such methods will be presented by appealing to the idea of a general class of evolutionary search algorithms which encompasses the major sub-dialects.

Early applications of EAs were mainly in engineering optimisation of one sort or another (see, e.g. Davis 1990; Goldberg 1989; Grefenstette 1987), but as the method became better known and sparked the imagination of many researchers, the range of applications became increasingly wide and soon encompassed creative and artistic domains, including music.

The deceptively simple biological analogy at the heart of EAs is highly attractive and provides a rich seam for further developments that many researchers have mined and are still busy mining today. As we shall see, this has resulted in a highly flexible framework, with far fewer restrictions on its application than for other comparable methods, allowing plenty of scope for creative work. This is one of the great strengths of the area and one of the reasons why it is attractive to musicians and artists.

The next section gives a succinct introduction to the technical details of EAs. This is followed by sections on two particularly popular areas for musical applications of evolutionary computing: composition and sound design. Important issues arising from the use of EAs in these areas are discussed. The chapter then continues with a wider discussion about the place of adaptive systems in music.

1.2. Evolutionary Search Algorithms

1.2.1. Some Biology

Most EAs are based squarely on the Neo-Darwinian framework from biology and borrow certain key nomenclature from it. Hence it will be helpful to outline that framework before launching into the details of EAs.

According to Charles Darwin's theory of natural selection (Darwin 1859), evolutionary change comes about because of the existence of variations in inheritable traits in every generation. Those individuals who survive, owing to a particularly well-adapted combination of inheritable characteristics, give rise to the next generation. The individuals fittest survive to pass on those traits that helped to make them fit.

Darwin knew very little about how these variations arose or what the mechanisms underlying inheritable traits were. It was modern genetics that provided the key to answering these problems. Hence Neo-Darwinism postulates that natural selection acts on the genetic variations within populations – genes being the units underlying inheritable characteristics. These variations are caused by genetic processes such as mutations (sometimes caused by mistakes in DNA replication) and recombination of genetic material from different sources (e.g. the two parents in sexual reproduction).

Natural selection is usually thought of as acting on the *phenotype*, the outwards expression of the genes (the *genotype*), such as physical characteristics or behaviour, the environment it inhabits and the interactions between them. This process, together with others such as genetic drift and speciation, is a key element of modern evolutionary theory.

1.2.2. The Basics

Fig. 1.1 outlines the general scheme of an EA. An initial population of structures representing solutions to the problem is first created. They might be completely

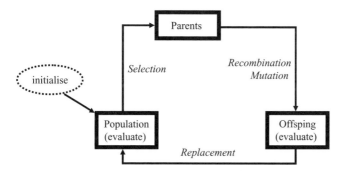

FIGURE 1.1. General scheme of an evolutionary algorithm.

random individuals or based on a prior solution or generated using heuristics that ensure that they have certain desirable characteristics. Each member of the population is evaluated so that it can be assigned a fitness (usually a numerical score). This will involve decoding the genetic representation (genotype) into a problem solution (phenotype) and testing its fitness using some method for determining how well it solves the problem. Parents are selected, with a bias towards fitter members of the population, for the creation of offspring by using artificial genetic operators such as mutation and recombination. The offspring are evaluated and certain of them are selected to take the place of existing members of the population chosen according to a replacement scheme (usually biased towards the least fit individuals). The cycle continues until a sufficiently fit individual emerges or some stopping criteria, such as number of cycles run, is met. Most parts of the cycle involve random, or stochastic, processes crucial to the success of the method.

We will now look at the operation of this scheme in more detail by examining the constituent parts of the EA. The main components of an evolutionary search algorithm are:

- genetic representation
- evaluation function
- population structure
- selection method
- genetic operators
- replacement scheme

1.2.2.1. The Genetic Representation

The structures making up the population, i.e., the artificial genotypes, are usually strings of numbers or symbols that represent solutions to the problem at hand. They might be a string of real numbers that are the parameters controlling a sound synthesis algorithm – and hence represent a sound – or they might be groups of numbers representing information such as musical note values and durations – and hence represent a piece of music. Complex encodings involving mixtures of numbers, symbols, rules and other data structures have also been successfully used; for example, the sub-field of genetic programming is concerned with the evolution of a particular form of LISP computer program (Koza 1992). It is also possible to use a fairly simple genotype in combination with a complex decoding scheme to translate it into the phenotype. Rather indirect routes to the end goal can be taken, for instance, the genotype may specify the design of a process, or abstract machine, which is then run to generate the end product of interest (e.g. a musical phrase). The genotypes can be of a fixed length or, where appropriate, they can be allowed to grow and shrink. The great flexibility available in designing a suitable representation is one of the major advantages over more traditional methods afforded by the EA framework. However, not all representations for a given problem will be equally good. In some cases the representation to use is fairly obvious and straightforward (e.g. a string of numbers acting as the parameters of a well-defined process or design), in others it may not be so clear. The representation defines the *genotype space* through which the EA searches looking for a combination of genes that defines a sufficiently fit phenotype. If the representation is badly designed the space may become impossibly convoluted and too difficult to search with any efficiency, rendering the EA useless. Throughout the remainder of this book concrete examples of representations suitable for musical systems will be found.

1.2.2.2. The Evaluation (Fitness) Function

EAs are a form of 'generate and test' algorithm (generate a new candidate solution and test it to see if it is any good) and the evaluation function – which operates on the phenotype – providing the necessary means to measure fitness. As such it defines the solution requirements and implicitly encapsulates the meaning of adaptation and improvement for the particular evolutionary system. The selection method relies on the evaluation function assigning relative fitness values to members of the population in order to preferentially choose the fitter individuals to produce the next generation. Fitness is often measured on some numerical scale, but as a minimum the evaluation function must be able to distinguish between relatively fit and unfit individuals.

The simplest form of evaluation method is a well-defined mathematical function or procedure whose variables are directly encoded on the genotype; these are fed into the function and a fitness value is thrown back (Eiben and Smith 2003). For more complex phenotypes, for instance, when the genotype encodes the design of a robot, evaluation often involves generating a computer model of the phenotype (e.g. the robot) and then testing its behaviour in a complex simulation (Jakobi 1998). In other cases an automated analysis of some characteristics of the phenotype is conducted in order to derive a fitness measure. For instance, an evolved musical composition might be analysed in terms of its closeness to some target piece, or by using some musicological theory or technique (Wiggins et al. 1998). If the phenotype is the design of a physical artefact, evaluation might entail analysing various functional and aesthetic properties of the design (Bentley 1999). In examples such as these, defining a satisfactory automated fitness measure is often highly problematic – how do we codify aesthetics, how do we formalise crucial parts of the creative process of an artist or composer? This important issue will be revisited in Section 1.3 and in later chapters of this book. One partial solution that is commonly used, having been pioneered in the application of EAs in visual art (Todd and Latham 1992; Sims 1991), is to employ a human's judgement as the fitness measure. The main problem with this method, sometimes referred to as *aesthetic selection* or *interactive evolution*, is the amount of time required to perform the fitness judgements. This can preclude running the evolutionary method for more than a relatively small number of cycles.

1.2.2.3. The Population Structure

In the simplest cases, the population is just a data structure containing the genotypes and their associated information, such as fitness. The population size is often fixed, but it can be variable. In some EAs the entire population is replaced on each cycle, which is then referred to as a generation. A more sophisticated variety of EA uses a *spatially distributed* population, alluding to the underlying conceptual model of the population spread out over a 2-D grid with each individual occupying its own cell. Members of the population interact only with those individuals that are sufficiently close to be in their *neighbourhood*. Hence selection and reproduction act asynchronously and locally allowing for highly parallel implementation of an EA (for instance, using a network of processors – one for each cell on the grid). This form of EA has been shown to be highly efficient (Collins and Jefferson 1991; Hillis 1990; Husbands 1993).

1.2.2.4. The Selection Method

Selection, whereby more credence is given to fitter population members, provides the dynamo that powers the algorithm. The fittest are *more likely* to pass on some of their genes to later generations. This probabilistic element – which is found in other parts of the method, e.g., the genetic operators – helps to account for the technique's power and robustness.

A simple and reasonably effective selection method is *roulette selection*. In this scheme each member of the population is assigned a probability of selection based on its relative fitness (its fitness value divided by the total population fitness). Parents are then selected according to this probability. This is analogous to dividing up a roulette wheel into N sectors, one for each member of the population – sizing them according to the relative fitness of the individual represented, and then spinning it to select parents. The bigger the relative fitness the more likely the individual is to be selected for breeding. Note that with this scheme no member of the population is excluded from breeding, they all have some chance of contributing to the next generation. However, this method can result in too strong a selective pressure in favour of individuals that are relatively good at the early stage but may actually be far from optimal; the population *prematurely converges* to be dominated by copies of such individuals.

Rank-based selection is a particularly straightforward alternative scheme that provides more control over the selective pressure and allows strong differentiation of the population, even at later stages when their fitness values are very close. Using this strategy the population is ranked, or ordered, according to the fitness values of its members. Selection is then performed by following a pre-determined probability distribution function, such as the ones shown in Fig. 1.2. This may be a simple linear function that constrains the first-ranked (fittest) individual to be twice as likely to be selected as the median-ranked individual, or something more complex.

An alternative form of selection, that makes most sense in the context of parallel EAs, was alluded to earlier – the use of *local selection rules*. Briefly, the idea is that a population is somehow split up into many subpopulations, either explicitly or implicitly (as in the case of the spatial distribution mentioned above) and selection occurs *locally*, that is, with reference only to the subpopulation and not to the

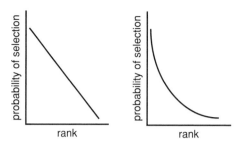

FIGURE 1.2. Typical rank-based selection probability distributions.

global population. Local schemes may be based on the methods described earlier or may be simpler. For a more detailed discussion of possible selection schemes see Eiben and Smith (2003) and Mitchell (1996).

Interactive EAs, employing human-based aesthetic selection, effectively dispense with a separate selection method: individuals are picked out by the user to act as parents for the next generation.

1.2.2.5. The Genetic Operators

The genetic operators maintain variation in the population and create new individuals from old ones. Myriad specialised operators have been developed over the years and there are numerous variation on the standard ones. Hence only a few of the most common generic operators will be outlined here. The two most common are *cross-over* and *mutation* (see Fig. 1.3). Like most widely used operators, they have strong stochastic elements to their operation. Simple cross-over involves choosing at random a cross-over point (some position along the string) for two mating chromosomes – two new strings are created by swapping over the sections lying after the cross-over point. Variations include two-point cross-over where randomly selected sections of the strings are swapped over and special operators that rearrange genes during the crossing over, either in order to keep the new solutions legal or to make them better (Michalewicz et al. 2004). Mutation changes the value of a gene to some other possible value. Depending on the encoding, this might entail assigning a new value at random from the entire range of possible

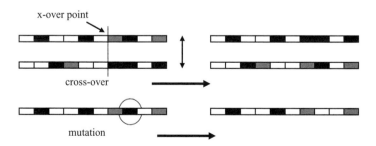

FIGURE 1.3. Schematic of popular genetic operators.

values for the gene, or randomly resetting to a value 'close' to the current one (*creep mutation*). Mutation operators can be heuristically guided, rather than completely blind (e.g. if a gene represents a note value in a piece of music, mutation operators might be designed to respect certain harmonic or melodic constraints – or perhaps more interestingly to *nearly always* respect them). For complex encodings, it often makes sense to have several different mutation operators acting in parallel. Other operators sometimes used are *inversion*, which is simply a matter of reversing a randomly chosen section of a single genotype; *translocation*, which involves moving a randomly selected section to another place on the genotype; and *duplication*, which entails adding extra copies of genes or groups of genes. The latter operator makes sense only in circumstances where a variable length encoding is being used; it often functions in tandem with a *deletion* operator. Specially designed cross-over operators can also be used to allow genotypes to grow and shrink (Harvey 1992). Special domain specific operators are regularly employed to good effect. For instance, in the application of EAs to musical composition operators based on musical transformations such as inversion and transposition can be very useful (Biles 1994).

The operators have assigned *rates* that determine how likely they are to be used. They are applied at the offspring creation stage according to a routine like the following: When two genotypes are selected for breeding, first apply crossover with some high probability to create two new genotypes. Next apply inversion to these with a medium probability. Finally, each gene on the resulting genotypes undergoes mutation (with a low probability). According to the encoding scheme and problem area, different combinations of operators with different rates are used. In some circumstances it makes sense to dispense with cross-over, for instance if it is difficult to devise an encoding that works with this operation, and just use one or more mutation operator. It is common to have to experiment with operator rates to find good settings, which can usefully be made to vary during the search – in some cases the rates themselves are put under genetic control (Back et al. 1991).

1.2.2.6. The Replacement Scheme

In some EAs enough offspring are produced on each cycle to replace the entire population in one go. In others, sometimes called *steady-state* algorithms, new individuals are introduced one at a time, as long as they are fitter than at least the worst member of the population which is then replaced. This allows a more gradual search. Other schemes use an inverse selection method to choose members of the current population to be replaced with a bias towards the least fit.

It should be clear from this brief outline of EAs that there are many choices to make in deciding how to apply them to any given domain and many parameters to tweak once the basic algorithm has been designed. The various elements of the EA must all work well together in order to achieve good results. The best choice of operators, genetic representation, evaluation function and so on can be either guided by what has been shown to work in the past or by experimentation with different settings and options. However, some appreciation of the growing theoretical understanding of how EAs work can be very helpful and save time spent down the blind allies of poor representations or inadequate fitness functions. EAs are complex nonlinear stochastic systems, which makes them extremely difficult to analyse. Hence the theoretical literature tends to be rather inconsistent and is often contradicted by empirical results. However, there is useful information to be gleaned and good sources include Schmitt (2001), Vose (1999) and Wright et al. (2005).

1.2.3. Related Developments

EAs have played an important part in the development of the related fields of Artificial Life, which is concerned with the synthesis and analysis of lifelike processes in artificial media (Langton 1995; Pollack et al. 2004) and adaptive behaviour, which studies the mechanisms underlying the generation of adaptive behaviour in real and artificial autonomous agents (Beer 1990; Schaal et al. 2004).

These areas have seen interesting explorations of phenomena and techniques that have found applications in artistic endeavours. For instance, coevolutionary systems, in which two or more 'species' compete (or possibly cooperate) over finite resources, have been exploited in Karl Sims' entertaining animations, in which primitive creatures wrestle with each other (Sims 1994), as well as in various engineering applications (Husbands 1993; Juillé and Pollack 1996). This is a direction which might hold some promise as far as computer music is concerned. Multiple species could represent different voices in a composition or it might be possible in some situations to have coevolving species of compositions and critics (who evaluate the compositions) developing towards some interesting end (Werner and Todd 1997, 1998; Hillis 1990).

Jon McCormack's Eden is an interesting example of an installation using ideas from these areas (McCormack 2003). In this system, simulated beings populate an artificial world in which they can move around and make and hear sounds. These sonic agents must compete for limited resources in their environment. The agents generate sounds to attract mates and also to capture the imagination of the audience, since its response has a direct affect on the virtual environment, particularly the growth rate of food. In this work McCormack has demonstrated the successful use of an open-ended automatic evolutionary process to generate a highly engaging interactive artwork. This system illustrates a more implicit approach to fitness evaluation, with a fairly oblique interaction element. Such pieces suggest a wealth of opportunities for musical developments.

1.2.4. Applications of Evolutionary Computing in Music

There is a growing body of work involving the use of EAs in musical applications (see Horner and Goldberg 1991; Burton and Vladimirova 1999; Bilotta et al. 2001; Miranda 2003 for representative examples), just as there is in the visual arts and in design (Bentley 1999). In music, the two areas that have attracted the most attention are composition and sound design. In the former, there have been a number of attempts to evolve musical pieces in the style of a particular composer, or within a specific idiom, which have met with some success (Biles 1994; Hodgson 1999, 2002). However, extending such work to more creative and original compositions is challenging, for reasons including those discussed in Section 1.3. In the area of sound design, researchers have demonstrated the efficacy of the technique in controlling sound synthesis methods, both to explore new sounds and to develop synthesis algorithms for existing target sounds (Johnson 1999; Dahlstedt 2001; Garcia 2001; Mandelis 2001).

Various aspects of these topics, in relation to specific systems, will be dealt with in detail in later chapters. Musical composition with EA will be discussed in more detail in Chapters 6–8 and EA in sound synthesis and design will be discussed in more detail in Chapters 3, 4 and 8. The remainder of this chapter is intended to raise a number of important issues in these areas as background and context to the rest of the book. Fitness evaluation turns out to be a particularly thorny issue in relation to compositional systems and it is not a trivial matter in sound design.

1.3. Evolutionary Computing in Musical Composition

1.3.1. Introduction

The main purpose of this section is not to attempt a comprehensive survey of evolutionary computational approaches to musical composition (see Burton and Vladimirova (1999) for a good overview as well as later chapters in this book) but rather to highlight some of the potential problems, apparent in the literature, of too close a marriage between the development of compositional computer programs, and an approach to musical form derived primarily from academic theory, rather than what many composers demonstrably do. This is a very real problem since textbook musical form is by its nature algorithmic and has often been seen as the ideal starting point for the development of composition programs, particularly those based on pre-existent models of compositional practice (see Wiggins et al. 1998). The main 'test case' for discussion in this section will be the sonata form, in theory and practice as this, in particular, is a type of composition that could well prove problematic if the creative process to be modelled is not based on a traditional textbook definition but rather, something paralleling an end product that significant composers actually produced. This is not to suggest that the production of an interesting sonata structure per se is a primary goal of more than a minority of practitioners in this field. Rather, that sonata form itself was a significant tool (whether algorithmic in nature or not) in the evolution of complex musical structure for more than 150 years in the history of Western Art Music. Its potential to encompass so many elements that inform the creative process – exploration, contrast, development, transformation, motivic mutation, etc. – make it an ideal context to examine the potential limitations of EA composition programs.

The musical forms generated by an EA-based system will be implicitly restricted and shaped by the design of the various components of the system – most importantly the genotype, the genetic operators and the fitness function. If an automatic fitness evaluation method is used, the desired musical outcome must be somehow formally codified. Deriving sets of rules to describe particular forms or styles is fraught with difficulties, as discussed below. If the automatic fitness function problem is sidestepped by using human evaluation, the search space defined by the genetic representation and operators must be sufficiently constrained to avoid impossible bottlenecks in the time needed to perform the evaluations (Biles 1994; Gartland-Jones and Copley 2003; 2005). As this will entail encoding musical knowledge into the representation and operators, the difficulties do not disappear.

1.3.2. Algorithmic Composition

In his book *The Algorithmic Composer*, David Cope stated that throughout the history of Western Art Music, composers have used algorithms as part of the creative process. His premise was that an algorithm could be defined as nothing more than 'a set of rules for solving a problem in a finite number of steps' (Webster 1991, p. 35; cited in Cope 2000, p. 1). Clearly, this is of crucial importance to anyone engaged in building Artificial Intelligence models of musical creativity and assuming Cope's premise is valid, algorithms of musical composition and form building would be central to the construction of such models. However, while it is perfectly possible to define some compositional processes as algorithmic, not all fall so neatly into this category. A necessary preliminary step would be to attempt a delineation of boundaries, as to what extent, which compositional processes can or cannot be so defined.

Cope stated, 'Most composers apply rules, steps, or sets of instructions when composing music, especially when composing music in a particular style' (Cope 2000, p. 2). Part of his support for this proposition is a series of examples of compositional processes defined as algorithmic. These include the tenor part of an isorhythmic motet (significantly, Cope omits discussion and illustration of the other voices, which are freely composed), Bontempi's *rota*, musical dice games and Johann Fux's *Gradus ad Parnassum* (Cope 2000, pp. 3–11). This is a wide-ranging set of examples although, with the exception of the motet, all bear only a peripheral relation to musical composition as actually practised by fully fledged composers. In the seventeenth century, Giovanni Bontempi proposed that his *rota* as a guide by means of which one thoroughly ignorant of the art of music can begin to compose; a sort of musical equivalent of painting-by-numbers. Musical dice games were similarly do-it-yourself kits for beginners, while in the eighteenth century, Fux's *Gradus ad Parnassum* was the standard instruction book for learning strict counterpoint for much of the eighteenth century – a useful tool for the elementary technical training of aspiring composers but bearing about the same relation to real music as a book of finger exercises, however advanced, would have to the performing repertoire of a professional concert pianist.

On the subject of form, Cope writes that

strict adherence to an established musical form constitutes yet another compositional use of musical algorithms. For example, imagining a song form of the medieval period, a dance form of the baroque, or a sonata allegro form of the classical period of Western music history as symbols in a flowchart – one way to describe an algorithm – does not seem unreasonable. (Cope 2000, pp. 3–4)

The problem arises with Cope's unstated but implied assumption that significant composers at all periods in the development of Western art music did indeed adhere strictly to *established* musical forms in their most original work, even granting that these forms were already in acknowledged existence at the time of writing, rather than being deduced after the event by historians or writers of textbooks on musical composition!

To return briefly to Fux, it is of course documented that composers Joseph Haydn, Wolfgang Amadeus Mozart and Ludwig van Beethoven, to name but three, worked assiduously through the exercises in the *Gradus ad Parnassum* or from textbooks of a similar nature; but it is equally demonstrable that they paid scant attention to the *letter* of the majority of Fux's rules in their compositional maturity. This is not to suggest that Fux is valueless as an example of a producer of musical algorithms, rather simply that the process of modelling anything more than the most elementary compositional process is rather more complicated than his citation by Cope might suggest. Historically, a large claim made for the benefit of strict counterpoint study of the Fuxian variety was that it provided what amounted to an algorithm for composing in the style of the composer Giovanni Pierluigi da Palestrina, who had been regarded for centuries after his death as a byword for purity of contrapuntal style. Unfortunately, this claim was largely unfounded and was completely exploded by Morris (1922) as far back as the 1920s:

Yet the rules of Mr Rockstro [*another author of a book on strict counterpoint*] are not peculiar. They are, more or less, the same as those found in almost every textbook of counterpoint. Who invented them, goodness only knows: why they have been perpetuated, it passes the wit of man to explain. Music written to meet their requirements is something altogether *sui generis*, a purely academic by-product. ... The rules of counterpoint are found to have no connexion with musical composition as practised in the sixteenth century: are we to abandon the rules or to abandon the sixteenth century? Follow Byrd and Palestrina, or follow Mr. Rockstro and Professor Prout? (Morris 1922, p. 2)

1.3.3. Is Sonata Form an Algorithm?

Sonata form expressed as an algorithm brings similar problems in its wake. Is the algorithm to be based on textbook definitions or on what significant composers actually produced? Furthermore, there remains the question of which variety of sonata form as practised is to be taken as the starting point. Many commentators (see, e.g. Rosen (1980, pp. 365–402) and Straus (1990, pp. 96–97)) are now in agreement that there exists a fundamental distinction between what could broadly be described as eighteenth- and nineteenth-century approaches. For a composer in the second half of the eighteenth century, the sonata form (not termed as such) was an elaborated binary structure characterised by differentiated key areas. The first part contained a tonic area and a dominant (or related key) area, although the first area could be characterised by a modulation to the tonality of the second area. The second part consisted of an area of rapid modulation or episode followed by a return to the home key in which tonality the movement remained until its end. The two-part view of sonata structure is confirmed by the prevailing eighteenth-century practice of repeating both sections, rather than just the first part, as is usually the case in contemporary performance.

What is set out above is just about the fullest extent of universal common ground in composing practice that can be extrapolated from the majority of later eighteenth century sonata structures and a composing algorithm extracted from this would be little different from one derived from baroque binary dance patterns, despite the two forms being in reality quite distinct from each other. The distinction between the two is the far greater proliferation and elaboration of material that the sonata framework came to accommodate – what could, in fact be termed 'free composition'. The beauty of the form lay in its flexibility. This minimum common ground, never at this stage delineated in any contemporaneous textbook on composition, could accommodate not only Haydn's largely monothematic and developmental approach but also Mozart's, which tended to explore the underlying unity of two or more distinct but nonetheless contrasting themes.

All this came to change in the nineteenth century, thanks initially to the theorising of Adolph Marx (1795–1866) and Karl Czerny (1791–1857), which was largely based on the sonata practice of Beethoven (in his 'middle period'), who had provided yet another distinct approach to the original but still evolving model. I give here Arnold Schoenberg's description of the form, which corresponds to the nineteenth-century theorists' view, which was concerned less with the delineation of key areas and more with thematic contrast, expressed in a ternary rather than a binary context:

This form ... is essentially a ternary structure. Its main divisions are the EXPOSITION, ELABORATION and RECAPITULATION. It differs from other complex ternary forms in that the contrasting middle section (ELABORATION) is devoted almost exclusively to the working out of the rich variety of thematic material 'exposed' in the first division. Its greatest merit, which enabled it to hold a commanding position over a period of 150 years, is its extraordinary flexibility in accommodating the widest variety of musical ideas, long or short, many or few, active or passive, in almost any combination. The internal details may be subjected to almost any mutation without disturbing the aesthetic validity of the structure as a whole. (Schoenberg 1967, p. 200)

Although Schoenberg proves himself a child of the nineteenth century in his thematic and ternary, rather than tonal and binary, view of sonata structure – perhaps in order to allow for his continuing to explore the form in non-tonal contexts – his description is still loose enough to accommodate a wide variety of approaches, including those of the later eighteenth century. The compositional algorithm that could be extrapolated from this description would, however, differ little from one derived from a simple ternary form.

For a truly distinctive sonata algorithm, resembling neither the simple binary nor the ternary model, we would need to turn instead to the traditional theorists, who would state that Sonata Form consists of firstly, an *exposition*, comprising first and second subject groups, respectively in the tonic and dominant (or related) keys and linked by a *transition* or *bridge passage*; secondly, a *development section*, in which the original thematic material will pass through a variety of related keys and may be extended by *episodes*; this will be followed (thirdly) by a *recapitulation*, in which the material from the exposition returns but is mostly confined to the original key. Various optional extras, such as *introductions*, *codettas* and *codas* can fill out the scheme and may be represented as byways on a flowchart, which is Cope's preferred method for setting out compositional algorithms in a non-computerised context.

Actually, this theoretical description does indeed correspond to more conservative later nineteenth century practice and this lends a depressing sameness – from a purely formal point of view to the majority of sonata-type structures from this period. The extraordinary paradox is that the romantic nineteenth century was far less free than the classical late eighteenth century in its interpretation of what might be termed 'the sonata principle', except in the case of more progressively minded composers, such as Franz Liszt, Hector Berlioz and Richard Wagner, who tended to abandon the form completely. It is difficult to avoid the conclusion that once the rules had been encapsulated in a detailed formal scheme or algorithm, the sonata began to lose its dynamic and developmental possibilities and its various sections took on the character of moulds into which appropriate music could be poured. Such an approach to potential sonata material would have been psychologically impossible for any major eighteenth or early nineteenth century composer of whose structure-building creativity generally went beyond simply following formulae devised by others.

1.3.4. The Dangers of Too Many and Too Few Rules

It may seem that several of the preceding paragraphs address issues more central to the concerns of musical historians, analysts and aestheticians than those of designers of computer programs for musical composition. However, if we are modelling musical creative processes to any degree of sophistication, it is crucial that we base our model on something close to what composers actually did, rather than on theoretical constructs, often established long after the creative event, that oversimplify or distort complex thought processes in the interests of pedagogical expediency. An excessively rule-based system stands in grave danger of producing little more than schoolroom exercises or, at best, stolid replications of good craftsmanship because no facility has been provided for expanding a given search space to accommodate the possibility, indeed the desirability of the unexpected, or even iconoclastic but still meaningful musical idea or development.

Although the explorative and stochastic nature of evolutionary search are help-ful, this is perhaps the most challenging problem facing the designer of an EA-based composition program, whether for general use or tailored to one particular set of preferences. The past decade and more has shown that an EA has no difficulty in replicating a composer in 'hard-work' (as opposed to 'inspired') mode (see Jacob 1996, p. 158). But without the most stringently defined search space an unman-ageably large amount of potential material, mostly unusable, is apt to be produced. Biles (1994) has described this situation as the fitness bottleneck. However, if the search space is too strictly defined – 'Strict adherence to an established musical form' (Cope 2000, pp. 3–4) – the unexpected and interesting permutation, which is what all the hard work is supposed to uncover may not emerge at all. As Werner and Todd (1998) pointed out:

More structure and knowledge built into the system means more reasonably structured musical output; less structure and knowledge in the system means more novel, unexpected output, but also more unstructured musical chaff. (p. 315)

What algorithm from textbook musical forms could have allowed for Haydn's unprecedented departure from the expected course of musical events in the de-velopmental extended coda that erupts into the final variation on a theme in the slow movement of his *String Quartet*, Op. 20 no. 4; Mozart's introduction of a modulatory and developmental theme that is *not*, contradicting all expectation, the second subject of the first movement of his *Haffner Symphony*; Beethoven's 'sonata structure, accommodating variation' (Keller 1987, p. 136) that forms the choral finale of his *9th Symphony*; or Franz Schubert's fusion, by thematic inte-gration of the four movement sonata scheme into a single continuous movement in his *Wanderer Fantasy*?

These are not isolated, eccentric examples but the essence of a truly creative use of form, wholly characteristic of their respective composers, which can lend musical compositions their enduring power to fascinate and hold the attention. It is this capacity to reinvent (or, particularly in the case of Haydn, to invent) form that is a fundamental difference between a Joseph Haydn and a Johann Baptist Vanhal; a Wolfgang Amadeus Mozart and a Karl Ditters von Dittersdorf; a Ludwig van Beethoven and an Anton Diabelli; or a Franz Schubert and a Johann Hummel. Meaningful contradiction of expectation is one expression of individuality that distinguishes specific pieces and composers from the more typical cultural products of whatever age in which they lived, giving the music an intrinsic value that can transcend time and place.

To attempt to model this level of creativity is asking much of a process still in a comparatively early stage in its development but it seems vital that the possibility of overriding rules must be provided for in composition programs with any preten-sions to model creative, rather than reproductive musical thought. The historical fact that theory so often followed, and in the process distorted, practice should in it-self be warning enough of the pitfalls of regarding compositional processes purely as algorithms. It is natural to have recourse to algorithms when modelling cre-ative processes, as every computer program ever devised is in essence algorithmic.

However, it must also be recognised that if the algorithm employed is reductive and constricting in relation to the process it is modelling, the musical interest of what emerges will be at best limited, if not utterly predictable.

1.3.5. IndagoSonus

Drew Gartland-Jones' *IndagoSonus* system is a very interesting approach to partially address some of these issues (Gartland-Jones 2003). The system uses virtual blocks, which have the ability to both play and compose music. As the blocks are arranged in various structures they interact with each other in ways that influence the emerging music. Each block has a pre-composed 'home' musical phrase and the ability to compose new phrases based on its home phrase and a phrase that is passed to it from another block. A block's compositional activity is aimed at producing a new musical section that has a thematic relationship to both of these pieces. To do this, it uses an EA that is initialised with the home music and has the incoming phrase as its compositional target, allowing the use of an automatic evaluation function that measures the closeness of fit to the target. The path taken by the EA generates intermediate material related to the home and target pieces. The user can stop the evolutionary processes at any stage and restart it with new incoming phrases, as well as set parameters that control how far the evolutionary process will travel between the two pieces. To quote the designer

any number of blocks may be chained or grouped in any 3D structure. If a block is passed some music from its neighbour, it first recomposes itself, and then passes its new music on to all of its neighbours, and so forth within a pre-specified range. It is important to clarify that each block holds on to its home music throughout, enabling any music composed by it to remain thematically related, despite the constant process of re-composition undertaken by each block. In this way the composer of the music for all blocks maintains a compositional thumbprint on the evolving musical structure. In effect, the listener/performer is able to shape the overall music by choosing to send musical fragment from blocks they like to influence other blocks. (Gartland-Jones and Copley, 2003, p. 53)

By this subtle mixing of automatic fitness evaluation and human intervention, not to mention the use of multiple interacting EAs, the system makes some headway in addressing the fitness bottle-neck problem while avoiding over constraining the search space.

1.4. Evolutionary Computing in Sound Design

The use of EAs at the sound level is concerned with the manipulation of parameters that define a sound, using a particular sound synthesis technique (SST), or with parameters that define a particular deformation on an input stream (sound effects).

There are two broad categories of EA application in this area: as an optimisation technique for deriving the parameters of an accurate model of a particular sound (usually a sampled sound) and for exploratory search in the investigation of new sounds. These areas are briefly introduced in this section while highlighting pertinent issues.

In the optimisation case a sample of sound, often from a traditional instrument, is used as a target waveform. An EA is put to work to derive the parameters of a particular SST to produce a sound as close as possible to the target. A fitness function that measures the difference between a candidate sound and the target is usually employed and there are many technical issues involved in how best to define this. There are a number of examples of successful uses of this approach (e.g. Garcia 2001). Sound definitions usually describe a singular point in the parameter space of the SST without explicitly detailing how this sound changes and deforms from that frozen point. Such deformations of sound, or movements in parameter space, are necessary for mapping the sampled instrument to a keyboard and note scale, and implementing other transformations that add expressivity to the sound. In order to map those dynamics from the original source of the sampled waveform, generally a large number of waveforms is needed. As an absolute minimal requirement, at least three distinct waveforms would have to be used for each degree of freedom of the original sound source. For instance, if the source is a piano sound, the degrees of freedom of the piano would include: the key position, velocity, aftertouch and so on. In practice most acoustic instrument sounds do not vary in a linear fashion along their axes of freedom and far more than three samples would have to be used for each axis. This can very easily result in a prohibitive number of samples, which places too high a computational demand on the EA. This can be a serious problem only if this technique is used to faithfully emulate an original sound source. In contrast, if such fidelity is not required, then some interesting possibilities may begin to emerge. For instance, if the specific parameters are derived from a single waveform, then any deviation from these parameters will create sounds that are similar to the original but with deformation characteristics that depend on the particular SST used. For example, if a piano sound is used to derive the parameters for a frequency modulation (FM) SST and a physical modelling SST, then the deformations afforded by the former would be unique to this particular implementation of FM and for the latter unique to the particular physical modelling used. In effect there would be two instruments that would sound very similar at some performance configuration, but at the same time they would behave very differently in terms of sound deformation when the performance configuration changes.

The second category of EA-based sound creation, that of developing new sounds, requires a somewhat different approach. Although there is a large body of knowledge that can at least act as a starting point in attempting to formalize the evaluation process of EA-based composition systems, in the area of new sound design, where the 'quality' of the sound is to be assessed, there is no equivalent source. This is partly because of the complexity and lack of transparency of SSTs and partly also because of the difficulty in modelling aesthetic judgements. In this domain, the subjective usually rules over the objective. Hence the use of human-based interactive selection is the norm (Dhalstedt 2001; Mandelis 2001; Mandelis and Husbands 2003; Yee-King 2000; Woolf 1999), which raises the issue of the evaluation bottle-neck already discussed in relation to composition; this issue will be discussed in Chapter 4. Although there are general problems such as maintaining a consistent judgement of quality, the time taken to evaluate a sound is usually considerably less than that for a composition. This means that it is often feasible to run the algorithm for a reasonable number of cycles. The less constrained approach necessitated by the lack of formalised knowledge allows for a powerful exploration of sound space – the user is free to navigate a world of sonic possibilities, turning up interesting and unexpected new forms that can be put to good artistic use.

Genophone (Mandelis 2001, 2002) is one such exploratory system, designed in part to allow a flexible exploration of sound spaces without the need for detailed understandings of SSTs. We will now briefly describe aspects of the system, focusing on general issues in the way evolutionary search is used. The system makes strong use of genetic recombination, which in biological systems is a creative process in itself. A biological analogy would be the breeding of animals or plants, which humans have done for millennia. When pigeons are bred, for example, it is not normal (at least not yet) to employ gene level manipulations via genetic engineering. Instead, manipulations such as artificial insemination or pair choices are enough to manipulate the genome as a whole and consequently the resulting off-spring. *Genophone* provides analogous macroevolutionary manipulations to those employed in organic breeding: parents can be selected by the user, particular traits can be encouraged and manipulated. In addition, via dataglove manipulations, it provides a local direct and interactive exploration that facilitates smaller changes when used as a performance tool.

The issue of an instrument's degrees of freedom and the movement in this parametric space as 'performance' (Pressing 1990; Rovan et al. 1997; Wessel and Wright 2000; Mulder 1994) was considered as an integral part of an instrument's (sound) definition during the design and implementation of the *Genophone* system. This was achieved by evolving the particular parameter values that produce a desired sound *along with* a performance mapping scheme, where a subset of those parameters is mapped onto manipulation devices (dataglove and keyboard controls) for use in performance (see Fig. 1.4).

The option of locking individual genes, or even whole sections of the genotype, provides an added layer of control over the evolutionary process that helps bridge the gap between a totally free-form search and the tight regulation offered by a manual sound editor. The inspiration for parameter locking came from the way genes are activated and deactivated in biological genomes, producing epigenetic evolutionary effects (Singh and Krimbas 2000).

An important difference between the way EAs are generally used in constrained searches towards fixed sound targets, on the one hand, and unconstrained exploration of sound spaces, on the other, is the choice of initial population. In constrained EAs, a population of random individuals is often used to jump-start the evolutionary process. This is partly to ensure no initial bias exists, which may direct the search away from the global maximum – the perfect match to the target. In the unconstrained exploratory case, this is not necessary; in fact experiments with *Genophone* have shown that it is not even desirable. These experiments indicated

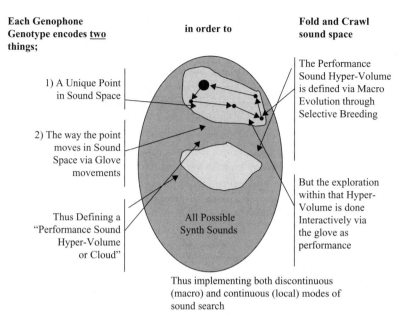

FIGURE 1.4. Exploration of sound and performance mapping spaces with Genophone (after Mulder 1994).

that it is preferable to seed the initial population with sounds that have been professionally hand-designed and are of some aesthetic quality. A large amount of knowledge is embedded in the parametric definitions of these sounds, information that ultimately encodes a set of aesthetic values, albeit in an implicit and not easily decipherable way. By using such hand-designed sounds as points of departure for the evolutionary search, this embedded knowledge can be exploited. Experiments with *Genophone* also revealed that starting from hand-designed origins does not necessarily mean that the resulting offspring would sound very much like their parents. In fact sometimes they can sound surprisingly dissimilar, yet somehow still retain some of the original quality of the hand-designed parents. It is also very easy at each generation to 'mate' a preferred offspring with a newly chosen hand-designed sound, thus rapidly diverging from the original parent set.

These two distinct uses of evolutionary computing for sound design have been described as the 'survival of the fittest' and as the 'survival of the prettiest', drawing an analogy with the biological processes of natural selection and sexual selection. The first one is in essence a convergent process, whereas the second one is divergent.

1.5. New Musical Possibilities Through Adaptive Systems

The themes of the previous two sections are broadened out in this section into a discussion of evolutionary and adaptive algorithms as tools for exploring new musical possibilities. In particular, it will be argued that adaptive systems can provide a rich interactive mechanism for performing as well as composing with the computer.

Musicians have always made use of, and arguably inspired, new technologies. The computer opens up an unimaginable scope for developing new sounds, new aesthetics and new composition and performance practices. Audio development programs and languages such as Max/MSP, PD and SuperCollider are broadening the community of computer music composers, and making the implementation of systems for exploring new musical possibilities easier and quicker. The challenge, of course, is to make something that anyone actually wants to listen to. Early computer music composers revealed formidable new worlds of acoustic textures that were impossible to achieve with acoustic instruments, but it has been suggested that the diminished audiences for 'serious' computer music may be associated with an over zealous enthusiasm for precise and elaborate formalisms (Garnett 2001). Eduardo R. Miranda has suggested that part of the problem for listeners is that these formal systems 'lack the cultural references that we normally rely on when appreciating music' (Miranda 2003, p. 1). Although lacking the hallmarks of any particular catalogued musical tradition, the organisational structures of the dynamics of some evolutionary and adaptive systems bear strong similarities with the morphologies and structures that appear across all musical styles. The behaviours of some models have an inherent liveliness that has been shown to effectively mimic certain musical phenomenon, and exhibit complex structural dynamics that have been shown to be musically effective at all levels, from timbral morphologies to long-term structure at the level of musical form. In addition, the responsive nature of some adaptive systems offers an appealing mechanism for interactive performances allowing us to integrate the aesthetically challenging possibilities of computer music within the traditions of human performance practice.

1.5.1. Generating Structure in Time

Superficially, an evolving population of digital genes may seem to have little in common with our concept of musical form. But this model of artificial evolution shares with music a very fundamental characteristic: it is a temporal process. That it exists in time is one of the few uncontroversially universal features of music, yet consideration of dynamic form is rarely a primary consideration in computer-assisted composition. A common problem reported by practitioners of computer-based approaches (such as rule-based systems and neural networks as well as some evolutionary systems) is that despite successfully creating specific elements, there is a lack of overall musical energy or flow. For example, while discussing constraint-based system for harmonisation Christoph Lischka notes: 'The harmonisations are (in a sense) correct. But they are not exciting. What is lacking is some kind of global coherency' (Lischka 1991, p. 237). This makes the creation of long term or hierarchical structure a real difficulty. It seems likely that these problems are associated with the fact that time-based structures are rarely a primary focus, a tendency that perhaps has deeper roots in the music theoretic principles from which many models are derived (for a discussion of the temporal paradox in musicology see Cook 1990).

There are myriad time-based models that could be used for generating music, and many composers have explored their possibilities. The fact that a process is formally defined as a function of time does not in any way ensure that the musical outcome will be engaging, nor even that the temporal dynamics can be appreciated by the listener. Just as the application of EAs demands careful formulation of representation schemes, fitness functions and operators, this approach relies on the inspired selection and implementation of a suitable model and the definition of a meaningful mapping from numerical output to musical space.

The implementation of a model is often motivated by an intuition that it shares an organisational structure with a particular musical phenomenon or effect. The musical success of the approach is then dependent upon mapping the numerical output into a suitable musical domain in a way that preserves the desired structure. In Chapter 8 Miranda describes various implementations of cellular automata (CA) models for musical applications. In one of these, *Chaosynth*, a chemical oscillator CA is used to parameterise a granular synthesis engine (Miranda 2000). The dynamics of the chemical oscillator CA rule, as it evolves from a random state to sustained oscillation, bear strong resemblance to the morphological evolution of sound in the voice and many acoustic instruments: their partials converge from a random distribution to a stable pattern of oscillation. The mappings used to parameterise the granular synthesis engine preserve these characteristics and so the sounds produced similarly bear these morphological features, capturing the *global* spectral evolution of an acoustic note onset. Using a complex dynamic model allows the description of the changes in amplitude of multiple frequencies over time as well as the relations between them. These multiple levels of related dynamic structures are not peculiar to the timbral level, indeed almost all polyphonic music can be conceived as a complex of distinct, but interdependent voices weaving spatio-temporal forms at many levels. The use of complex dynamic systems enables the generation of these sorts of rich spatio-temporal structures seen at all levels of musical organisation.

Besides modelling musical form, specific musical phenomenon can be modelled using time-based systems, which would be difficult or impossible to capture using other approaches. Tim Blackwell's work on Swarm music (presented in Chapter 9) is motivated by the similarity between the self-organisation exhibited by the swarm algorithm and the self-organisation, or structure that emerges in improvised ensembles of live musicians:

The development of higher level musical structure arises from interactions at lower levels, and we propose here that the self-organisation of social animals provides a very suggestive analogy. (Blackwell and Young 2004, p. 137).

The swarm system used by Blackwell is an extension of Craig Reynolds' *Boids* algorithm (Reynolds 1987) which mimics the behaviour of a flocking birds. In this simple model, Reynolds shows that the global organisation of the flock can arise from simple rules which determine the movements of each bird relative to each other, without the need of any leader or pre-devised plan. The model is based on three simple principles: separation, alignment and cohesion. Separation means each bird must steer to avoid bumping into each other or any other object in the environment. Alignment keeps each individual moving in a similar path by taking the average heading of local flockmates. Cohesion keeps the flock together as each bird steers towards the average position of local flockmates. Blackwell has employed a similar algorithm to parameterise a granular synthesis engine, creating an eerily lifelike movement of sound swarming through time.

1.5.2. Integrating the Interactive Machine

In the *Boids* algorithm outlined above, note that the future position of each agent is described in terms of the current state of the other agents: the agents are sensitive to, and respond to changes in their environment. This is obvious when we consider what happens to a real, or simulated flock when it encounters an obstacle: the flock will part to avoid it before rejoining. In addition to mapping the behaviour of the flock into musical space then, we can apply the mapping in reverse so that sound events (created by live musicians) in the real world can be mapped into the virtual world to influence the behaviour of the flock. This provides a novel and interesting mechanism for interaction which extends the classic approaches to interactive music.

Traditional approaches to interactive music are based on models of interaction derived from existing musical practices, either allowing performers to control aspects of a predetermined score (Machover 1991) mimicking interpersonal relations in performance (Winkler 1991), or extending the performer's relation with their instrument (Machover and Chung 1989). The interesting thing about the use of adaptive systems in an interactive context is that the system amalgamates the characteristics of all these categories, creating at once a responsive composition and a dynamic, behaving instrument, which in performance can feel like another, albeit digital, performance partner. Other practitioners have been exploring adaptive models in improvised performance (Eldridge 2005; Bown and Lexer 2006) and performances made with systems such as homeostatic networks and continuous time recurrent neural networks demonstrate the success of the approach in integrating an experimental machine aesthetic within the rich traditions of live performance.

1.6. Concluding Remarks

In addition to providing a short introduction to evolutionary computing techniques, this chapter has described a variety of ways in which they can be used in musical settings, highlighting a number of important issues that arise. At a technical level it is crucial to appreciate the significance of appropriately designed components for any EA-based system, but in an artistic endeavour such as musical composition it is also imperative to engage fully with the wider community:

In order to assess the usefulness of [evolutionary computing] in musically creative tasks however, more general discussion of the musical output needs to be conducted. It needs to be recognised that the task is not simply one of computer science, but must include discussion in the relevant domain. This will require the skills and engagement of the wider musical academic community, and an increased number of interdisciplinary research projects. (Gartland-Jones and Copley 2003, p. 54)

Keeping the composer and/or performer firmly in the loop is one way to help encourage this. The development of tools to allow composers to sympathetically exploit appropriate properties of adaptive algorithms as well as the integration of adaptive systems within live performances, are very promising directions.

It is early, yet there is significant potential for exciting and fruitful developments of evolutionary and adaptive computing in music.

References

Back, T., Hoffmeister, F. and Schwefel, H. (1991). A survey of evolution strategies. In R. Belew and L. Booker (Eds.), *Proceedings of the 4th International Conference on GAs*. Morgan Kaufmann, San Fransisco, CA, pp. 2–9.

Back, T. and Schwefel, H.-P. (1993). An overview of evolutionary algorithms for parameter optimization. *Evolutionary Computation* **1**(1): 1–23.

Bagley, J. (1967). *The Behaviour of Adaptive Systems that Employ Genetic and Correlation Algorithms*. PhD Thesis, University of Michigan.

Beer, R.D. (1990). *Intelligence as Adaptive Behaviour: An Experiment in Computational Neuroethology*. Academic Press, New York.

Bentley, P.J. (Ed.) (1999). *Evolutionary Design by Computers*. Academic Press, London.

Biles, J. (1994). Genjam: A genetic algorithm for generating jazz solos. In *Proceedings of the International Computer Music Conference*. Aarhus, Denmark. pp. 131–137. Available online at http://www.it.rit.edu/-jab/Genjam94/Paper.html.

Bilotta, E., Miranda, E. R., Pantano, P. and Todd, P. (Eds.) (2001). *Proceedings of the ALMMA 2001: Artificial Life Models for Musical Applications Workshop, ECAL 2001*.

Blackwell, T. and Young, M. (2004). Self-organised music. *Organised Sound* **9**(2): 137–150.

Bown, O. and Lexer, S. (2006). Continuous-time recurrent neural networks for generative and interactive musical performance. In F. Rothlauf et al. (Eds.), *Applications of Evolutionary Computing: Proceedings EvoWorkshops 2006*, LNCS 3907, Springer, Berlin, pp. 652–664.

Burton, A.R. and Vladimirova, T. (1999). Generation of musical sequences with genetic techniques. *Computer Music Journal* **23**(4): 59–73.

Collins, R. and Jefferson, D. (1991). Selection in massively parallel genetic algorithms. In Belew, R. and Booker, L. (Eds.), *Proceedings of the 4th International Conference on GAs*. Morgan Kaufmann, San Fransisco, CA, pp. 249–256.

Cook, N. (1990). *Music, Imagination, and Culture*. Clarendon Press, Oxford.

Cope, D. (2000). *The Algorithmic Composer*. A-R Editions, Wisconsin.

Dahlstedt, P. (2001). Creating and exploring huge parameter spaces: Interactive evolution as a tool for sound generation. In *Proceedings of the International Computer Music Conference*. Habana, Cuba.

Darwin, C. (1859). *The Origin of Species*. John Murray, London.

Davis, L. (1990). *The Handbook of Genetic Algorithms*. Van Nostrand Reinhold, Princeton, NJ.

Eiben, A.E. and Smith, J.E. (2003). *Introduction to Evolutionary Computing*. Springer, Berlin.

Eldridge, A.C. (2005). Cyborg dancing: Generative systems for man machine musical improvisation. In *Proceedings of the Third Iteration*. Melbourne, Australia.

Fisher, R.A. (1930). *The Genetical Theory of Natural Selection*. Clarendon Press, Oxford.

Fogel, L.J., Owens, A.J. and Walsh, M.J. (1966). *Artificial Intelligence through Simulated Evolution*. John Wiley, New York.

Garcia, R. (2001). Growing sound synthesizers using evolutionary methods. In E. Bilotta, E. R. Miranda, P. Pantano, and P. M. Todd (Eds.), *Proceedings of ALMMA 2001 Workshop on Artificial Life Models for Musical Applications*, Cosenza, Italy. Editoriale Bios, pp. 99–107.

Gartland-Jones, A. (2003). Music box: A real-time algorithmic composition system incorporating a distributed interactive genetic algorithm. In G. Raidl et al. (Eds.), *Proceedings of the EvoWorkshops/EuroGP 2003*. Springer, Berlin, pp. 490–501.

Gartland-Jones, A. and Copley, P. (2003). The suitability of genetic algorithms for musical composition. *Contemporary Music Review* 22(3): 43–55.

Gartland-Jones, A. and Copley, P. (2005). Musical form and algorithmic solutions. In *Proceedings of the Creativity and Cognition Conference, Goldsmiths College, London*. ACM, pp. 226–231.

Garnett, G.E. (2001). The aesthetics of interactive computer music. *Computer Music Journal* 25(1): 21–33.

Goldberg, D. (1989). *Genetic Algorithms*. Addison-Wesley, Reading, MA.

Grefenstette, J. (Ed.) (1987). *Proceedings of the 2nd International Conference on GAs*. Lawrence Erlbaum, Hillsdale, NJ.

Haldane, J.B.S. (1932). *The Causes of Evolution*, Longman, Green, London.

Harvey, I. (1992). Species adaptation genetic algorithms: A basis for a continuing SAGA. In F.J. Varela and P. Bourgine (Eds.), *Proceedings of the 1st European Conference on Artificial Life*. MIT Press/Bradford Books, Cambridge, MA, pp. 346–354.

Hillis, W.D. (1990). Co-evolving parasites improve simulated evolution as an optimization procedure. *Physica D* 42: 228–234.

Hodgson, P. (1999). Modelling cognition in musical improvisation through evolution. In A. Patrizio, G.A. Wiggins and H. Pain (Eds.), *Proceedings of the AISB'99 Symposium on Musical Creativity*. SSAISB, Brightom, pp. 15–19.

Hodgson, P. (2002). Artificial evolution, music and methodology. In *Proceedings of the 7th International Conference on Music Perception and Cognition*. Sydney, pp. 244–248.

Holland, J. (1962). Outline for a logical theory of adaptive systems. *Journal of the Association of Computing Machinery* 3: 297–314.

Holland, J. (1966). Universal spaces: A basis for studies of adaptation. In E. Caianiello (Ed.), *Automata Theory*. Academic Press, New York, pp. 218–231.

Holland, J. (1975). *Adaptation in Natural and Artificial Systems*. University of Michigan Press, Ann Arbor, MI.

Horner, A. and Goldberg, D. (1991). Genetic algorithms and computer assisted music composition. In R. Belew and L. Booker (Eds.), *Proceedings of the 4th International Conference on GAs*. Morgan Kaufmann, San Fransisco, CA, pp. 437–441.

Husbands, P. (1993). An ecosystems model for integrated production planning. *International Journal of Computer Integrated Manufacturing* 6(1/2): 74–86.

Huxley, J.S. (1942). *Evolution: The Modern Synthesis*. Allen and Unwin, London.

Jacob, B. (1996). Algorithmic composition as a model of creativity. *Organised Sound* **1**(3): 157–165.

Jakobi, N. (1998). Evolutionary robotics and the radical envelope of noise hypothesis. *Adaptive Behaviour* **6**: 325–368.

Johnson, C. (1999). Exploring the sound-space of synthesis algorithms using in interactive genetic algorithms. In A. Patrizio, G. Wiggins and H. Pain (Eds.), *Proceedings of the AISB'99 Symposium on AI and Musical Creativity*. SSAISB, Brighton.

Juillé, H. and Pollack, J.B. (1996). Co-evolving intertwined spirals. In *Proceedings of the Fifth Annual Conference on Evolutionary Programming*. MIT Press, Cambridge, MA, pp. 461–468.

Keller, H. (1987). *Criticism*. Faber & Faber, London.

Koza, J.R. (1992). *Genetic Programming: On the Programming of Computers by Means of Natural Selection*. MIT Press, Cambridge, MA.

Langton, C. (1995). *Artificial Life: An Overview*. MIT Press, Cambridge, MA.

Lischka, C. (1991). Understanding music cognition: A connectionist view. In G. De Poli, A. Piccialli and C. Roads (Eds.), *Representations of Musical Signals*. MIT Press, Cambridge, MA, pp. 417–445.

Machover, T. (1991). *Program Notes for the International Computer Music Conference*. International Computer Music Association, San Fransisco.

Machover, T. and Chung, J. (1989). Hyperinstruments: Musically intelligent and interactive performance and creativity systems. In *Proceedings of the 1989 International Computer Music Conference*. International Computer Music Association, San Francisco, pp. 186–190.

Mandelis, J. (2001). Genophone: An evolutionary approach to sound synthesis and performance. In E. Bilotta et al. (Eds.). Proceedings of ALMMA Workshop, pp. 37–50. Available online at http://www.cogs.susx.ac.uk/users/jamesm/Papers/ECAL(2001)ALMMAMandelis.ps.

Mandelis, J. (2002). Adaptive hyperinstruments: Applying evolutionary techniques to sound synthesis and performance. In *Proceedings of the NIME 2002: New Interfaces for Musical Expression*. Dublin, Ireland, pp. 192–193. Available online at http://www.cogs.susx.ac.uk/users/jamesm/Papers/NIME(2002)Mandelis.pdf.

Mandelis, J. and Husbands, P. (2003). Musical interaction with artificial life forms: Sound synthesis and performance mappings. *Contemporary Music Review* **22**(3): 69–77.

McCormack, J. (2003). Evolving sonic ecosystems. *Kybernetes: The International Journal of Systems & Cybernetics* **32**(1/2): 184–202.

Michalewicz, Z. and Fogel, D.B. (2004). *How to Solve It: Modern Heuristics*. Springer, Berlin.

Miranda, E. R. (2000). The art of rendering sounds from emergent behaviour: Cellular automata granular synthesis. In *Proceedings of the 26th EUROMICRO Conference*. Maastricht, The Netherlands (published by IEEE Computer Society).

Miranda, E.R. (2003). On the music of emergent behaviour: What can evolutionary computation bring to the musician? *Leonardo* **36**(1): 55–59.

Mitchell, M. (1996). *An Introduction to Genetic Algorithms*. MIT Press, Cambridge, MA.

Morris, R.O. (1922). *Contrapuntal Technique In The Sixteenth Century*. Oxford University Press, Oxford.

Mulder, A. (1994). Virtual musical instruments: Accessing the sound synthesis universe as a performer. In *Proceedings of the First Brazilian Symposium on Computer Music*. Caxambu, Brazil, pp. 243–250.

Pollack, J., Bedau, M., Husbands, P., Ikegami T. and Watson R. (Eds.) (2004). *Artificial Life IX: Proceedings of the Ninth International Conference on the Simulation and Synthesis of Living Systems.* MIT Press, Cambridge, MA.

Pressing, J. (1990). Cybernetic issues in interactive performance systems. *Computer Music Journal* **14**(1): 12–25.

Rechenberg, I. (1965). *Cybernetic Solution Path of an Experimental Problem.* Royal Aircraft Establishment Translation No. 1122, Ministry of Aviation, Farnborough.

Reynolds, C.W. (1987). Flocks, herds, and schools: A distributed behavioral model. *Computer Graphics* **21**(4): 25–34.

Rosen, C. (1980). *Sonata Forms.* Norton, New York.

Rovan, J.B., Wanderley, M.M., Dubnov, S. and Depalle, P. (1997). Instrumental gestural mapping strategies as expressivity determinants in computer music performance. Presented at *Kansei—The Technology of Emotion Workshop.*

Schaal, S., Ijspeert, A., Billard, A., Vijayakumar, S., Hallam, J. and Meyer, J.-A. (2004). *From animals to animats 8: Proceedings of the Eighth International Conference on the Simulation of Adaptive Behavior.* MIT Press, Cambridge, MA.

Schmitt, L.M. (2001). Theory of genetic algorithms. *Theoretical Computer Science* **259**: 1–61.

Schoenberg, A. (1967). In G. Strang (Ed.), *Fundamentals of Musical Composition.* Faber & Faber, London.

Sims, K. (1991). Artificial evolution for computer graphics. In *Proceedings of the Siggraph '91.* pp. 319–328.

Sims, K. (1994). Evolving 3D morphology and behavior by competition. In R. Brooks and P. Maes (Eds.), *Proceedings Artificial Life IV.* MIT Press, Cambridge, MA, pp. 28–39.

Singh, R.S. and Krimbas, C.B. (2000). *Evolutionary Genetics: From Molecules to Morphology.* Cambridge University Press, Cambridge.

Straus, J.N. (1990). *Remaking the Past.* Harvard Press, Cambridge, MA.

Todd, S. and Latham, W. (1992). *Evolutionary Art and Computers.* Academic Press, New York.

Turing, A.M. (1950). Computing machinery and intelligence. *Mind* **LIX**(236): 433–460.

Vose, M.D. (1999). *The Simple Genetic Algorithm: Foundations and Theory.* MIT Press, Cambridge, MA.

Werner, G.M. and Todd, P.M. (1997). Too many love songs: Sexual selection and the evolution of communication. In P. Husbands and I. Harvey (Eds.), *Fourth European Conference on Artificial Life.* MIT Press/Bradford Books, Cambridge, MA, pp. 434–443.

Werner, G. and Todd, P. (1998). Frankensteinian methods for evolutionary music composition. In N. Griffith and P. Todd (Eds.), *Musical Networks: Parallel Distributed Perception and Performance.* MIT Press/Bradford Books, Cambridge, MA, pp. 313–339.

Wessel, D. and Wright, M. (2000). Problems and prospects for intimate musical control of computers. *Computer Music Journal* **26**(3): 11–22.

Wiggins, G., Papadopoulos, G., Phon-Amnuaisuk, S. and Tuson, A. (1998). Evolutionary methods for musical composition. In *Proceedings of the CASYS98 Workshop on Anticipation, Music and Cognition.* Liege, Belgium. Available online at http://www.soi.city.ac.uk/-geraint/papers/CASYS98a.pdf.

Winkler, T. (1991). Interactive signal processing for acoustic instruments. In *Proceedings for the 1991 International Computer Music Conference.* Computer Music Association, San Francisco, CA.

Woolf, S. (1999). *Sound Gallery: An Interactive Artificial Life Artwork*. MSc Thesis, School of Cognitive and Computing Sciences, University of Sussex, UK.

Wright, A.H;, Vose, M.D.; De Jong, K.A.;nd Schmitt, L.M. (Eds.) (2005). *Foundations of Genetic Algorithms: 8th International Workshop, FOGA 2005*. Lecture Notes in Computer Science, Vol. 3469, Springer, New York.

Yee-King, M. (2000). *AudioServe—An Online System to Evolve Modular Audio Synthesis Circuits*. MSc Thesis, School of Cognitive and Computing Sciences, University of Sussex, UK.

2
Evolutionary Computation for Musical Tasks

JOHN A. BILES

2.1. Introduction

If the preceding chapter was an introduction to evolutionary computation (EC) for musicians, this chapter is intended as an introduction to music as a problem domain for EC researchers. Since we cannot hope to provide even a bare-bones treatise on music appreciation, much less music theory, we assume that the reader is at least somewhat familiar with music, if not as a producer, at least as a consumer. We will start by trying to define some musical terms to work with, including 'music' itself, which will lead us to a brief excursion into human–computer interaction as a metaphor for musical performance. We will then conduct an informal task analysis of music to define the tasks musicians perform and survey how EC has been applied to facilitate (or obfuscate, in some cases) the performance of those tasks. We will then summarize the various approaches that have been taken in representation, fitness and genetic operators.

2.2. What Is Music?

Everybody knows what music is. That is not to say that everybody agrees on what music is. Rather, everybody has a personal conception of what music is, and that conception informs how they process the sounds they experience in their lives. Since one person's conception is likely very different from another's, this leads to disagreement over whether or not a given aural experience is good music, or even whether or not it's music at all. A common expression of derision is 'That's not music; it's *noise!*' While we might agree that 'noise' is the antithesis of 'music', we probably would not agree on which aural experiences belong to each category. Another commonly heard expression is 'I may not know music, but I know what I like'. Often, people who say this really mean '...I like what I know'. The implication is that people have differing conceptions and opinions about music, and while they are often deeply committed to these beliefs, they may find it difficult to explain or even understand them. This clearly marks music as a subjective domain, but it is *emphatically* subjective, with belief systems rising to almost religious levels. This is one reason why music is a difficult domain for computational methods. Not only is a clear operational definition of 'good' music hard to come by, a definition of 'music' is often arbitrary at best.

However, there are two defining characteristics of music on which most would agree. First, music is an aural medium – it must be heard to be experienced fully. Second, music is a temporal medium – it must be experienced in real time. For our purposes, then, we will operationally define music as *temporally organized sound*. This rather inclusive definition certainly covers the typical music we hear on the radio, which is not a bad definition of sounds that have acquired some societal consensus as 'music', but it also includes bird songs, babbling brooks, even the ambient sounds of daily life.

To help focus this rather nebulous definition of music as temporally organized sound, we will examine four key properties or aspects of music – pitch, rhythm, timbre and form. For each aspect we will define some standard terms, primarily for the non-musician. An in-depth or even a cursory treatment of music theory is clearly beyond the scope of this book and so our discussion is intended to provide operational definitions of musical terms that we will use in surveying EC-based music systems.

2.2.1. Musical Terminology

Pitch is to ear, as frequency is to oscilloscope. This is a bit oversimplified, but the point is that *pitch* is a perceptual notion, not a physical notion (Pierce 1999). Not all sounds have a specific perceivable pitch (striking a crash cymbal, for example), but we usually can determine 'higher' pitch versus 'lower' (striking a splash versus a crash cymbal, for example). In the realm of traditional western musical instruments, like piano or trumpet, pitch has been well codified as the notes available on a piano, specifically 12 equally spaced *pitch classes* per octave. When pitches are arranged in a horizontal sequence, one sounding after another, we refer to this as a *melody*, and we refer to the difference in adjacent pitches in a melody as a *horizontal interval*. A melodic theme or idea that serves as a seed for later development is called a *motif*. When pitches are arranged vertically, so that two or more pitches sound simultaneously, we refer to this as *harmony*, and we refer to the difference between pitches in harmony as a *vertical interval*.

Rhythm essentially refers to timing, both how long sound events last and when they are scheduled to occur. The timing and length of each pitch in a melody defines that melody's rhythm. We are used to thinking of rhythm as 'the beat' of a piece of music, and it is true that almost all of the music heard on the radio has an easily discernable beat that we often track by tapping a foot or some other appendage. Other rhythms, however, are too slow to tap one's foot to, like the rhythm of day and night, or too irregular, like the frantic cascades of sound produced by an avant garde jazz group in full flight. Music, then, may be *beat-oriented* or *pulsed*, but it need not be. If it is beat-oriented, then it usually exhibits a *meter*, which is basically the number of stressed and unstressed beats in a repeating pattern. For example, both Sousa marches and disco music are typically 'in four', meaning that there

TABLE 2.1. Musical time scales (after Roads 2001).

Time scale	Time period	Musical examples
Infinite	Infinity	Ideal sine waves of Fourier theory
Supra	Days, months, years, centuries	Concert, album, musical style
Macro	Minutes to hours	Individual composition
Meso	Seconds to minutes	Phrase structures, sections of a piece
Sound object	Fraction of a second to seconds	Note, discernable sound event
Micro	Milliseconds	Sound particle, grain
Sample	Microseconds (sampling rate)	Individual digital sample
Subsample	Nanoseconds	Events above Nyquist frequency
Infinitesimal	0	Ideal impulse function

are four beats per repeating pattern, and those beats happen at a *tempo* of around 110 beats per minute. The span of the repeating pattern is referred to as a *measure* or *bar*. While the 'arrhythmic' music of the avant garde jazz group has no fixed pulse, it definitely has rhythm in that events are organized in time. In other words, even arrhythmic music is rhythmic.

Timbre refers to the quality, identity or origin of a sound. We are used to thinking of the timbres of traditional orchestral instruments as the colours available in the palette of the composer. While this evolving palate has stood composers in good stead for centuries, it is a tiny fraction of the timbres we hear every day, and a smaller fraction still of the possible (or impossible) sounds that can be realized through synthesis techniques. Timbre space, then, is indeed vast.

Form refers to the organization of sounds into higher-level structures. These structures may be prescribed, as with a 12-bar blues or sonata form, which usually leads to a top–down method of composition. Chapter 1 in this volume provided an excellent discussion of form as it relates to EC-based composition systems, using sonata form as an example. Many composers ignore standard forms and build structure bottom-up from lower-level components. Some composers even allow structures to emerge from random events or from interactions among lots of low-level agents, as in cellular automata music (see Chapter 8).

Regardless of how planned or unplanned a compositional form is, musical structures tend to be hierarchical. It is easy to recognize that a specific piece is made up of sections or choruses, which are made up of phrases which in turn are made up of notes. However, the temporal hierarchy extends beyond this in both directions. Roads (2001) describes a comprehensive model of time scales in music, which range from the infinitesimally brief to the infinitely long. His model defines nine time scales for music, which are listed in Table 2.1.

The macro, meso and sound object time scales are familiar to traditional musicians. The macro time scale represents the form or architecture of an individual piece. The meso time scale includes motifs, traditional phrase structures, and melodic, harmonic and rhythmic development. The sound object time scale deals with the individual notes or sound events that can be perceived individually.

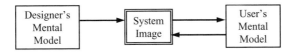

FIGURE 2.1. Donald Norman's model for user interaction.

The micro time scale is the realm of transients, granular synthesis and other phenomena that occur below the threshold of individual perception (see Chapters 8 and 9 in this volume). The sample and subsample time scales reflect the dominance of digital audio representations, in that they exist at and above the boundary of frequencies that can be represented digitally. At the extremes are the ideal mathematical notions of no duration and infinite duration, which appear in musically useful theoretical models. Finally, the supra time scale extends beyond the length of an individual composition to include a concert, a stylistic period or a career. EC has been applied at time scales ranging from the supra down to the sample level.

One ambiguity of form/organization is whose organization are we talking about – the composer's or the listener's? Composers often invest considerable time and effort in constructing complex structures that interrelate in subtle and elegant ways. These structures, when grasped in their totality, can be stunning, but do listeners grasp the same deep structures as the composer? Probably not, which, believe it or not, motivates a brief discussion of human–computer interface (HCI) design.

2.2.2. Music as HCI

Donald Norman's *Design of Everyday Things* (Norman 1988) is one of those books that keeps cropping up in surprising contexts. Among other things, he proposes an elegant model of human interaction with technology, which serves as a useful model for how listeners experience music. Norman's model focuses on the designer of a system, the user of a system, and the system image that the designer creates and the user accesses (see Fig. 2.1).

The *designer* of a system works from a mental model of the system, which guides the construction of the *system image*. The system image is accessed by the *user*, who forms his or her own mental model of the system, which guides how the user will use the system. In the context of interface design, this simple model elegantly highlights where many interfaces go wrong – the mental model of the user is often inadequate to enable access to the functionality intended by the designer, usually because the system image is not transparent enough to show clearly what functionality is available and how to access it.

One misinterpretation of Norman's model of interaction is the contention that the mental model of the designer and the mental model of the user should be the same. In all but the simplest systems, that goal is not just unrealistic – it is pathological. The mental model of the designer includes all kinds of internal details that are at best irrelevant to the system's use. If the user has to understand all those details in order to use the system, then the system is either trivial or its interface is inadequate. A user-centered design seeks to help users build mental models that facilitate the use of the system to perform the tasks they are trying to perform.

Applying Norman's model to music, the designer is the composer, the users are the audience and the system image is the piece being performed, with all of its accompanying material. This includes the actual performance of the piece, the title and any program notes, the venue (concert hall, coffeehouse, elevator), the appearance and behavior of any performers, the review in last Sunday's newspaper, even the score, if it is available – in short anything perceivable by the audience. An individual listener uses the system image to augment his or her prior musical knowledge and experience to yield a mental model that informs how he or she processes the piece, and that model evolves over the course of the piece. The mental model of the composer includes the deep structure of the piece in all its levels and subtlety, underlying melodic motifs and how they have been developed, and myriad other details that may or may not be perceived or even be perceivable by the audience. If the mental model of a listener is sufficiently rich, he or she will stay more or less engaged during the performance and, hopefully, will have something to say about the piece over coffee after the performance. If the mental model of a listener is not rich enough, then he might merely say, 'What was that?', implying that he simply 'did not get it'. In either case, each listener will likely come away with something different from what the composer intended. This is unavoidable and probably one reason why we enjoy music – it speaks (or sings) to us individually.

Norman's mental models have a lot to do with the 'organized' part of 'temporally organized sound'. The issue really becomes: whose organization are we considering? In standard musical genres, like jazz, for instance, a listener may understand that the tunes tend to include improvization, that the rhythm typically 'swings' and that the form is often theme–variations–theme. Another listener, without that knowledge, may not understand that the middle of the tune is improvized, or even what improvization is, in which case that listener will not 'get' that aspect of the performance. However, he or she may still find the performance enjoyable or even compelling. These listener mental models of improvization are discussed in detail in Chapter 7 in this volume.

In the case of random or emergent organization, the mental model of the composer operates at a meta-level – the specific form is not determined ahead of time but emerges spontaneously. If listeners understand this, then they will not be deterred by an 'aimless quality' and may focus on textures or other aspects of the music, or they may be stimulated by the whole concept of emergent or random structure. A listener who does not get the concept of random or emergent structure may simply zone out and find the music inaccessible. The goal of 'music appreciation', then, is to help initialize listeners' mental models sufficiently to enable them to 'get' at least some of what the composer is trying to convey.

Getting back to our definition of music as temporally organized sound, the organization can be intended by a composer and/or inferred by a listener. Sometimes the composer's and listener's organizations are similar; sometimes they are not. Sometimes one is missing entirely. Even ambient sounds can be organized. Bird songs are clearly organized by the bird/composer, and a babbling brook can be organized by a hiker/listener in the absence of any composer. Temporally organized sound, then, simply means sounds organized in time, regardless of who does the organizing.

2.3. Musical Tasks

Now that we have some basic concepts, let us describe what musicians do. This is basically an informal task analysis of music, and the goal is to identify musical tasks so that we can focus on how EC has been applied to facilitate the performance of those tasks. This will help us organize the ways in which EC has been applied to music and summarize the approaches researchers have taken in bending EC to fit the musical domain. Organizing the discussion around musical tasks instead of EC dimensions (Biles 2003; Burton and Vladimirova 1999) will hopefully convey a more musical perspective.

We shall start with a high-level task, specifically the task of producing a concert of original music performed by a high school jazz ensemble to feature a well-known guest artist. This is, in fact, an annual event at the high school attended by the author's son and daughter, which commissions six to eight original compositions per year for various performing groups to feature a visiting jazz artist (PMCP 2005). We will perform a decomposition of this high-level task and, along the way, point out subtasks to which EC has been applied. After that, we will summarize the numerous variations in genetic representation, genetic operators and fitness approaches that have been tried and we will present recommendations for which approaches work best in musical tasks.

The first level of decomposition of our concert task could be to break up the concert into individual commissioned pieces, which basically shifts us from the supra time scale of the concert to the macro time scale of individual compositions. Each piece, then, can be treated as an independent task, which can be decomposed further into four subtasks as summarized in Fig. 2.2. This decomposition highlights the different participants in the concert and reflects the tasks they perform.

In the first task, the composer composes the piece, producing a score. This score is submitted to the organizing committee of the concert, which selects the winning compositions for the concert.

The main performing group, a high school jazz ensemble in this case, then renders the score into sound: first in rehearsal and ultimately at the concert. The featured soloist also consults the score in preparing to perform the piece, but does

Composer, <u>composes</u> score
Performers <u>perform</u>, rendering score into sound
"*Sound* guy" <u>processes</u>/records sound
Audience <u>listens</u> to the concert, buys a CD

FIGURE 2.2. Very high-level musical task decomposition.

so separately before arriving at the high school a day or two before the event. The only time the soloist rehearses with the jazz ensemble is at a brief rehearsal the day before the concert. Since the soloists' improvizations will be spontaneous during the concert, this brief 'run through' is intended only to insure that the soloist and jazz ensemble are both literally 'on the same page' and that there is no confusion about how the piece will proceed in performance. This illustrates how the score, as an abstraction of the piece, is sufficient to enable a performance but is necessarily less detailed than the actual performance. In jazz, the details provided by the improvizers in real time are obvious, but even in non-improvizational genres, the interpretation of the performers adds content that cannot be notated completely. Only in computer-generated 'tape music', where the composer generates an audio 'tape', is there no interpretation because the composer generates all aspects of the piece, including the digital representation of the sound.

This brings up the issue of synthesis technology, which is an important domain in which EC has been applied, but which is not a part of our jazz concert scenario. Imagine that instead of a concert for jazz ensemble, we have a concert of electronic 'tape' music. In that case the rendering of the composer's score to sound will be done by digital synthesis, not human performers. As Chapters 3 and 4 in this volume will amply demonstrate, synthesis is a fertile domain for EC.

Returning to our jazz concert, the 'sound guy' processes the public performance by managing sound reinforcement and making a digital recording. Sound reinforcement includes microphone placement to capture sound produced by the ensemble and the soloists, application of sound processing effects like equalization, compression and reverberation, and mixing the resulting channels to yield balanced sound, both for the live audience and for the recording. In a tape piece, the 'sound guy' is often the composer, who can extend control of the piece to the actual sonic experience by diffusing the sound in the performance space.

In the final task in our scenario, the audience listens to the performance at the concert, responds with enthusiastic applause, and buys the locally produced CD, when it becomes available.

Each of the four tasks identified in this crude task decomposition (five if synthesis is included as a separate performance or processing task) is a domain in which EA has been applied. While the composition subtask is by far the most explored task area in which EC has been applied, the surface has at least been scratched in the others. We will continue our musical task analysis with the composition task.

2.3.1. Composition

Most of the EC applications that have been reported in the literature relate to the composition task. Some comprehensive systems have attempted to generate complete compositions (Jacob 1995, 1996), while many others have focused on compositional subtasks. Fig. 2.3 breaks down composition into several interacting subtasks that serve as useful categories of EC-based systems. The order of these subtasks is arbitrary and does not necessarily imply a 'waterfall model' of music

Generate melodic motifs/ideas
    Pitch sequences without rhythm
    Rhythm sequences without pitches
    Sequences with both pitch and rhythm
Develop (extend, enhance) melodic ideas
    Generate variations and countermelodies
    Combine melodic fragments into longer lines
Harmonize
    Generate harmony parts
    Generate chord changes
Arrange
    Define individual parts for specific performers
    Assign parts to instruments in the target ensemble
Structure
    Adhere to a given structure top-down
    Build or evolve a structure bottom-up
    Do both (inside-out)

FIGURE 2.3. Subtasks of composition.

design. A better model would be the star model from interface design (Hartson and Hix 1993), where these subtasks are iterated typically in opportunistic ways.

EC has been applied to *melody generation* more frequently than to any other musical task. In fact, GA-based melody generators are becoming a popular class project in EC and artificial intelligence courses (Milkie and Chestnutt 2001). The task essentially boils down to evolving populations of short, monophonic melodic fragments or motifs, which typically range from one to eight or so measures in length. This task breaks down further into generating pitch sequences and duration sequences. Some systems evolve both pitches and durations concurrently (Biles 1994; Jacob 1996; Marques et al. 2000), others evolve pitches and rhythm separately (Prerau 2001), and still others ignore rhythm entirely and only evolve pitch sequences (Ralley 1995; Johanson and Poli 1998). As we shall see when we summarize representation, fitness and operator choices, the proliferation of these systems has led to a wide diversity of EC techniques in melody generation.

Some systems evolve only rhythm sequences, usually one-measure percussion patterns that can be combined and looped to generate the drum part of a tune (Horowitz 1994; Burton 1998; Tokui and Iba 2000). Most of these systems are inspired by the ubiquitous drum machine – a MIDI-based device that stores digitally represented drum sounds and provides an interface to allow the 'programming' of one or more measures that can be looped and sequenced to provide a rhythmic foundation for a tune. While these systems do not really generate melody, in that the 'pitches' in their sequences map to different percussion instruments rather than different notes, their architectures tend to be similar to those used in simple melody generators.

Melodic development has the distinction of being the first musical domain to which EC was applied (Horner and Goldberg 1991). The specific task for this inaugural EC music system was thematic bridging, where an initial motif is morphed through a series of transforms into a target motif. Melodic development systems extend or enhance melodies by generating variations on a motif (Ralley 1995; Jacob 1995, 1996) or a rhythm pattern (Ariza 2002), combining motifs to create longer melodic lines (Jacob 1995, 1996), or generating melodic counterpoint (Polito et al. 1997). What all these systems have in common is that they start with motifs at their lowest level, rather than notes, and tend to build larger or higher level structures. This places them up the compositional hierarchy, relative to the simple melodic generators.

Harmonization is one compositional subtask that may be approached more productively with non-EC techniques. The classic task is to generate standard four-part harmony for soprano, alto, tenor and bass voices (SATB) for a given melody. The tricky part is that each of the four horizontal voices must be 'singable' as individual melodies and the vertical harmonies must make sense. This essentially reduces to a scheduling problem, which is made easier by the fact that there are well-codified rules for voice leading and harmonic progressions that can serve as convenient constraints. Consequently, SATB harmonization is one of the few musical tasks that can be productively considered an optimization problem. When the input to the system is both the melody to be harmonized and the chord changes to be navigated, the problem is relatively easy (Horner and Ayres 1995). However, when the input is only the melody to be harmonized, and the system must evolve the chords as well as the voice leading for SATB (McIntyre 1994), the problem is much more difficult, and other approaches, like rule-bases or neural networks, seem to be preferable (Phon-Amnuaisuk and Wiggins 1999).

Arranging a tune typically involves assigning parts to instruments in an ensemble and usually generating or developing those parts. Aside from the aspects of this task covered by melodic development and harmonization, EC has not been used to attack this task directly, but arranger components have appeared in some composition systems (Jacob 1995).

The structuring task is probably the most difficult compositional task to get a handle on, as described in Chapter 1 in this volume. Most EC-based composition systems are very low level and seldom rise above the 'phrase' level. However, some systems have gone all the way to full-blown compositions (Jacob 1996), which has necessitated their working up the compositional hierarchy all the way to the root of the tree (see also Chapter 6). Most of these are collaborative systems that allow (or require) the user to either perform the higher-level structuring by hand (Unemi 2002) or serve as the fitness function for an IGA 'Arranger' (Jacob 1995, 1996). The most exciting work in this area is the emergent systems using communicating agents, Cellular Automata or swarms, where compelling forms can emerge from simple elements (Gartland-Jones 2003; Gartland-Jones and Copley 2003). Cellular Automata and swarms will be discussed in more detail in Chapters 8 and 9, respectively.

2.3.2. Performance

The expressive performance of a score is an ongoing research area in musicology and the psychology of music (Gabrielsson 1999), and it has proven to be a difficult task for computers (Widmer and Goebl 2004). Some researchers have used EC to attack aspects of this task; an example is presented in Chapter 5.

Grachten et al. (2004) used a genetic algorithm to optimize parameter values in the cost function for a performance annotation system based on edit distance. The edit distance between a source (score) and target (performance) sequence of notes is the sequence of edit operations that generates the target from the source with minimum cost. The set of available edit operations include insertion and deletion of notes as well as transformation and ornamentation operations that represent how notes could be performed, and each operation has an associated cost. The GA was used to find parameter settings for the cost function that yielded the most accurate annotations of jazz ballad performances.

Madsen and Widmer (2005, 2006) studied performance styles of 12 different pianists performing the same Schubert piano piece. They first used a self-organizing map algorithm to extract 25 performance templates, each of which encodes a two-dimensional, loudness-tempo trajectory for a short performance segment. A specific performance is then represented by a sequence of these templates, and an evolutionary algorithm is used to evolve approximate matches of subsequences of the performances, both to examine stylistic tendencies of an individual performer and to look for similarities among performers.

In addition to studying how music is performed by musicians, EC has impacted the audience's experience of performances. Biles and Eign (1995) coined the term 'audience-mediated performance' to refer to a performance in which the content is directly influenced by the audience. In EC music performances, this usually takes the form of the audience serving as a collective fitness function for an interactive genetic algorithm. This 'fitness as performance' concept has been used in live concert settings (see the author's chapter on *GenJam* in this volume) and on the Internet, where websites appear from time to time that allow visitors to rate individuals in a population of melodic fragments, which evolves over time under the guidance of this online audience. The first of these web-evolved systems by Putnam (1996) appeared in 1994 and was widely recognized, as evidenced by the large number of links to his website that persisted long after the site was deleted.

Audience-mediated performance is a natural goal for sound installations. The Sound Gallery (Woolf and Yee-King 2003) uses sensors to track the movements of audience members in a sound space. Each corner in the space contains a separately evolving population of evolvable hardware specifications, which are used to drive a loudspeaker. As audience members cluster around one speaker, the fitness of its current hardware specification increases. Periodically, the best individuals from one corner (island) migrate to another, and individuals age and eventually die out in order to avoid convergence.

Similarly, the Hewlett-Packard Disc Jockey (Graham-Rowe 2001) uses biofeedback units worn by clubbers in a disco to provide ongoing fitness for a GA-based DJ that selects, sequences and mixes dance tracks. The HPDJ apparently passed a "Turing test" for about a third of the audience, who thought the DJ was a human. It was not reported, however, what proportion of the audience believed that the DJ was a musical performer.

2.3.3. Processing

It is rare these days for a musical performance to be exclusively acoustic. Many instruments are electronic and make use of synthesis technology, and even performances by acoustic instruments are likely to be amplified to fill the performance space. Audio processing, then, is a significant task in creating a musical experience, and EC has played a role in this task. We will briefly mention two domains in which EC has been applied to audio processing – mixing and synthesis.

Mixing includes the application of audio effects like equalization and reverberation. Both of these are delay-based effects that are implemented with filters. Filter design, then, is a foundation of audio signal processing, and it has been accomplished successfully with EC (Sharman and Esparcia-Alcazar 2003). Reverberation has also been approached with EC, specifically the optimization of reverb parameters to match the characteristics of a specific room (Mrozek and Wakefield 1996).

EC has been applied extensively in the synthesis domain, as amply demonstrated by other chapters in this volume. Chapter 3 focuses on EC applications to evolve optimal parameter settings to match target sounds for a variety of synthesis methods, and Chapter 4 looks at EC as a tool in the search for interesting timbres. We shall divert discussion on EC applied in the synthesis domain to those chapters.

2.3.4. Listening

Except for musicology, which will be covered in Chapter 10, the listening task has not received much direct attention from EC researchers, probably because the emphasis in EC music applications has been on generating music, not listening to it. Federman (2003) used a learning classifier system (LCS) to predict the next pitch is a melodic sequence. Her LCS used a GA to learn new classification rules, and the system was tested on simple nursery tunes and chorales. While this is a relatively primitive form of listening, it is a successful attempt to model listener expectations.

Some composition systems have included coevolved listeners that serve as evolving fitness agents. Jacob's composition system contains an 'ear' module, which is an interactive genetic algorithm that evolves a population of filters to judge the harmonic suitability of melodic material produced by a 'composer' module, which is also implemented as a GA (Jacob 1995, 1996). The composed material that survives the ear is then grouped together by an 'arrange' module (yet another GA), which produces actual compositions.

Similarly, Todd and Werner (1999) focused on the creator–critic loop by coevolving male singers and female critics in a system inspired by birdsongs. Each male 'sings' a 32-note song, which a set of females critique, based on the horizontal intervals used in the song. Each female then selects the male with the best intervals and the pair survives to the next generation. 'Best' in this case was defined in three different ways: local transition preferences, which scored each horizontal interval in the song and computed a sum; global transition preferences, which compared the state-transition table of the song of the male to a similar table representing the expectations of the female; and surprise preference, which rewards songs that begin by meeting expectations and then violate those expectations, thereby surprising the female. The most interesting, musically, was the surprise preference, demonstrating that variety is the spice of artificial as well as real life. This work will be discussed in more detail in Chapter 10.

2.4. Evolutionary Tools and Techniques

Now that we have described musical tasks to which EC has been applied, let us survey the wide variety of EC tools and techniques that have been tried in EC-based systems. This summary represents a compendium of approaches across scores of studies. We will organize this discussion around EC issues, rather than musical issues, specifically representation, fitness and genetic operators.

2.4.1. Representation Schemes

As every EC practitioner knows, the design of a genetic representation (genotype) and its mapping into the actual problem domain (phenotype) is critical to the efficacious use of EC. This is certainly true in representing music. Two representational dimensions have emerged from the literature, one dealing with how to represent individual pitches and durations, and the other with how to represent sequences or other structures in 'chromosomes'.

2.4.1.1. Pitch and Duration Representations

There have been three primary approaches to representing pitch: absolute, relative and scale-offset. *Absolute* representations provide an unambiguous mapping to a specific pitch or pitch class plus octave, and include standard note names (like Bb4 or F#5), MIDI pitch codes (0–127, with 60 being middle C) or actual frequencies (concert A is supposed to be 440 Hz). *Relative* pitch schemes represent pitches as intervals from some reference pitch. The reference pitch might be the previous pitch in the sequence, the pitch at the beginning of the current phrase, the root of the current chord in the harmonic progression, the tonic note of the current section or the entire piece, or some other pitch that can serve to anchor the chain of intervals in a sequence to some specific pitch. The *scale-offset* approach has aspects of both absolute and relative schemes. Here, pitches are represented as offsets into scales that will change as the chords change in the underlying harmonic progression. A given scale offset may map to a Bb using one scale or an A using another. In the simplest case, when there is no harmonic motion, the scale-offset scheme reduces to an absolute scheme using a single scale that avoids dissonant chromatic notes, like a standard major scale.

Each approach has its advantages. The absolute scheme has the advantage of being conceptually simple and works well with 'toy' melody generators, especially when a simple tonality is enforced by using a diatonic scale (e.g., only the white keys on a piano) or a pentatonic scale (e.g., only the black keys). Absolute frequency is necessary if the piece is microtonal, i.e. it uses pitches that 'fall in the cracks' of the piano. The relative schemes are particularly useful when melodic material will be transposed or manipulated in other general ways. The scale-offset scheme always plays notes that are 'on key', even when the key changes, which can make it preferable when a non-trivial harmonic context will be either supplied *a priori* or generated as part of the composition system.

2.4.1.2. Event Sequence Representations

There have been two primary approaches to represent durations: beat-oriented and absolute. *Beat-oriented* representations use traditional note length values like quarter note or dotted half note, while absolute durations use actual times, usually in milliseconds. Beat-oriented approaches are preferable with pulsed music, with a meter and tempo, especially when the tempo might change. *Absolute* times are likely preferable when the piece is not pulsed, i.e. sound events occur at specified times, but there is no beat.

Chromosome structures for representing melodic lines fall into three categories – position based, order based and tree based. *Position-based* chromosomes typically represent measures or phrases, usually in a pulsed rhythmic scheme. The desired granularity of time resolution multiplied by the number of beats per measure will indicate the number of genes in the chromosome. For example, to represent sixteenth notes in a 3/4 measure, one would need 12 genes in a measure–length chromosome (four subdivisions of a beat times three beats per measure). Similarly, if we want to represent four bars in 4/4 time with eighth-note granularity, we would need 32 genes (four measures of four beats, with each beat subdivided into two event windows.

The genes in this scheme could represent pitches and/or note onsets. For example, a rhythmic line on a single drum could be represented with a single bit for each gene, where a '1' could map to 'hit the drum at that point in the measure' and a '0' could map to 'don't hit the drum'. If we want a position-based chromosome of pitches, we could use three bits and map '0' to be a rest and '1' through '7' to be notes in a diatonic scale. In our four-bar chromosome above, this would yield a 96-bit chromosome that could represent any sequence of eighth notes and rests. We could not represent quarter notes or half notes with this scheme, but if we interpreted the '0' as a 'hold' event, which simply held the note from the previous gene, we could have note lengths of any multiple of an eighth note. The obvious next step is to encode both a rest and a hold so that we can have notes and rests of any length that is a multiple of an eighth note. We will see this scheme in *GenJam* (Biles, 1994), which is detailed in Chapter 7.

Order-based representations address the note–length problem by representing notes as pitch–duration pairs. Any of the above choices for pitch and duration representations are fair game, and the various combinations provide more or less leverage, depending on the kind of music desired. For example, absolute frequency and absolute times in an order-based representation provide maximum 'freedom' in that literally any physical pitch can sound for any length of time, which might be terrific for ethereal soundscapes but would provide no leverage at all for standard tunes.

Tree-based representations come, not surprisingly, from genetic programming (Spector and Alpern 1994; Johanson and Poli 1998). When representing melodic material, the terminal (leaf node) symbols typically map to pitches or a rest, possibly with a duration included. The functions (interior nodes) map to musical operators like sequence, repetition, chord and so on. One obvious advantage of tree-based representations is that they can be extended to higher-level structures that could represent the deep structure of a piece. The *GPmuse* system (Polito et al. 1997) used genetic programming in three interacting agents operating at different levels to compose sixteenth-century counterpoint. Some EC researchers have extended tree-based representations to grammatical evolution of musical hierarchies (Fox 2006; de la Puente et al. 2002).

2.4.2. Fitness

Undoubtedly the most difficult issues in applying EC to music arise from how to implement fitness. In a few musical tasks, like SATB harmonization, which was discussed earlier, and tweaking a synthesizer to match a target sound, which is detailed in Chapter 3, fitness can be implemented algorithmically. However, in most compositional tasks fitness boils down to deciding the merit of a piece of music, and this is inherently subjective. Three general approaches have been used to implement fitness: automatic, interactive and no fitness.

2.4.2.1. Automatic Fitness

Automatic fitness schemes are of three species: heuristic features, rule-based and learned. Dozens of *heuristic features* have been devised for describing melodic material (Towsey et al. 2001; Ames 1992). These include the range and variety of pitches or horizontal intervals, direction or stability of melodic contours, note versus rest density, rhythmic variety and syncopation, and a host of other readily computable functions. Some features have a basis in traditional music theory; others come from other theoretical perspectives like the Zipf-Mandelbrot Law (Manaris et al. 2003); and still others fall into the category of 'let's see if this works . . . '. The overall fitness for a given melodic individual, then, combines a set of features, usually using some kind of weighted sum of feature values or differences relative to a set of ideal feature values. Unfortunately, these global difference polynomials tend to be weak or brittle (Towsey et al. 2001), and the features themselves have questionable validity. Consequently, this approach seldom yields music that sounds good (Phon-Amnuaisuk and Wiggins 1999).

Rule-based approaches implement knowledge-based systems, often grounded in music theory. Usually, the rules take the form of constraints, as in the case of species counterpoint, which is a highly specified genre (Polito et al. 1997; McIntyre 1994). While these constraints can weed out things that are theoretically bad, they are powerless to identify things that sound especially good. This leads to both false positives (some music is theoretically correct but sounds bad) and false negatives (some music is good *because* it breaks the rules in compelling ways). In short, music theory may help explain *why* a piece of music sounds good, but it ultimately cannot decide *whether* a piece sounds good. Whether music sounds good is ultimately up to the listener, based, as was discussed earlier, on his or her musical mental model.

Learned fitness schemes typically apply adaptive techniques to hopefully yield more robust fitness values by learning from a training set of acceptable examples. K-means techniques have been employed to learn optimal weights for feature vectors, but the dominant technique has been to use a *neural network*. The input layer of the neural network could be a feature vector, using the types of features described earlier (Biles et al. 1996), or the musical sequence itself (Gibson and Byrne 1991; Johanson and Poli 1998). Obviously, the choice of a training set is critical. One approach to choosing a training set is to select exemplars from a specific style that is to be emulated (Burton 1998). Another approach is to train on population individuals that have emerged as musically meritorious from interactive training (Biles et al. 1996; Johanson and Poli 1998).

While neural network fitness is intuitively appealing, it never turns out to be an unqualified success. For example, attempts to train a neural network on the successful survivors of an interactive breeding regimen typically result in a network that does not generalize beyond the exemplar set, if it can even recognize all the exemplars successfully (Biles et al. 1996). The problem likely stems from the lack of validity of easily computable features, in the case of feature vectors as the input layer, or lack of information, in the case of the melodic material itself as the input layer. In short, the results are seldom deemed musical.

2.4.2.2. Interactive Fitness

If automatic fitness methods turn out to be depressingly inadequate, then the obvious alternative is to let a human decide. *Interactive* fitness uses a human *mentor*, who must experience each individual in a population and somehow indicate, minimally, which individuals should survive to the next generation. The justification for using a mentor is obvious – if we need a human's aesthetic judgement, and we cannot model that judgement process algorithmically, then just let the human make that judgement. This sounds simple, and it can be, but there are a host of issues around using a mentor, most of which are HCI issues and many of which force a retooling of the EC machinery in general and genetic operators in particular.

Interactive EC systems originated with Richard Dawkins in the graphics domain (Dawkins 1986), and received a significant boost from Sims (1991). In graphics, the paradigm is clear – the mentor views thumbnail images of the entire population and inputs some indication of merit for the individuals. The mentor then turns the EC crank to generate a new generation, and the process repeats. This sounds simple, but let us look deeper. First, how many individuals are in the population? In typical EC-based systems population, sizes range from dozens to hundreds. Imagine a population on the smaller end of that continuum, say 48 individuals. Now, imagine viewing 48 individual thumbnail images, let us say arranged in six rows of eight images each. How many pixels can we allocate to each image? 120 by 80 would seem near the upper limit, given the resolution of a typical laptop today and the need for some screen real estate in which to place buttons and other interface objects within the application window. Images that are 120 by 80 pixels are not too hard to see individually, but there are 48 of them. Suppose that your job as mentor is to rank the images, 1 to 48. That is probably an unreasonable task to perform, so we will just ask the mentor to assign a 1 to 100 rating to each one, which should be easier, but is still not simple. To simplify it more we could reduce our ratings to three categories – keeper, loser or do not care. Those that we mark 'keeper' will definitely survive to breed; those we mark 'loser' will be eliminated, and the remainders may or may not survive.

We have achieved something that might be workable, albeit for a relatively small population, by traditional EC standards. Now let us make this a musical example. Instead of thumbnail images, each of our 48 population members will be represented by a button, which, when clicked, will play the musical fragment mapped from that individual chromosome. Now, imagine trying to rank or rate these 48 individuals. One issue is that you cannot hear the entire population all at once the way that you can see it all at once in the image example. Another issue is that you have to listen to each individual one at a time, by itself, in real time. Just going through the population once to get the lay of the land is pretty time consuming, and making judgements as to whether one individual is better than another is downright daunting. We could make the interface a little more usable if we retained our prior image size for the buttons and used that space to graph a melodic contour or maybe traditional music notation of the individual, but such a representation is pretty abstract, especially if the mentor does not read music in his mind's ear. The obvious solution is to shrink the population to a more manageable size, typically nine to 16 individuals in most applications of this type (Horowitz 1994; Unemi 2002).

What we have experienced here is a classic demonstration of the *fitness bottleneck* (Biles 1994). If a mentor has to experience and evaluate each individual in a population, it takes time. If the domain is *temporal*, as is the case with music, it takes real time, pun intended. The fitness bottleneck for temporal domains, then, is especially narrow. Beyond the time it takes the mentor to evaluate individuals in a population, we also need to examine the toll it takes on the mentor. Listening carefully and critically to music requires a level of concentration that most people seldom demonstrate. Any recording engineer will testify to the need for 'fresh ears' when engaged in a mixing session, and the neighborhood piano teacher can be slightly disoriented after a full day of 'creative' Suzuki interpretations. But the task of the mentor is harder than the engineer's or the music teacher's. The engineer and the music teacher are listening to improve something they have already heard before, so they can focus on subtleties, but each iteration is essentially a refinement of the same content. On the other hand, the mentor must make more fundamental judgements about whether each individual musical fragment, which he may be hearing for the first time, has enough potential to deserve survival. As we have seen, there is no template for 'good' music, because if there were, we would have quit after the discussion of automatic fitness.

The task of the mentor in this scenario is especially difficult because the individual musical fragments are experienced outside of a larger musical context. If individuals in the population map to short melodic fragments, say a measure in length, then the mentor can feel like she is playing a variant of *Name That Tune*; I can rate that music in five notes. The advantage of short individuals is that they take less time to hear; the disadvantage is that they are harder to evaluate validly. For example, if we increase the length of the individuals to a four-bar phrase, then the phrases will be easier for the mentor to evaluate, but they will take longer to listen to. If the individuals represent entire tunes, then their context is more complete, but they take even longer to listen to, and we introduce the granularity problem, when the mentor really likes one section and really hates another section of the same individual. In standard EC crossover might eventually fix that, but in our scenario, the mentor probably does not want to wait for the EC machinery to stumble across the 'right' crossover point. This brings up the notion of collaborative hybrid systems (Unemi 2002; Thywissen 1999).

If automatic fitness does not seem to work and interactive fitness introduces a fitness bottleneck, maybe we should just eliminate fitness altogether. This is not as farfetched as it seems at first, but we will defer any real discussion of EC without fitness to Chapters 6 and 7 in this volume.

2.4.3. Genetic Operators

Genetic operators fall into five standard categories: initialization, selection, crossover, mutation and replacement. In the music domain, these operators often behave in ways that are outside the EC mainstream, to say the least. For each class of operator we will survey approaches that have been used and, as we did for representation schemes, try to point out advantages for each approach.

2.4.3.1. Initialization

There have been two main families of initialization schemes for EC-based music systems: random and sampled. Random schemes basically start from scratch by initializing individuals with random gene values. Many systems use a standard uniform random number generator to initialize notes in melodic chromosomes (Burton and Vladimirova 1997; Johanson and Poli 1998). While this is an obvious choice from a standard GA perspective, it tends to lead to an initial population of melodic individuals that is very unmusical, due to the large horizontal intervals that result. This makes the task of the mentor especially onerous, as nearly all the individuals in early generations will be pretty bad, and the mentor will have to lower the aesthetic bar to get anything remotely musical. The fitness bottleneck never seems as narrow as when nothing seems to make it through.

A more musical initial generation will generally result by using a fractal generator or a Markov chain trained on 'real' melodic material; see the Chapter 7 in this volume. Fractals have been used as music generators ever since it was noticed that the power spectrum of a classical music station exhibited fractal properties (Voss and Clark 1978). The reasoning was that if music is fractal, maybe fractals are musical (Gardner 1978). Markov chain music dates back even earlier (Hiller and Isaacson 1959). The goal of these 'smarter' random generators is to generate an initial generation that, at least statistically, more closely resembles the desired finished product, in an effort to reduce the volume of sludge that has to pass through the fitness bottleneck.

Sampled initialization operates by seeding the initial population with individuals that are already acceptable. These can come from the user, who supplies melodic motifs for the system to develop (Ralley 1995; Jacob 1996), or they can come from a corpus of analyzed works in the desired style (Prerau 2001); see also Chapter 6. One could argue that systems employing this scheme are really doing melodic development rather than pure composition, but the goal is once again to start with an initial generation that is more musical and to reduce the volume through the fitness bottleneck.

2.4.3.2. Selection

Three primary selection schemes have been employed in composition systems – fitness-based, musically aware and random. Traditional fitness-based selection is the obvious choice for maintaining EC purity and is the predominant selection method in EC-based music systems. Standard schema theory advises that we select in proportion to fitness in order to provide selection pressure and move the evolutionary process forward towards better and better solutions. Over succeeding generations, the population will tend to converge on one or more highly fit individuals as exploitation overtakes exploration in the search process (Goldberg 2002). When we are looking for one best solution to emerge from the population (the optimization model), this is not a problem. However, in most music systems the goal is not to find one best motif, but instead to build a diverse population of good motifs. The tendency of the EC machinery to converge can be disastrous because the result will be minor variations on one or two motifs, which in turn will yield a very boring tune. This yet again highlights the difference between optimization and exploration, an issue we shall revisit later.

An alternative to standard fitness-based selection methods is to use intelligent or musically aware selection. In this scheme, individuals are selected to breed based on their compatibility or because they were matched by the mentor/composer (Unemi 2002). As we have seen before, collaborative systems, in which the user plays many roles in the evolutionary process, provide more opportunity for exploration guided by the mentor, by the author.

Finally, we can make selection totally random, which certainly would be appropriate if we have no fitness. Clearly, if there is random selection, there will be no selection pressure, so diversity should not be an issue. On the other hand, how can the population improve if fitness is not considered, and selection is random? Rodney Waschka's *GenDash*, described in Chapter 6, and the autonomous version of the author's *GenJam*, described in Chapter 7, provide answers to this question.

2.4.3.3. Crossover

Crossover provides a mechanism for blending material from two or more individuals. The goal is to combine the best parts of different individual parents into an individual child whose fitness is higher than the fitness of either parent. In traditional EC, crossover operates on the genotype, and the choice of crossover point, or points, is random. This means that most crossovers do not meet the goal of generating better individuals, and the resulting low fitness of a genetic failure will result in its demise from the population. Over the course of many generations, however, better individuals will eventually emerge, survive and breed their own children, and eventually, acceptable, if not optimal, solutions will emerge. Crossover, then, is a great mechanism for exploiting the best potential of a population.

This traditional scenario is appropriate for the few musical tasks that reduce to optimization problems, like timbre matching and SATB harmonization, as mentioned earlier. However, in many musical tasks, the goal is not to simply generate a new individual that might sound good; the goal is to develop melodic material that will sound good. This results in intelligent or musically aware crossovers that can greatly enhance the chances of breeding children that are at least no worse than their parents. That intelligence appears both in the choice of crossover point and the way in which material from the parents is exchanged.

The choice of crossover point (or points, if more than one is allowed) can be made more intelligent by limiting it to musically advantageous points in the parent chromosomes, often by starting with crossover points in the phenotype rather than the genotype. Many chromosome structures in musical applications represent sequences of notes with each note represented by a bit string. When the bit strings are concatenated together, the resulting bit string for the note sequence represents the genotype of the sequence. If crossovers are allowed at any point in the bit string (genotype), then crossovers could occur within a note, which might not be a bad thing but could generate an unattractive note at the crossover point. However, by restricting crossover points to fall on note boundaries in the bit string, which essentially means selecting crossover points from the phenotype, the parents' notes are guaranteed to survive in the children. Chapter 7 presents an extensive example of this type of crossover, including an intelligent selection scheme to select the best crossover point from among the musically fruitful choices.

The way in which material is exchanged between parents is another opportunity for intelligence. The traditional single-point crossover, which simply exchanges material after the crossover point in the parents' genotypes is a reasonable approach for simple bit-string-based chromosome structures. However, many musical EC systems use chromosome structures that encode multiple layers of information. For example, various systems have represented notes with some of the following attributes: pitch class, chromatic inflection, octave, duration, loudness, articulation and timbre. Multi-attribute structures offer opportunities for variations of uniform crossover, like exchanging the octaves of a sequence of notes in the parent chromosomes without changing the pitch classes (Marques et al. 2000). A form of uniform crossover that resulted in multi-point crossover at the genotype level was used by Gary Lee Nelson in his *Sonomorph* system (Nelson 1993).

2.4.3.4. Mutation

Mutation is intended to insure that a population does not converge prematurely on a suboptimal result. In other words, mutation attempts to insure that the solution space is explored sufficiently, which complements crossover's role of exploiting promising individuals (Goldberg 2002). In traditional EC-based systems mutation is implemented by an occasional bit flip in the genotype, which over the course of many generations is sufficient to insure adequate exploration, provided the probability of mutation is set appropriately. Like crossover, however, this traditional approach seldom works in non-optimization music applications, where the goal is often to develop musical material, not just try something different. In short, an intelligent exploration is in order, which has led many researchers to invent intelligent mutations that effectively constrain exploration to musically promising avenues (Biles 1994; Ralley 1995; Papadopoulos and Wiggins 1998; Thywissen 1999; Marques et al. 2000; Ariza 2002). Again, Chapter 7 in this volume details the development of musically meaningful mutations (Biles 1994) on measure and phrase level individuals, so we will defer an in-depth discussion of intelligent mutation operators to that chapter.

The ultimate in intelligent mutation, however, is user intervention. Some collaborative systems allow users to alter individuals by hand (Unemi 2002). While some EC purists would call this 'cheating', it is very appropriate if the goal of the EC-based system is to help its user create good music, rather than demonstrate what EC can do autonomously.

2.4.3.5. Replacement

Replacement is another operation that a user might perform in a collaborative system. In a traditional EC-based system, though, replacement is often paired with selection by adding the newly generated children to the existing population, computing fitness values for new individuals, and then culling out enough individuals, usually low performing ones, to restore the population to a desired size. Most systems use some form of elitism, where the best individuals from the previous generation are guaranteed to survive into the next generation.

Two styles of replacement have emerged: generational and continuous. In generational replacement, the entire population is turned over after all the new children have been created for a generation. In continuous replacement new children replace low performing individuals as they are generated, one or two at a time, and there is no clear generational boundary. EC-based music systems have used both styles.

One use of an intelligent replacement is to increase diversity in the population by insuring that each individual to be inserted in the population is unique with respect to the individuals already present in the population. This is important in systems where the entire population is used to generate musical content, as is the case in the *GenDash* and *GenJam* systems, which are described in Chapters 6 and 7, respectively.

2.5. Final Thoughts

EA has become a useful tool for composers, performers, musicologists and other musicians, as the existence of this volume demonstrates. Like any maturing technology, the focus inevitably shifts from demonstrating that the technology actually works, to finding domain areas in which it can be applied successfully, to adapting the technology away from its theoretical roots and towards the needs of problem domains. In other words, the needs of applications domains eventually overtake the need to adhere to theoretical dogma. In the music domain, EC is showing the first signs of making that final transition. Music has clearly been established as a domain in which EC can be useful, but it remains to be seen how much the musical domain will alter EC as a technology.

References

Ames, C. (1992). Quantifying Musical Merit. *Interface* **21**: 53–93.

Ariza, C. (2002). Prokaryotic groove: Rhythmic cycles as real-value encoded genetic algorithms. In *Proceedings of the 2002 International Computer Music Conference*. ICMA, San Francisco.

Biles, J.A. (1994). GenJam: A genetic algorithm for generating jazz solos. In *Proceedings of the 1994 International Computer Music Conference*. ICMA, San Francisco.

Biles, J.A. and Eign, W. (1995). GenJam *Populi*: Training an IGA *via* audience-mediated performance. In *Proceedings of the 1995 International Computer Music Conference*. ICMA, San Francisco.

Biles, J.A., Anderson, P.G. and Loggi, L.W. (1996). Neural network fitness functions for a musical IGA. In *Proceedings of the International ICSC Symposium on Intelligent Industrial Automation (IIA'96) and Soft Computing (SOCO'96)*. ICSC-NAISO Academic Press, Canada/The Netherlands, pp. B39–B44.

Biles, J.A. (2003). GenJam in perspective: A tentative taxonomy for GA music and art systems. *Leonardo* **36**(1): 43–45.

Burton, A.R. (1998) *A Hybrid Neuro-Genetic Pattern Evolution System Applied to Musical Composition*. PhD Thesis, University of Surrey, School of Electronic Engineering. Available online at http://www.tony-b.freeuk.com/phd.html.

Burton, A.R. and Vladimirova, T. (1997). Genetic algorithm utilizing neural network evaluation for musical composition. In *Proceedings of the 1997 International Conference on Artificial Neural Networks and Genetic Algorithms*. Springer-Verlag, Berlin.

Burton, A.R. and Vladimirova, T. (1999). Generation of musical sequences with genetic techniques. *Computer Music Journal* **23**(4): 59–73.

Dawkins, R. (1986). *The Blind Watchmaker: Why the Evidence of Evolution Reveals a Universe Without Design.* WW Norton, New York.

de la Puente, A.O., Alfonso, R.S. and Moreno, M.A. (2002). Automatic composition of music by means of grammatical evolution. In *Proceedings of the 2002 conference on APL.* ACM Press, New York.

Federman, F. (2003). The NEXTPITCH learning classifier system: Representation, information theory and performance. *Leonardo* **36**(1): 47–50.

Fox, C. (2006). Genetic hierarchical music structures. In *Proceedings of the 19th International FLAIRS Conference.* AAAI Press, Menlo Park, CA.

Gabrielsson, A. (1999). Music performance. In D. Deutsch (Ed.) *Psychology of Music, 2nd ed.* Academic Press, San Diego, pp. 501–602.

Gardner, M. (1978). White and brown music, fractal curves and one-over-f fluctuations. *Scientific American* **238**(4): 16–27.

Gartland-Jones, A. (2003). MusicBlox: A real-time algorithmic composition system incorporating a distributed interactive genetic algorithm. In *Applications of Evolutionary Computing: EvoWorkshops 2003.* LNCS 2611, Springer, Berlin, pp. 490–501.

Gartland-Jones, A. and Copley, P. (2003). The suitability of genetic algorithms for music composition. *Contemporary Music Review* **22**(3): 43–55.

Gibson, P.M. and Byrne, J.A. (1991). NEUROGEN: Musical composition using genetic algorithms and cooperating neural networks. In *Proceedings of the IEE Second International Conference on Artificial Neural Networks.* IEE, London, pp. 309–313.

Goldberg, D.E. (2002). *The Design of Innovation: Lessons from and for Competent Genetic Algorithms.* Kluwer Academic, Boston.

Grachten, M., Arcos, J.L. and Lopez de Mantaras, R. (2004). Evolutionary optimization of music performance annotation. In U.K. Wiil (Ed.), *Computer Music Modeling and Retrieval: Second International Symposium, CMMR 2004.* Lecture Notes in Computer Science 3310. Springer, Berlin, pp. 347–358.

Graham-Rowe, D. (2001). Computer DJ uses biofeedback to pick tracks. *New Scientist.* Available online at http://www.newscientist.com/article.ns?id=dn1563.

Hartson, H.R. and Hix, D. (1993). *Developing User Interfaces.* John Wiley, New York.

Horner, A. and Goldberg, D.E. (1991). Genetic algorithms and computer-assisted music composition. In R. Belew and L. Booker (Eds.), *Proceedings of the Fourth International Conference on Genetic Algorithms.* Morgan Kauffman, San Francisco.

Horner, A. and Ayres, L. (1995). Harmonisation of musical progression with genetic algorithms. In *Proceedings of the 1995 International Computer Music Conference.* ICMA, San Francisco.

Horowitz, D. (1994). Generating rhythms with genetic algorithms. In *Proceedings of the 1994 International Computer Music Conference.* ICMA, San Francisco.

Hiller, L.A. and Isaacson, L.M. (1959). *Experimental Music: Composition with and Electronic Computer.* McGraw-Hill, New York.

Jacob, B. (1995). Composing with genetic algorithms. In *Proceedings of the 1995 International Computer Music Conference.* ICMA, San Francisco.

Jacob, B. (1996). Algorithmic composition as a model of creativity. *Organised Sound* **1**(3): 157–165.

Johanson, B. and Poli, R. (1998). Gp-music: An interactive genetic programming system for music generation with automated fitness raters. In *Proceedings of the 3rd International Conference on Genetic Programming, GP'98.* MIT Press, Cambridge, MA.

Madsen, S.T. and Widmer, G. (2005). Exploring similarities in music performances with an evolutionary algorithm. In *Proceedings of the 18th International FLAIRS Conference*. AAAI Press, Menlo Park, CA.

Madsen, S.T. and Widmer, G. (2006). Exploring pianist performance styles with evolutionary string matching. *International Journal of Artificial Intelligence Tools* **15**(4): 495–514.

Manaris, B., Vaughan, D., Wagner, C., Romero, J. and Davis, R.B. (2003). Evolutionary music and the Zipf-Mandelbrot law: Developing fitness functions for pleasant music. In *Lecture Notes in Computer Science, 2611*, Springer-Verlag, Heidelberg, pp. 522–534.

Marques, M., Oliveira, V., Vieira, S. and Rosa, A.C. (2000). Music composition using genetic evolutionary algorithms. In *Proceedings of the IEEE Conference on Evolutionary Computation 2000*. IEEE Press, New York, NY.

McIntyre, R.A. (1994). Bach in a box: The evolution of four-part baroque harmony using the genetic algorithm. In *Proceedings of the IEEE Conference on Evolutionary Computation, 14(3)*. IEEE Press, New York, NY, pp. 852–857.

Milkie, E. and Chestnutt, J. (2001). *Fugue Generation with Genetic Algorithms*. Available online at http://www.cs.cornell.edu/boom/2001sp/milkie/.

Mrozek, E.M. and Wakefield, G.H. (1996). Perceptual matching of low order models to room transfer functions. In *Proceedings of the 1996 International Computer Music Conference*, ICMA, San Francisco.

Nelson, G.L. (1993). Sonomorphs: An application of genetic algorithms to the growth and development of musical organisms. In *Proceedings of the Fourth Biennial Art and Technology Symposium*. Connecticut College, pp. 155–169.

Norman, D.A. (1988). *The Design of Everyday Things*. Doubleday, New York.

Papadopoulos, G. and Wiggins, G. (1998). A genetic algorithm for the generation of jazz melodies. In *Proceedings of STeP 98, Jyväskylä, Finland*. Available online at http://www.soi.city.ac.uk/~geraint/papers/STeP98.pdf.

Phon-Amnuaisuk, S. and Wiggins, G. (1999). The four-part harmonisation problem: A comparison between genetic algorithms and a rule-based system. In *Proceedings of AISB 99*. Edinburgh, Scotland, 1999.

Pierce, J. (1999). Introduction to pitch perception. In P.R. Cook (Ed.), *Music, Cognition and Computerized Sound: An Introduction to Psychoacoustics*. MIT Press, Cambridge, MA.

PMCP. (2005). *Penfield Music Commission Project*. Available online at http://www.penfield.edu/phs/default.asp?section=show_page&id=158.

Polito, J., Daida, J. and Bersano-Begey, T.F. (1997). Musica ex machina: Composing 16th-century counterpoint with genetic programming and symbiosis. In P.J. Angeline, R.G. Reynolds, J.R. McDonnell, R. Eberhart (Eds.), *Evolutionary Programming VI: Proceedings of the Sixth Annual Conference on Evolutionary Programming, 1213*. Springer-Verlag, Heidelberg.

Prerau, M. (2001). On the possibilities of an analytic synthesis system. In *Proceedings of the European Conference on Artificial Life 2001 Workshop: Artificial Life Models for Musical Applications*. Prague, Czech Republic.

Putnam, J.B. (1996). A grammar-based genetic programming technique applied to music generation. In L.J. Fogel, P.J. Angeline and T. Baeck (Eds.), *Evolutionary Programming V: Proceedings of the Fifth Annual Conference on Evolutionary Programming*. MIT Press, Cambridge, MA, pp. 277–286.

Ralley, D. (1995). Genetic algorithm as a tool for melodic development. In *Proceedings of the 1995 International Computer Music Conference*. ICMA, San Francisco.

Roads, C. (2001). *Microsound*. MIT Press, Cambridge, MA.

Sharman, K. and Esparcia-Alcazar, A. (2003). Evolutionary methods for designing digital filters. *Contemporary Music Review* **22**(3): 5–19.

Sims, K. (1991). Artificial evolution for computer graphics. In *Proceedings of SigGraph '91*. pp. 319–328.

Spector, L. and Alpern, A. (1994). Criticism, culture, and the automatic generation of artworks. In *Proceedings of the Twelfth National Conference on Artificial Intelligence, AAAI-94*. AAAI Press/The MIT Press, Menlo Park, CA, Cambridge, MA. Available online at http://hampshire.edu/%7ElasCCS/genbebop.html.

Thywissen, K. (1999). GeNotator: An environment for exploring the application of evolutionary techniques in computer-assisted composition. *Organised Sound* **4**: 127–133.

Todd, P. and Werner, G. (1999). Frankensteinian methods for evolutionary music composition. In N. Griffith and P. Todd (Eds.), *Musical Networks: Parallel Distributed Perception and Performance*. MIT Press, Cambridge, MA.

Tokui, N. and Iba, H. (2000). Music composition with interactive evolutionary computation. In *GA2000, Proceedings of the Third International Conference on Generative Art*, Milan, Italy.

Towsey, M., Brown, A., Wright, S. and Diederich, J. (2001). Towards melodic extension using genetic algorithms. *Educational Technology & Society* **4**(2): 54–65.

Unemi, T. (2002). SBEAT3: A tool for multi-part music composition by simulated breeding. In *Proceedings of the Eighth International Conference on Artificial Life (A-Life VIII)*. MIT Press, Cambridge, MA.

Voss, R.F. and Clarke, J. (1978). 1/f noise in music: Music from 1/f noise. *Journal of the Acoustic Society of America* **63**(1): 258–263.

Widmer, G. and Goebl, W. (2004). Computational models of expressive music performance: The state of the art. *Journal of New Music Research* **33**(3): 203–216.

Woolf, S. and Yee-King, M. (2003). Virtual and physical interfaces for collaborative evolution of sound. *Contemporary Music Review* **22**(3): 31–41.

3
Evolution in Digital Audio Technology

ANDREW HORNER

3.1. Introduction

Replicating musical instruments is a classic problem in computer music. A systematic collection of instrument designs for each of the main synthesis methods has long been the El Dorado of the computer music community. Here is what James Moorer, the pioneering computer music researcher at Stanford University and later director of the audio project at Lucasfilm, had to say about it (Roads 1982):

There is another musical project we have talked about but have never done. It is an enormous project, the fabled 'Lexicon of Analyzed Tones'. One could make the argument that cataloguing orchestral instruments is an obsolete sort of thing to do. However, I could make the counterclaim that the orchestral instruments give us immediately a wide variety of musically interesting timbres. I would like to see someone go through the entire pitch range of each orchestral instrument at several dynamics and articulation styles and analyze and categorize each tone. I would like to give several synthesis algorithms for each instrument; that is, a frequency modulation algorithm, an additive synthesis algorithm, a wavetable synthesis algorithm and so on. This lexicon would be the kind of Rosetta stone for computer music we have all been looking for. Most of the computer musician's time is spent looking for sounds and the lexicon would help to reduce that effort.

The main reason why computer musicians struggle looking for sounds is that most synthesis techniques require parameter optimization to replicate a musical instrument. The notable exceptions are additive and sampling synthesis, but even additive synthesis usually requires data reduction of the amplitude envelopes to make them easier to handle and sampling synthesis requires smooth loop points for sustained sounds.

During the 1970s and 1980s, before sampling became popular and memory became cheap, replicating musical by instruments using techniques such as frequency modulation (FM) was one of the 'holy grails' of music synthesis. Synthesizers such as the Yamaha DX7 allowed users great flexibility in mixing and matching sounds, but they were notoriously difficult to make sound like a given instrument. Instrument design wizards practiced the mysteries of their 'dark art'. Other methods, such as wavetable synthesis, were less mysterious but were limited to production of rather static organ-like sounds. With a single wavetable, one could easily attain a trumpet-like sound, but a realistic trumpet was still out of reach.

Then, sampling came along and soon even cheap synthesizers could sound like realistic pianos and trumpets, as long as the desired articulations happened to match those of the original recorded samples. Sample libraries quickly replaced sound wizards.

Ironically, about the same time FM declined, researchers started applying evolutionary algorithms to optimize parameters for FM and wavetable synthesis. The results were about as realistic as sampled sounds, with the added benefits of increased spectral and temporal control. In one instance, a synthesized French horn even managed to pass for the real thing when a fake audition tape was submitted to a well-known summer music program in the United States (Horner 1999). The virtual horn player was accepted and even offered a scholarship when the initial offer was discretely declined.

This chapter will focus on the use of evolutionary algorithms to evolve parameters for music synthesis. It will discuss the use of genetic algorithms and other related techniques to evolve synthesis configurations and optimize parameter settings to replicate traditional instruments. The next section describes the fundamentals of each synthesis method, followed by a review of parameter optimization for the method, with a special emphasis on evolutionary methods. We also discuss other digital audio applications where evolutionary algorithms have proved fruitful.

3.2. Music Synthesis and Processing

There are numerous music synthesis techniques with various degrees of control and accuracy for replicating musical instruments. This section describes each of the main synthesis methods and how its parameters are derived by traditional optimization methods and evolved by evolutionary methods. Some music-processing techniques modify rather than generate a sound, such as artificial reverberation and sound localization. Because they require filter optimization they are discussed in the Subtractive/Filter Synthesis section.

3.2.1. Additive Synthesis

Additive sine wave synthesis is one of the most straightforward and powerful synthesis methods. It adds a series of harmonically related sine waves, each with its own amplitude and frequency envelope. Fig. 3.1 shows a block diagram of the additive synthesis model. A short-time Fourier transform of a musical tone determines the amplitude and frequency envelopes (Roads 1996, pp. 117–133). If there is no modification of the envelope parameters, additive synthesis can reconstruct the original waveform exactly. However, the difficulty of manipulating so many parameters often necessitates some sort of data reduction. Piecewise-linear approximation of additive synthesis amplitude and frequency envelopes is

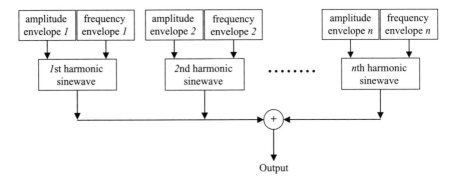

FIGURE 3.1. Additive synthesis block diagram.

one of the most common data reduction techniques used in sound synthesis. For each envelope, a series of line segments are connected at breakpoints. Examples of commercial digital synthesizers using additive synthesis with piecewise-linear envelopes include the Fairlight CMI (1979), the Kurzweil 150 Fourier Synthesizer (1986) and the Lyre Fourier Digital Synthesizer (1986).

A closed-form solution to the line segment approximation problem does not exist because the problem is nonlinear; moving just one breakpoint changes how well the approximation matches the original envelope over the length of the neighbouring segments. Several researchers have reported fitting amplitude and frequency envelopes by hand (Risset and Mathews 1969; Grey and Moorer 1977; Chamberlin 1980) and at least three have proposed automated methods for reducing the approximation error below some pre-determined threshold (Beauchamp 1969; Strawn 1980; Serra, Rubine and Dannenberg 1990).

Moorer and his colleagues (Moorer, Grey and Snell 1977; Moorer, Grey and Strawn 1977, 1978) gave hand-fitted line segment approximations for amplitude and frequency envelopes to various instrument tones (violin, clarinet, oboe and the trumpet). Engineers have since used this data extensively to test various real-time digital synthesizers.

Beauchamp's LINSEG method automatically determined line segment approximations with each amplitude envelope optimized separately (Beauchamp's 1969). After smoothing each envelope to remove micro-variations, the procedure used a series of least-squares-fit straight lines to approximate the data. LINSEG used the longest lines that kept the absolute difference error below a pre-determined threshold. For complex envelopes, this method tended to generate many more line segments than a comparable 'hand-fit' would.

Instead of reducing the error below a pre-determined threshold, another approach is to determine the best possible approximation for a specified number of line segments. For example, to design an instrument patch for a keyboard synthesizer constrained to only five line segments per envelope, an automatic procedure is needed to specify how to best utilize the line segments. Strawn's procedure (ADJUST) attempted this, but it required an initial estimate of the solution and the solution it ultimately found was usually only slightly improved over the initial guess (Strawn 1980). This is because ADJUST used a hill-climbing procedure to improve the initial guess, thus simply converging to a nearby local optimum.

An alternative approach to using independent breakpoints for each envelope is to pick the N best breakpoints that are common to all harmonics. Using common breakpoints has the advantage that it requires less storage and runs faster, since wavetable interpolation can be used instead of additive synthesis to crossfade pairs of wavetables. The Prism, built by Kinetic Systems in the early 1980s, was the first known synthesizer based on linear interpolation between wavetables. Also, Chamberlin (1980) employed this method for microcomputer real-time synthesis during the same period. The method was explored in detail by Serra et al. (1990), who devised a technique for adding breakpoints until the maximum mean-squared error was brought below a prescribed threshold.

Horner and Beauchamp (1996; see also Horner, Cheung and Beauchamp 1995), introduced the use of genetic algorithms (GA) to solve the piecewise-linear approximation problem for determining the best N breakpoints. They compared the GA performance to other breakpoint picking methods such as greedy and hill-climbing algorithms. The GA consistently outperformed the other methods for both amplitude and frequency envelopes. The results held true for both independent and shared breakpoints, as well as linear and quadratic approximations. They found that for hardware synthesis, where the number of breakpoints is typically quite limited, the GA approach was clearly the best. With ten or more breakpoints, the greedy method also performed well. Since the greedy method was much faster, they concluded that the greedy approach was perhaps best for software synthesis since faster results might be more important than using a few extra breakpoints. The GA approach served as an important benchmark in reaching this conclusion.

3.2.2. Wavetable Synthesis

The popular music industry currently uses the term *wavetable synthesis* synonymously with *sampling synthesis*. However, in this chapter, *sampling* means recording an entire note and playing it back, while *wavetable synthesis* means storing only one period of a waveform in an oscillator table and scaling the table output by an amplitude envelope. A sum of harmonic sine waves generates the waveform and the set of harmonic amplitudes defines the *basis spectrum* of the wavetable.

The main advantage of wavetable synthesis is its efficiency at generating periodic waveforms. The disadvantage of wavetable synthesis is that each wavetable produces only a static spectrum, while real sounds produce dynamic spectra. Wavetable synthesis requires several wavetables mixed together to produce dynamic spectra (see Fig. 3.2).

Wavetable matching finds the best set of parameters to synthesize a musical instrument tone using wavetable synthesis. A number of investigators have explored methods for optimizing wavetable basis spectra and their amplitude envelopes. For example, Maher and Beauchamp (1990) used wavetable matching in their investigation of vocal vibrato synthesis. They selected their basis spectra at the low

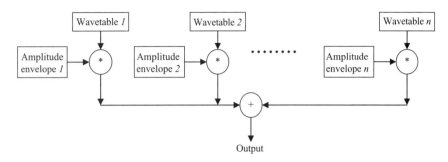

FIGURE 3.2. A multiple wavetable block diagram.

and high points in the vibrato of a tenor tone and cross faded the wavetables as a function of the vibrato.

Spectral interpolation uses pairs of cross-fading wavetables (Chamberlin 1980; Serra, Rubine and Dannenberg 1990). Spectral interpolation divides the signal into a series of interpolated basis spectra. Synthesis proceeds by gradually cross fading one spectrum with the next. When a basis spectrum has ramped down to zero, a new basis spectrum immediately replaces it and begins fading up. Serra et al. (1990) gave two algorithms for determining spectral interpolation basis spectra and amplitude envelopes. The first uses piecewise linear interpolation of basis spectra drawn from the original tone. The second uses a linear regression algorithm to statistically compute the basis spectra. Holding the spectral error below a user-specified threshold determines how many basis spectra to use. These algorithms change the basis spectra between 5 and 20 times per second. As an alternative approach, a genetic algorithm can select a pre-determined number of the best wavetables (Horner and Beauchamp 1996) rather than the user specifying a threshold. Genetic algorithms have also optimized wavetable interpolation with more than two wavetables (Horner 1996a), but where at most one wavetable cross fades at a given time. Mohr (2002; Mohr and Li 2005a, b) solved the problem for two or more wavetables by using the single-source acyclic weighted shortest path algorithm.

Group additive synthesis (Kleczkowski 1989) is another wavetable variant at the opposite extreme of spectral interpolation. Group additive synthesis uses nonintersecting sets of harmonics for the various wavetables. As an example, one wavetable might contain only the even harmonics while the second only the odd. Subsequent to Kleczkowski's initial study, researchers have optimized group additive synthesis parameters using an automated clustering scheme (Oates and Eaglestone 1997) and GA (Cheung and Horner 1996; Horner and Ayers 1998; Lee and Horner 1999). Horner and Ayers (2002) give a complete set of group additive synthesis designs for the woodwinds and brass.

Researchers have also used GA to match the multiple wavetable model shown in Fig. 3.2 (Horner, Beauchamp and Haken 1993a; Horner 1995). One approach to wavetable matching uses a genetic algorithm to select spectral snapshots from the original tone as the basis spectra (Horner, Beauchamp and Haken 1993a). This approach is intuitive and it generates an exact match at the time points of the selected snapshots and usually excellent matches at neighbouring points as well. The relative spectral error between the original and matched spectra typically serves as a fitness function to guide the GAs search for the best solution. Most matched instruments required three to five wavetables for a good match – a considerable saving compared to additive synthesis.

Wavetable synthesis is an inherently harmonic synthesis method. Handling tones that are nearly harmonic, such as the stretched octaves of piano tones and plucked string tones, requires some tricks. By grouping partials with similar frequency deviations, genetic algorithms have successfully optimized group additive synthesis parameters to simulate piano (Lee and Horner 1999) and string tones (So and Horner 2002, 2004).

Another refinement is to consider the effect of simultaneous frequency masking in wavetable parameter optimization (Wun and Horner 2001). Masked partials can be omitted from the fitness function to give a more accurate reflection of perceptual spectral differences.

Insights gained from having initially explored a problem with GA have often led to finding a better or simpler solution. Wavetable matching is such an example. Instead of using the GA to approximate the best match to all the spectral snapshots of the original tone, an alternative method is to find the best match for a subset of the spectral snapshots (Horner 2001; Ng and Horner 2002). It turns out that this approach is about as effective and efficient as the GA method and much simpler. Other methods such as local search (Wun, Horner and Ayers 2004; Wun and Horner 2005a) and iterative methods (Wun, Horner and Ayers 2003; Wun and Horner 2005b) have also been shown to give effective results.

Each of the various types of wavetable synthesis has its strong points, depending on the given situation. For simplicity, group additive synthesis has the advantage of being intuitive, since each harmonic is only in one wavetable. For memory-constrained systems where instruments have to compete for limited wavetable space, wavetable matching is a very good choice. Conversely, for real-time systems where memory is not a problem, wavetable interpolation is a good choice.

3.2.3. Subtractive/Filter Synthesis

Subtractive synthesis is the complement to additive synthesis. Instead of building up a complex sound from many simple sounds (sine waves), a complex source sound is fed into a filter which sculpts the sound as desired (see Fig. 3.3). This source–filter relationship is why subtractive synthesis is also known as filter synthesis.

Subtractive synthesis is probably most commonly used in linear predictive coding (LPC), especially for speech synthesis (Atal and Hanauer 1971; Flanagan 1972; Markel and Gray 1976). LPC has also been used in music synthesis (Cann 1979–1980; Moorer 1979; Lansky and Steiglitz 1981; Lansky 1989; Dodge 1989). LPC and related techniques are effective tools for designing linear filters, but they

source sound

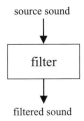

filter

filtered sound

FIGURE 3.3. Subtractive/filter synthesis block diagram.

cannot be applied to nonlinear filters. Only a few researchers have considered nonlinear filter optimization in music synthesis (Smith 1983; Massie and Stonick 1992).

Chu (1990) was among the first to use genetic algorithms to optimize nonlinear filters. He used the GA to configure stack filters in a non-music application. His goal was to configure the filter so that it removed as much corrupting noise from the signal as possible. The fitness value was based on the filter's effectiveness in suppressing impulsive noise.

Horner and colleagues described a *timbre breeding* method for evolving instrument designs (Horner, Beauchamp and Packard 1993; Beauchamp and Horner 1998). The user initially selects a source sound for breeding. A series of random filtering and time warping operations modifies the source, where spectral snapshots of the second tone are used as filter transfer functions. The filtered tone is then compared to its parent and the user decides which sound survives to the next generation. The process continues until the user is satisfied with the evolved sound. An interesting set of timbres was obtained by breeding a trumpet tone with a rubbed glass sound. Mating a cello and bass clarinet resulted in a bizarre sound that resembled a cello being played through a resonant bass clarinet.

Mrozek and Wakefield (1996) used a GA to optimize artificial reverberation. The GA was used to search for low-order filter parameters so that the generated impulse response best matched that of a target room transfer function. They used perceptually-based error criteria to compare the impulse responses. They compared N-segment all-pass reverberators and found a four-stage reverberator gave results as good as a seven-stage reverberator. Mrozek and Wakefield outlined several possible extensions of this method, including characterizing the perceptual effectiveness of the error criteria, generalizing the method to other types of rooms and fitting room impulse responses for binaural realization over headphones.

Another application of filtering is sound localization in 3D sound systems. Such systems simulate auditory cues that humans rely on to determine the position of a sound. Among these cues, head-related transfer functions (HRTFs) provide important spatial cues and are widely used in 3D sound systems. HRTFs describe the spectral filtering that occurs between a source sound and the listener's eardrum. Typically, a large set of HRTFs must be used, each representing a different azimuth and elevation. Some researchers have used statistical techniques to data reduce HRTFs (Martens 1987; Kistler and Wightman 1992), though the output can be difficult to interpret and modify because it is a statistical construct without a physical basis.

Cheung, and colleagues applied GAs to this data reduction problem by selecting representative basis functions from the set of original HRTFs (Cheung, Trautmann and Horner 1998). This makes the output much more intuitive to work with. A least squares solution was used to compute the optimal combination of linear weights to represent the individual HRTFs at different azimuths and elevations. An average relative spectral error was used as the fitness function. They found that only three basis functions were required to closely match the original HRTFs while achieving a 50-fold data reduction.

Ng and Horner (2000) investigated the computation and memory tradeoffs in matching acoustic instruments with a hybrid wavetable-filter model. They tried to find the best combination of wavetables followed by a time-varying filter for computation and storage efficiency. They found that the optimal computation and memory use of the model simplified to a wavetable model without the filter. The filter only gave marginal improvement in this particular model and was not worth the extra computation and memory. Adding one wavetable to the match was equivalent to increasing the filter order by at least five. This somewhat surprising result confirmed the effectiveness of wavetable matching at efficiently capturing the overall spectral shape and evolution. The result does not mean that filters are not useful for sculpting sound, but that adjusting the wavetable parameters was a more efficient means of control for this particular model.

Schatter, and colleagues used GA and fuzzy sets to generate subtractive synthesis parameters for particular target sounds (Schatter, Züger and Nitschke 2005). The set of fuzzy controllers was used to map between the user-interface and sound generator. GAs were used to optimize the subtractive synthesis parameters in best approximating the target sound.

3.2.4. Sampling Synthesis

Sampling is the most popular music synthesis technique used in current synthesizers and sound cards. It produces high-quality tones by simply playing back the originally recorded samples (Roads 1996). For sustained sounds, it continuously loops over a segment of the samples until the note is released. The looping can be considered a simple form of wavetable synthesis with a single wavetable. The quality of the original recording and the effectiveness of its looped sustain are the main criteria for success in sampling and the method is computationally cheap. The disadvantages of sampling are its memory requirements and limited flexibility. For example, a single piano tone of 4.3 s requires about 388 kB of memory at a CD-quality sample rate. If we use two notes per octave over six octaves, then more than 4 MB of memory is needed just for the piano alone. Another disadvantage of sampling is its lack of flexibility, especially at time scaling. We can loop the sustain, but stretching the attack and decay is very difficult with sampling.

To overcome these difficulties, Serra and colleagues first suggested a hybrid sampling-wavetable model in their paper on wavetable interpolation (Serra et al.

1990). The idea is to use sampling synthesis for the perceptually critical attack and wavetable synthesis for the more gradually changing steady-state and decay. The resulting tone thus has high-quality attacks, with only modest memory requirements. The wavetable match of the steady-state and decay also improves, since no wavetables need to be devoted to modelling the attack. Thus the hybrid model attempts to integrate the advantages of sampling and wavetable synthesis. The model is especially appropriate for instrument tones with short but complex attacks such as piano, percussion and plucked string tones.

Yuen and colleagues (Yuen and Horner 1997; Yuen, Chan and Horner 1996) implemented and evaluated the hybrid sampling-wavetable model using GA optimization of the wavetable parameters. The method minimizes phase cancellations during the crossfade between sampling and wavetable synthesis. The method was used to effectively and compactly match piano, harp, glockenspiel and temple block tones. A piano design requiring 4 MB of memory for sampling synthesis was data reduced to 300 kB of memory for the hybrid model.

A possible future application of GA to sampling would be to find pairs of suitable loop points in sustained tones. By using different loop points each time through the loop, perhaps the spectral dynamics can be made more natural. By making the spectral variations less predictable, at least some of the most annoying looping artefacts can be avoided.

3.2.5. Frequency Modulation (FM) Synthesis

Like wavetable synthesis, FM synthesis generates interesting sounds efficiently. There are several types of FM, including those with multiple parallel modulators, nested (serial) modulators and feedback (Fig. 3.4). Like multiple wavetable synthesis, FM can combine several carrier-modulator pairs in parallel, as in Fig. 3.5. During the height of FMs popularity in the 1980s, synthesizers such as the Yamaha DX7 allowed users great flexibility in mixing and matching these models.

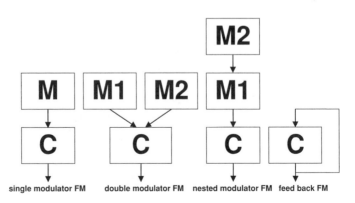

FIGURE 3.4. Block diagrams of several types of FM.

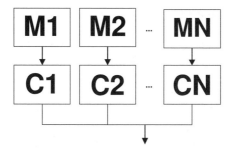

FIGURE 3.5. Block diagram of multiple-carrier single-modulator FM.

Chowning's original FM equation used for music synthesis consisted of a single sine wave modulating a carrier sine wave in a vibrato-like fashion (Chowning 1973). In fact, with sub-audio modulator frequencies, the result is vibrato. However, with an audio-rate modulator frequency, the result is frequency modulation. A Bessel function difference determines the amplitude values of FM-produced harmonics.

A modulation index controls the amount of modulation and the precise shape of the spectrum. The spectrum bandwidth generally increases as the modulation index increases, although a great deal of oscillation accompanies this growth. Time-varying modulation indices produce dynamically changing spectra from a single FM carrier-modulator pair. Wavetable synthesis with a single table lacks this control. Unfortunately, spectral components often fade in and out too dramatically as the modulation index changes. This is not characteristic of the spectral evolution of musical tones.

A harmonic tone results if the carrier frequency is an integer multiple of the modulator frequency, a special case named *formant FM*, since the spectrum spreads out, like a formant, around the carrier frequency.

Like wavetable synthesis, FM synthesis is very efficient in terms of computation and storage. A single carrier-modulator FM instrument requires about the same amount of computation as a pair of wavetables. However, FM can store a single sine waveform for all the carriers and modulators. FM is thus more storage efficient than wavetable synthesis. Also, if the modulation index is not time-varying, the carrier's output will be a static spectrum. The FM model provides similar control to that found in wavetable synthesis. However, unlike wavetable synthesis, the spectrum produced by FM is not arbitrary, but restricted to a subset of possible spectra.

One of the factors leading to FM's decline in popularity is that matching an arbitrary musical instrument tone is difficult, much more difficult than wavetable matching. A closed-form analytical solution for determining the best set of FM parameters does not exist and some form of optimization is necessary. Most previous work on FM has used *ad hoc* and semi-automated techniques for matching instrument tones. However, hand-tuning of multiple carriers quickly exceeds the limits of human ability and endurance.

Chowning's original paper on FM included some hand-tailored instruments (Chowning 1973). He gave parameters appropriate to various classes of instruments based on simulating properties of those instruments. For instance, the brightness of a brass tone is usually proportional to its overall amplitude. Chowning simulated this behaviour by taking advantage of the fact that the brightness of FM spectra generally increases as the modulation index increases. He then varied the modulation index in direct proportion to the amplitude of the carrier to approximate a brass instrument. He produced woodwind-like tones and percussive sounds using similar methods. Chowning also discussed a double carrier instrument near the end of his paper.

Morrill's study of FM trumpet tones (Morrill 1977) followed Chowning's lead in trying to determine parameters based on detailed knowledge of the trumpet. Morrill outlined single and double carrier instrument designs for the trumpet and clearly identified the limitations of single carrier instruments. His double carrier instrument set the carrier frequencies to the fundamental and sixth harmonic, the latter corresponding to a known upper formant region in the trumpet. He also pointed out the difficulty in predicting the spectral output of the double carrier instrument.

Beauchamp (1982) developed a frequency-domain method to find FM parameters as part of a larger study on brightness (spectral centroid) matching. He used a single carrier-modulator pair with a centroid-controlled modulation index to match the time-varying spectral centroid of the original signal. Though the level of control was too coarse to provide a good perceptual match, the technique was notable in its attempt to perform an automated spectral match.

In recent years, researchers have introduced evolutionary matching techniques for the various FM models, first applying them to formant FM (Horner, Beauchamp and Haken 1993b). A genetic algorithm procedure was used to optimize the modulation indices and carrier and modulator frequencies for various numbers of carriers. The GA found invariant modulation indices because time-varying modulation indices cause harmonics to fade in and out, a spectral property not at all characteristic of acoustic instruments. Using invariant indices also avoids index discontinuities and the considerable extra expense of optimizing time-varying indices. As in wavetable matching, the relative spectral error between the original and matched spectra served as fitness function in guiding the GAs search for the best FM parameters. Most matched instruments required three to five carriers for a good match, similar to the wavetable matching results.

A few years after Chowning's original work, Schottstaedt (1977) introduced a double modulator FM model with two parallel modulators. If the carrier and modulator frequencies are all related by integer multiples of the fundamental, a harmonic tone results. Double FM-produced harmonics depend on a sum of Bessel function differences and products. This is a more complicated relationship than the single modulator FM, where each carrier's harmonics depend on a single Bessel function difference. This complexity makes double FM parameter optimization a more difficult task than the formant FM parameter optimization.

In a later study, Chowning (1980) designed a double carrier FM instrument to simulate a singing soprano voice. Like Morrill's FM trumpet, Chowning centred the first carrier at the fundamental and the second at an upper formant, intuitively deriving the parameters of the instrument. He identified vibrato as critically important in achieving a voice-like sound.

Schottstaedt (1977) changed the basic FM instrument design by using two modulators to simultaneously modulate the frequency of a single carrier. After describing the spectral behaviour of the double modulator FM model, he gave parameters for simulating the piano and string instruments. Schottstaedt used instrument characteristics and trial-and-error to find the parameters. He found small modulation indices to be the most useful.

Tan et al. (1994) introduced an enumerative procedure for optimizing a steady-state double modulator FM model. Because this model only produced static spectra, it did not effectively match instruments with dynamic spectra. Since then, genetic algorithms have successfully optimized the double FM problem (Horner 1996b; Lim and Tan 1999; Tan and Lim 1996;). The GA optimized invariant modulation indices and found relatively small modulation indices. Double FM matches were worse than formant FM matches when compared against the same number of table lookups. However, double FM matches were better than formant FM matches for the same number of carriers, an advantage when double FM hardware is available.

Justice (1979) introduced the nested modulator FM model with serial modulators. Like double FM, if the carrier and modulator frequencies are all related by integer multiples of the fundamental, a harmonic tone results. Writing the nested modulator FM equation in terms of Bessel functions results in an infinite set of sums, which is a much more complicated relationship than the Bessel function expansion of double FM. This complexity makes nested FM parameter optimization more difficult than double FM parameter optimization.

Justice (1979) also outlined a Hilbert transform procedure to decompose a signal into parameters for a single carrier FM instrument. The procedure attempted to produce a matched FM signal close to the original, leaving the user to tweak the parameters as desired. However, Justice matched FM-generated signals and not those of acoustic musical instruments.

Payne (1987) extended Justice's technique to a pair of carriers with nested modulators. Each carrier contributed to an independent frequency region, giving a more accurate match than with a single carrier. In addition to matching contrived FM signals, Payne matched a cello sound. The result was reportedly string-like, but lacking properties of liveliness. Payne reported that the matching procedure was computationally very expensive.

Delprat and her collaborators used a wavelet analysis and a Gabor transform to find spectral trajectories to estimate the modulation parameters (Delprat, Guillemain and Kronland-Martinet 1990; Delprat 1997). This approach is similar to that used by Justice and Payne except that it breaks the frequency range into more component parts. Thus, it is also computationally expensive. Delprat gave examples for a saxophone and trumpet using five carrier-modulator pairs, an indication that precise spectral control requires multiple carriers.

Horner (1998) also applied the GA to nested modulator FM matching, optimizing invariant modulation indices. Like double FM matching, the optimized parameters for nested modulator FM had relatively small modulation indices. The results showed that if nested modulator FM hardware is already available, then double or triple modulator FM gives the best results of all the FM models for the same number of carriers.

Another FM variant that proved useful in synthesizers in the 1980s was feedback FM (Mitsuhashi 1982; Tomisawa 1981). The output of the carrier modulates the following sample, scaled by a modulation index. When the modulation index is less than about 1.5, a monotonically decreasing spectrum results (Tomisawa 1981). Because of this, feedback FM is potentially more easily controlled than the other forms of FM, where the harmonics oscillate in amplitude as the modulation index changes. Another advantage of feedback FM over other forms of FM is that its harmonic amplitudes are strictly positive when the modulation index is less than 1.5 (other forms of FM produce both positive and negative amplitudes). This avoids cancellation when adding multiple carriers together. The monotonically decreasing spectrum of feedback FM has a disadvantage as well. Many musical instruments have strong formants at upper harmonics, but feedback FM's monotonic spectrum cannot model these formants. Ring modulation of the feedback FM carrier with a cosine wave overcomes this limitation and allows formant simulation (Dodge and Jerse 1997, pp. 92–94).

GAs have also been applied to feedback FM matching using time-varying modulation indices (Horner 1998). Like double FM, the optimized parameters for feedback FM had relatively small modulation indices. Feedback FM often gave the best matches of all the FM models when compared against the same number of table lookups, indicating feedback FM is a good choice for software synthesis where computation is the main factor.

Overall, FM synthesis provides real-time flexibility over wavetable synthesis when wavetable memory is limited, though wavetable matching is simpler and more effective than FM matching in general (Horner 1997). Among the various types of FM, the best method depends on the given situation. For simplicity and ease of control, formant FM is best. For software synthesis where computation is the main factor, feedback FM is best. If FM hardware is available, nested modulator FM is best.

3.2.6. Waveshaping Synthesis

Risset was the first to experiment with what is now known as waveshaping synthesis or nonlinear distortion (Risset and Mathews 1969). Arfib (1979) and LeBrun (1979) independently established the method as an alternative to FM synthesis. Like FM synthesis, waveshaping allows dynamic control of the spectrum with only a few parameters and it allows more precise spectral control in some ways.

The basic idea is to pass a sine wave of variable amplitude through a shaping function, which distorts the signal. The sine wave amplitude envelope has the effect of scaling the input signal, which indirectly controls the level of distortion. Typically higher-amplitude values result in more distortion and a richer spectral output, somewhat the way many acoustic instruments increase in brightness with increasing amplitude. Lebrun and Arfib showed that by restricting the shaping function to Chebyshev polynomials, the output steady-state spectrum can be predicted. In waveshaping, the amplitude of the input sine wave is thus used to control timbre, rather than overall loudness. Instead, a second amplitude envelope is applied to the output of the shaping function to control overall loudness. Roads (1996, pp. 252–260) gives a more detailed overview of waveshaping synthesis.

To match an acoustic instrument sound there are, therefore, three parameters: The shaping function, the sine wave amplitude envelope and the loudness amplitude envelope. Arfib (1979) and Beauchamp (1982) showed how to set these parameters for a simple waveshaper. These results are similar in nature and quality to that of optimizing a simple formant FM module with time-varying modulation index. Beauchamp (1979) added a high pass filter to the waveshaping output to better simulate brass instruments by matching their brightness evolution.

Beauchamp and Horner (1992) used GA optimization of filter and waveshaping parameters with multiple waveshapers. Because of the large number of parameters, an iterative strategy was used. First, parameters were found for a single waveshaper and high pass filter. They then subtracted the resulting spectrum from the original spectrum to obtain a residual spectrum. Parameters for a second waveshaper and filter were then found to best match the residual spectrum. Average errors were reduced by 25% and 50% for two and three waveshapers, respectively.

3.2.7. Discrete Summation Synthesis

Discrete summation synthesis is a relatively unknown cousin of FM synthesis and was first described by Moorer (1976, 1977). Like FM, discrete summation synthesis generates a complete set of harmonic sine waves from only a small number of them (usually two to five). The price paid for this computational efficiency is that only a subset of possible spectra can be produced. More spectral control can be obtained by using multiple ring-modulated discrete summation synthesis modules, each with its own amplitude envelope (Dodge and Jerse 1997). The spectrum of each module is controlled by three parameters: The amplitude decay factor, carrier frequency and modulating frequency. The discrete summation synthesis parameters have a more straightforward effect than FM parameters. The output spectrum of each module has double sidebands centred on a peak at the carrier frequency, with partials in each sideband decaying exponentially according to the decay factor. Like formant FM, if the carrier and modulating frequencies are suitably constrained, the resulting sidebands will form a harmonic series.

Most work on discrete summation synthesis has been limited to theoretical discussion about the discrete summation synthesis formulas, with the parameters left to the user to pick by hand. An exception is the work by Chan and colleagues (Chan and Horner 1996; Yuen, Chan and Horner 1996), which used genetic algorithm optimization of discrete summation synthesis parameters. They found that three to five discrete summations were adequate to give good matches. They also compared the performance of discrete summation matching with wavetable matching. Wavetable matching always gave better results, but the difference was relatively small when more modules were used.

Overall, discrete summation synthesis is an excellent choice when wavetable memory is limited (e.g. in mobile phones) since it only requires a single sine wave. Discrete summation synthesis also provides more real-time flexibility than wavetable synthesis. Compared to FM synthesis, the spectra of discrete summations have a straightforward roll off, which makes them more intuitive to work with than FM-generated spectra.

3.2.8. Granular Synthesis

Granular synthesis builds up a complex sound from a cloud of very short grains of simple sounds (Xenakis 1971; Roads 1978, 1985; Roads 1996). Typically, each grain is about 10 to 100 ms and composed of simple waveforms, FM waveforms (Truax 1988; Roads 1985; Waschka and Ferreira 1988) or sound samples (Jones and Parks 1988; Truax 1989, 1993). Aside from the waveform, other grain parameters include amplitude, frequency and duration. Precise control of the grains is cumbersome because there are typically hundreds of them combined at each instant to build up a sound cloud.

To overcome this difficulty, several high-level approaches have been devised to regulate the multitude of parameters, including cellular automaton (Bowcott 1989; Orton, Hunt and Kirk 1991), population modelling (Bowcott 1990), nonlinear functions (Hamman 1991) and neural networks (Nagashima 1992).

Bowcott (1990) used an evolutionary algorithm to generate granular synthesis events. The chromosome of each grain includes its synthesis type and a list of parameters for the synthesis type. The events change in time as the evolution process unfolds and the grains respond to one another.

Fujinaga and Vantomme (1994) used genetic algorithms to regulate granular synthesis parameters. They considered each grain an individual in the GA population and mapped the grain's parameters to the chromosome bitstring. Each population represents a time frame in the overall evolution of the cloud. Change can be controlled in the grain population by dynamically varying the GA crossover rate, mutation rate, population size and the fitness function itself. Since the application is free from the usual GA constraints such as the need to converge, composers can freely modify the GA parameters to explore the granular sound space. The same idea can be applied with other evolutionary processes that have populations of individuals.

In another approach, Johnson (2003) implemented a system for exploring sound spaces with interactive GAs. The system acts as an interface to FOF synthesis (Roads 1996), which Johnson classifies as a special case of granular synthesis. The user is presented with an interface consisting of a series of buttons, each representing a current member of the population. The user rates the sounds with a slider and when finished, signals the population to advance to the next generation. Johnson found that it only took a small number of generations to converge the population to one particular region in the sound space.

3.2.9. Physical Modelling Synthesis

Physical modelling synthesis uses mathematical models of an instrument's physical acoustics. The advantages of physical modelling include scalability (being able to produce a family of instruments from a single instrument model), more realistic note and timbre transitions and the ability to naturally produce performance accidents such as split notes and squeaks. Physical models can be computationally expensive, but some relatively efficient algorithms such as waveguides have been devised based on DSP operations such as delay lines, filters and table lookup (Roads 1996). This efficiency is gained at the expense of accuracy, with results that are often instrument-like rather than near-perfect matches.

Even these efficient physical models contain a large number of parameters. There are many effective methods for the estimation of these parameters for linear models, but estimation of parameters for nonlinear models is very difficult (Smith 1983).

Vuori and Välimäki (1993) used a simulated evolution algorithm for parameter estimation of nonlinear physical models. The technique was applied to estimate the steady-state parameters of their real-time DSP flute model, which consisted of three delay lines and appropriate digital filters between them. The simulated evolution algorithm converged smoothly and effectively to the desired level. Vuori and Välimäki noted the same approach could be used for the parameter estimation of other nonlinear models as well.

Cook (1995) used physical models of a flute for both sound synthesis and animation. For the sound synthesis part, he used a series of cylindrical waveguides with tonehole junctions and filters, a coupled-noise model to more accurately model noise components and low-order filters to model the inertial characteristics of the flute player's fingers. Controlling this complex instrument through the parameters was very difficult. Cook set the initial parameters from physical measurements and first principles. He then randomized the parameters around the initial values and used a GA to optimize the parameters through evolution. The synthesis model was then combined with ray-tracing animation to create the sonic and visual experience of 'driving around outside and inside the flute'.

3.2.10. Waveform Synthesis

Most of the synthesis techniques mentioned previously are frequency-domain techniques, where the spectrum of the instruments is optimized or manipulated. An alternative approach is to work with the time-domain waveform directly, which can be called signal matching rather than spectral matching. Signal matching is generally much more difficult than spectral matching since both the spectrum and the phase must be matched in signal matching, whereas most spectral matching research only matches the spectrum.

Stapleton and Bass (1988) applied a spectrum matching technique for waveform synthesis of musical instrument tones. Their method, based on the Karhunen-Loeve (KL) transform, determines time-domain basis functions from the signal itself. The approach requires phase alignment of the basis waveforms as well as their amplitude envelopes. The procedure is expensive (due to the computational cost of finding phase alignments) and has phase cancellation problems when the amplitude envelopes are changed during resynthesis. These are major obstacles in the practical application of this technique.

In a completely different approach, Magnus (2004) designed an algorithm to evolve waveforms. The goal was to produce genetically evolved music that gradually moves toward a user-specified target waveform. Thus, the emphasis is on the process rather than the result. In this work, chromosomes are time-domain waveforms. To avoid clicks that would result from mutation or crossover of individual samples, each gene represents a waveform segment between zero crossings. Fitness is based on similarity to a target waveform. During evolution, all the waveforms in the population are written to a single sound file with each individual waveform weighted by its fitness. The weighting causes individuals closest to the target waveform to be most prominent. Thus, the musical output is greatly varied at the beginning, with some fit individuals emerging within a few generations and gradually the population takes on properties of the target waveform, perhaps even converging to it. Magnus experimented with different types of mutation including segment amplification, exponentiation, reversal, removal, repetition and swapping. She found that each mutation type has its own characteristic sound. For example, repetition allows the target waveform to be most readily identified. Magnus incorporated her algorithm in a compositional framework where a world is defined in which the waveforms evolve. The world is characterized by a number of loudspeaker locations, each with its own target waveform and mutation probabilities.

A very similar form of waveform synthesis by evolutionary processes was investigated in papers by Fornari and colleagues (2001a, b, c). Their system also created an evolutionary sequence of waveforms that gradually converge to a target population. A genetic algorithm applied waveform transformations using customized crossover and mutation operators. A Hamming window was used to smooth waveform segments selected for crossover to avoid clicks. Mutation was implemented as a modulation of the initial waveform. For each generation, only the best waveform in the population is sent to the output sound file. The sonic evolution tends to converge to a static sound when the target population remains unchanged, but the user is allowed to intervene and replace the target population at any time, thus pushing evolution in a different direction.

3.2.11. Synthesis System Design

Synthesis system design is a generalization of parameter optimization where the sound synthesis method itself is optimized as a parameter.

Takala et al. (1993) used *timbre trees* to represent sound signals, where each node in the tree represented an arithmetic operation, analytic function or noise generator. Vectorized operations were also provided for compact representation of additive synthesis. They used interactive GA to mutate timbre trees, with users guiding the evolution. Using these tools, they produced a class of bee-like sounds ranging from mosquitoes to chain saws, as well as a class of police sirens ranging from the realistic to the bizarre. They also varied the parameter values to allow sound morphing over the full range of bee-like and chainsaw-like sounds. This system can be viewed as the first application of genetic programming to sound design.

Garcia (2000, 2001) extended and generalized this genetic programming approach to automating the design of sound synthesis algorithms. The system used expression trees to represent sound synthesis algorithms. Evolutionary methods were used in two stages: (1) for suggesting how the trees should be structured and (2) for optimizing the parameters within the tree. The main idea is to allow the evolutionary method to suggest which form of synthesis (FM, LPC, filter synthesis, etc.) is most effective at representing the target sound. For a fitness function, Garcia used phase information as well as spectral information. He also used a psychoacoustic model of simultaneous frequency masking in some of his experiments. He tested his system on a simple FM woodwind instrument and verified that it could generate an expression tree with close similarity to that of the target equation (Garcia 2001). The spectrum agreed with the target in general but had higher energy at high frequencies. He also tested a piano tone sampled from a synthesizer with modest success, managing to evolve a tone that sounded like a 'string hit by a hammer' (Garcia 2005).

It would be interesting to see if synthesis system design can more successfully replicate acoustic instruments without phase optimization. GAs are good for problems that are big, but not too big. If there are too many parameters, the GA may not find a promising region of the search space. The system might work better if at least the general synthesis type is specified in advance by the user (FM synthesis, wavetable synthesis/interpolation, filtering, etc.). As an example, if the user selects FM synthesis, the system could then determine which form of FM gives the best representation (e.g. formant FM, multiple modulator FM, nested modulator FM or feedback FM). In any case, synthesis system design is an area with good potential for further exploration.

3.3. Other Digital Audio Applications

In addition to music synthesis and processing, evolutionary algorithms have also been used in a variety of other digital audio applications. Music recognition in particular includes a wide range of musical applications. Optical recognition of music notation and musical instrument recognition are two music recognition applications where genetic algorithms have been used. Another GA application is the tuning of musical scales.

3.3.1. Optical Music Recognition

Automatic recognition of musical notation is called optical music recognition. Typically, such a system uses various features such as height, width, area and central moments of the musical symbols (Fujinaga 1996). The feature vectors of a given sample are compared to those of previously classified samples, to determine the class of the closest match. The k-nearest neighbour (k-NN) classifier assigns the class represented by the majority of the k-nearest neighbours to the given sample.

Fujinaga (1996) combined the k-NN classifier and a genetic algorithm to form an exemplar-based learning system. The system can learn to recognize new music symbols and handwritten music notation. It continuously improves by adjusting the weighting of each feature. The weights are coded as genes in the GA. Fujinaga's experiments with the system showed dramatic improvements in the recognition rate.

3.3.2. Music Instrument Recognition

Another classification problem is that of timbre recognition, which has become very popular in recent years (Herrera-Boyer 2003). Similar to their optical musical recognition work, Fujinaga and his co-authors again used an exemplar-based learning system with a k-NN classifier enhanced by a genetic algorithm (Fujinaga 1998; Fraser and Fujinaga 1999; Fujinaga and MacMillan 2000). In his first experiment, Fujinaga (1998) selected features from the steady-state portion of the sound. The features included spectral centroid and higher order moments such as skewness. The recognition rate was 50% for a 39-timbre group and 81% for a 3-timbre group. In a second experiment (Fraser and Fujinaga 1999), two improvements were made. First, features were selected from the attack rather than steady-state portions of the sound. Second, dynamic spectral features were added such as spectral centroid velocity and its variance. The recognition rate increased to 64% for the 39-timbre group and to 98% for the 3-timbre group. In a third experiment (Fujinaga and MacMillan 2000), the system was implemented in real time and spectral irregularity and tristimulus were added as spectral envelope features. The recognition rate increased further to 68% for the 39-timbre group.

3.3.3. Musical Tuning

Another digital audio application is the search for optimal tuning of musical scales. The idea is to tune a harmonic progression so that the harmonic intervals are as beat-free as possible. The assumption is that minimizing beats results in better tuning.

While it is possible to tune some simple chord sequences without beats using a fixed just tuning (Doty 1993), for other sequences it is not. Considerable previous work has focused on fixed tunings such as just, Pythagorean, meantone, Werkmeister, Vallotti and equal temperament (Lloyd and Boyle 1979; Partch 1974; Lindley 1984; Carlos 1987; Chalmers 1993). For instance, assuming that the worst tuning errors among thirds and fifths must be minimized, the best fixed tuning for a mostly diatonic piece tends to be close to one-fourth comma meantone tuning and the best tuning for an adventurously chromatic piece tends to be close to equal temperament (Hall 1980).

If a fixed pitch centre is sacrificed, a wider range of chord sequences can be tuned without beats using an adaptive just tuning of the notes (Sethares 1994). An adaptive tuning allows the pitch of a particular note to vary according to its context. For example, a middle C might be tuned to 260 Hz on one note and 258 Hz on another. Creating a composition through software synthesis allows the use of adaptive tunings.

Sethares (1994) introduced an adaptive just tuning method for harmonic timbres based on maximizing consonance, an idea mentioned in Polansky (1987). The technique customizes tunings based on the music and also on the timbre of the instruments playing it.

Even with an adaptive just tuning, the intervals in many musical examples cannot be tuned without beats. In such cases, some form of optimization is needed to minimize beats. Horner and Ayers (1996) used a genetic algorithm to optimize adaptive tunings for chord sequences. The method makes the thirds and fifths as beatless as possible. The GA results were significantly better in a number of musical examples compared to just intonation, with its commas and other standard tunings, such as meantone and equal temperament.

Of course, making thirds and fifths as beatless as possible may run counter to the composer's intention of creating tension in the equal tempered beating of particular chords. Adaptive tuning is probably best suited for pre-equal tempered music and contemporary music written specifically for it, though it can give attractive results in many kinds of music.

3.4. Conclusions

We have reviewed the application of evolutionary algorithms to music synthesis, music processing and other digital audio applications. GAs in particular have proved effective in evolving parameters for nearly every form of music synthesis. They have also been used in a variety of other digital audio applications including artificial reverberation, sound localization, music recognition and musical tuning.

GA solutions are often much more intuitive to work with than statistically-generated solutions. For example, in wavetable parameter optimization the basis spectra are selected from the original spectral snapshots rather than being statistically-generated. The same holds true in HRTF data reduction in sound localization. These solutions have a physical basis that users can intuitively understand.

The optimized parameters for the various music synthesis techniques provide an interesting point of departure for instrument designers in applications such as *timbral interpolation* (Grey 1975; Beauchamp and Horner 1998). Timbral interpolation crossfades the parameters of one spectral match to that of another. The smoothness of the transformation depends on the synthesis technique. For example, wavetable synthesis gives a smoother interpolation than FM synthesis, since interpolating distantly spaced FM index values will likely produce wildly changing spectral results during the interpolation due to oscillation of the Bessel functions. However, such interpolations may be musically interesting and useful.

Genetic and evolutionary algorithms are a great way to optimize digital audio problems with many interacting variables, but even GAs can fail to find good solutions when there are too many variables or their interactions are too complex. For example, phase optimization in time waveforms must take into account phase cancellations which are subtle and complex. While finding a good group of phases is possible for a single waveform period (Horner 2000; Horner and Wun 2005), tracking time-varying changes in the phase is indeed difficult (Garcia 2000, 2001, 2005). While this threshold will gradually rise as CPU speeds continue to increase in the future, nevertheless some problems will remain intractable.

Evolutionary algorithms are a great way to solve a problem when no problem-specific approach is obvious. As we saw with wavetable parameter optimization, once a GA solution was in place, other methods emerged and could be tested against this benchmark (Horner 2001; Mohr 2002; Ng and Horner 2002; Wun, Horner and Ayers 2003; Wun, Horner and Ayers 2004; Mohr and Li 2005a, b; Wun and Horner 2005a, b). Another example was finding line segment approximations of amplitude envelopes for additive software synthesis, where a greedy approach could find solutions about as good as GA and much faster.

Evolutionary algorithms have attractive characteristics that make them well suited to digital audio problems. As parameter optimizers, they are easy-to-use, flexible and effective. As natural processes, they are an appealing way to evolve musical timbres. As learning algorithms, they are a great way to gracefully adapt to new situations in music recognition applications. Evolutionary algorithms will surely prove useful in many other digital audio applications in the future.

Acknowledgements

The Hong Kong Research Grant Council's Projects HKUST6167/03E and HKUST6135/05E supported this work.

References

Arfib, D. (1979). Digital synthesis of complex spectra by means of multiplication of non-linear distorted sine waves. *Journal of the Audio Engineering Society,* **27**(10): 757–779.

Atal, B. and Hanauer, S. (1971). Speech analysis and synthesis by linear prediction of the speech wave. *Journal of the Acoustical Society of America,* **50**(2): 637–655.

Beauchamp, J.W. (1969). A computer system for time-variant harmonic analysis and synthesis of musical tones, In H. von Foerster and J.W. Beauchamp (Eds.), *Music By Computers.* John Wiley & Sons, NY.

Beauchamp, J.W. (1979). Brass-tone synthesis by spectrum evolution matching with non-linear functions, *Computer Music Journal,* **3**(2): 35–43. Revised and updated version In C. Roads and J. Strawn (Eds.), *Foundations of Computer Music,* MIT Press, Cambridge, MA: pp. 95–113.

Beauchamp, J.W. (1982). Synthesis by amplitude and 'brightness' matching of analyzed musical instrument tones.*Journal of the Audio Engineering Society,* **30**(6): 396–406.

Beauchamp, J.W. and Horner, A. (1992). Extended nonlinear waveshaping analysis/synthesis techniques, In *Proceedings of the 1992 International Computer Music Conference,* San Jose, CA, pp. 2–5.

Beauchamp, J.W. and Horner, A. (1998). Spectral modeling and timbre hybridization programs for computer music. *Organised Sound,* **2**(3): 253–258.

Bowcott, P. (1989). Cellular automation as a means of high level compositional control of granular synthesis. In *Proceedings of the 1989 International Computer Music Conference,* Columbus, OH, pp. 55–57.

Bowcott, P. (1990). High level control of granular synthesis using the concepts of inheritance and social interaction." In *Proceedings of the 1990 International Computer Music Conference,* Columbus, OH, pp. 50–52.

Cann, R. (1979–1980). An analysis/synthesis tutorial, *Computer Music Journal,* **3**(3): 6–11; **3**(4): 9–13; **4**(1): 36–42.

Carlos, W. (1987). Tuning: At the crossroads. *Computer Music Journal,* **11**(1): 29–43.

Chalmers, J. (1993). *Divisions of the Tetrachord.* Hanover, NH: Frog Peak Music.

Chamberlin, H. (1980). Advanced real-timbre music synthesis techniques. *Byte Magazine,* April: 70–94 and 180–196.

Chan, S.K. and Horner, A. (1996). Discrete summation synthesis of musical instrument tones using genetic algorithms. *Journal of the Audio Engineering Society,* **44**(7): 581–592.

Cheung, N.M. and Horner, A. (1996). Group synthesis with genetic algorithms. *Journal of the Audio Engineering Society,* **44**(3): 130–147.

Cheung, N.M., Trautmann, S. and Horner, A. (1998b). Head-related transfer function modeling in 3-d sound systems with genetic algorithms. *Journal of the Audio Engineering Society,* **46**(6): 531–539.

Chowning, J. (1973). The synthesis of complex audio spectra by means of frequency modulation. *Journal of the Audio Engineering Society,* **21**(7): 526–534.

Chowning, J. (1980). Computer synthesis of the singing voice, *Sound Generation in Wind, Strings, Computers.* Stockholm: The Royal Swedish Academy of Music.

Chu, C.H.H. (1990). A genetic algorithm approach to the configuration of stack filters. In *Proceedings of the 3rd International Conference on Genetic Algorithms and their Applications.* Arlington, VA, pp. 219–224.

Cook, P. (1995). Integration of physical modeling for synthesis and animation. In *Proceedings of the 1995 International Computer Music Conference.* Banff, Canada, pp. 525–528.

Delprat, N., Guillemain, P. and Kronland-Martinet, R. (1990). Parameter estimation for nonlinear resynthesis methods with the help of a time-frequency analysis of natural sounds. In *Proceedings of the 1990 International Computer Music Conference.* Glasgow, pp. 88–90.

Delprat, N. (1997). Global frequency modulation law extraction from the gabor transform of a signal: A first study of the interacting components case. *IEEE Transactions on Speech and Audio Processing,* **5**(1): pp. 64–71.

Dodge, C. (1989). On speech songs. In M. Mathews and J. Pierce (Eds.), *Current Directions in Computer Music Research.,* Cambridge, MA, MIT Press, pp. 9–17.

Dodge, C. and Jerse, T. (1997). *Computer Music.* Schirmer Books, NY.

Doty, D. (1993). *The Just Intonation Primer.* Other Music, San Francisco, p. 38.

Flanagan, J.L. (1972). *Speech Analysis, Synthesis, and Perception.* Springer-Verlag, NY.

Fornari, J., Manzolli, J., Maia, A. and Damiani, F. (2001a). *The Evolutionary Sound Synthesis Method*. ACM Multimedia, Ottawa, Ont, Canada, September 2001.

Fornari, J., Manzolli, J., Maia, A. and Damiani, F. (2001b). Waveform synthesis using evolutionary computation. In *Proceedings of the V Brazilian Symposium on Computer Music*. Fortaleza, Brazil.

Fornari, J., Manzolli, J., Maia, A. and Damiani, F. (2001c). The Evolutionary Sound Synthesis Method. *SCI Conference*. Orlando, FL.

Fujinaga, I. and Vantomme, J. (1994). Genetic algorithms as a method for granular synthesis regulation. In *Proceedings of the 1994 International Computer Music Conference*. Aarhus, Denmark, pp. 138–141.

Fujinaga, I. (1996). Exemplar-based learning in adaptive optical music recognition system. In *Proceedings of the 1996 International Computer Music Conference*, Hong Kong, pp. 55–56.

Fujinaga, I. (1998). Machine recognition of timbre using steady-state of acoustic musical instruments. In *Proceedings of the 1998 International Computer Music Conference*. Ann Arbor, MI, pp. 207–210.

Fraser, A. and Fujinaga, I. (1999). Toward real-time recognition of acoustic musical instruments. In *Proceedings of the 1999 International Computer Music Conference*. Beijing, pp. 175–177.

Fujinaga, I. and MacMillan, K. (2000). Realtime recognition of orchestral instruments. In *Proceedings of the 2000 International Computer Music Conference*. Berlin, pp. 241–243.

Garcia, R. (2000). Towards the Automatic Generation of Sound Synthesis Techniques: Preparatory Steps. *109th Convention. Audio Engineering Society*. Los Angeles, CA, Preprint 5186.

Garcia, R. (2001). *Automatic Generation of Sound Synthesis Techniques*. M.S. Thesis. Cambridge, MA: Media Lab, MIT.

Garcia, R. (2005). http://www.ragomusic.com/research/ml/.

Grey, J. (1975). *An Exploration of Musical Timbre*. Ph.D. Dissertation. Stanford, Department of Music, Stanford University.

Grey, J. and Moorer, J. (1977). Perceptual evaluation of synthesized musical instrument tones. *Journal of the Acoustical Society of America*, **62**: 454–462.

Hall, D. (1980). *Musical Acoustics: An Introduction*. Wordsworth Publishing, Belmont, CA.

Hamman, M. (1991). Mapping complex systems using granular synthesis. In *Proceedings of the 1991 International Computer Music Conference*. Montréal, Canada, pp. 475–478.

Herrera-Boyer, P., Peeters, G. and Dubnov, S. (2003). Automatic classification of musical instrument sounds. *Journal of New Music Research*, **32**(1): 3–21.

Horner, A., Beauchamp, J.W. and Haken, L. (1993a). Methods for multiple wavetable synthesis of musical instrument tones. *Journal of the Audio Engineering Society*, **41**(5): 336–356.

Horner, A., Beauchamp, J.W. and Haken, L. (1993b). Machine tongues XVI: Genetic algorithms and their application to fm matching synthesis. *Computer Music Journal*, **17**(4): 17–29.Horner, A., Beauchamp, J.W. and Packard, N. (1993). Timbre breeding. In *Proceedings of the 1993 International Computer Music Conference*. Tokyo, pp. 396–398.

Horner, A. (1995). Wavetable matching synthesis of dynamic instruments with genetic algorithms. *Journal of the Audio Engineering Society*, **43**(11): 916–931.

Horner, A., Cheung, N.M. and Beauchamp, J.W. (1995). Genetic algorithm optimization of additive synthesis envelope breakpoints and group synthesis parameters. In *Proceedings of the 1995 International Computer Music Conference.* Banff, Canada, pp. 215–222.

Horner, A. (1996a). Computation and memory tradeoffs with multiple wavetable interpolation. *Journal of the Audio Engineering Society,* **44**(6): 481–496.

Horner, A. (1996b). Double modulator fm matching of instrument tones. *Computer Music Journal,* **20**(2): 57–71.

Horner, A. and Ayers, L. (1996). Common tone adaptive tuning using genetic algorithms. *Journal of the Acoustical Society of America,* **100**(1): 630–640.

Horner, A. and Beauchamp, J.W. (1996). Piecewise linear approximation of additive synthesis envelopes: A comparison of various methods. *Computer Music Journal,* **20**(2): 72–95.

Horner, A. (1997). A comparison of wavetable and fm parameter spaces. *Computer Music Journal,* **21**(4): pp. 55–85.

Horner, A. (1998). Nested modulator and feedback fm matching of instrument tones. *IEEE Transactions on Speech and Audio Processing,* **6**(4): 398–409.

Horner, A. and Ayers, L. (1998). Modeling acoustic wind instruments with contiguous group synthesis. *Journal of the Audio Engineering Society,* **46**(10): 868–879.

Horner, A. (1999). Fake horns: Experiments in taped auditions. *The Horn Call: Journal of the International Horn Society,* **30**(1): 61–65.

Horner, A. (2000). Low peak amplitudes for wavetable synthesis. *IEEE Transactions on Speech and Audio Processing,* **8**(4): 467–470.

Horner, A. (2001). A simplified wavetable matching method using combinatorial basis spectra selection. *Journal of the Audio Engineering Society,* **49**(11): 1060–1066.

Horner, A. and Ayers, L. (2002). *Cooking with Csound Part 1: Woodwind and Brass Recipes.* Madison Wisconsin, A-R Editions, Computer Music and Digital Audio Series.

Horner, A. and Wun, C.W. (2005). Low peak amplitudes for group additive synthesis. *Journal of the Audio Engineering Society,* **53**(6): 475–484.

Johnson, C. (2003). Exploring sound-space with interactive genetic algorithms. *Leonardo,* **36**(1): 51–54.

Jones, D.L. and Parks, T. (1988). Generation and combination of grains for music synthesis. *Computer Music Journal,* **12**(2): 27–34.

Justice, J. (1979). Analytic signal processing in music computation. *IEEE Transactions on Acoustics, Speech, and Signal Processing,* **27**(6): 670–684.

Kistler, D. and Wightman, F. (1992). A model of head-related transfer functions based on principal components analysis and minimum-phase reconstruction. *Journal of the Acoustical Society of America,* **91**: 1637–1647.

Kleczkowski, P. (1989). Group additive synthesis. *Computer Music Journal,* **13**(1): 12–20.

Lansky, P. and Steiglitz, K. (1981). Synthesis of timbral families by warped linear prediction. *Computer Music Journal,* **5**(3): 45–49.

Lansky, P. (1989). Compositional applications of linear predictive coding. In M. Mathews and J. Pierce (Eds.), *Current Directions in Computer Music Research.* Cambridge, MA, MIT Press, pp. 5–8.

LeBrun, M. (1979). Digital waveshaping synthesis. *Journal of the Audio Engineering Society,* **27**(4): 250–266.

Lee, K. and Horner, A. (1999). Modeling piano tones with group synthesis. *Journal of the Audio Engineering Society,* **47**(3): 101–111.

Lim, S.M. and Tan, B.T.G. (1999). Performance of the genetic annealing algorithm in DFM synthesis of dynamic musical sound samples. *Journal of the Audio Engineering Society,* **47**(5): 339–354.

Lindley, M. (1984). Temperaments. In S. Sadie (Ed.), *The New Grove Dictionary of Musical Instruments*. Macmillan, London.

Lloyd, L. and Boyle, H. (1979). *Intervals, Scales and Temperaments*. St. Martins Press, NY.

Magnus, C. (2004). Evolving electroacoustic music: The application of genetic algorithms to time-domain waveforms. In *Proceedings of the 2004 International Computer Music Conference*. Miami, pp. 173–176.

Maher, R. and Beauchamp, J.W. (1990). An investigation of vocal vibrato for synthesis. *Applied Acoustics*, **30**: 219–245.

Markel, J. and Gray, A. (1976). *Linear Prediction of Speech*. Springer, NY.

Martens, W. (1987). Principal components analysis and re-synthesis of spectral cues to perceived direction. In *Proceedings of the 1987 International Computer Music Conference*. Urbana, IL, pp. 274–281.

Massie, D. and Stonick, V. (1992). The musical intrigue of pole-zero pairs. In *Proceedings of the 1992 International Computer Music Conference*. San Jose, CA, pp. 22–25.

Mitsuhashi, Y. (1982). Musical sound synthesis by forward differences. *Journal of the Audio Engineering Society*, **30**(1/2): 2–9.

Mohr, J. (2002). *Music Analysis/Synthesis by Optimized Multiple Wavetable Interpolation*. Ph.D. Dissertation. Edmonton, Alberta, Canada, Department of Computer Science, University of Alberta.

Mohr, J. and Li, X. (2005a). Optimized multiple wavetable interpolation. *WSEAS Transactions on Information Science and Applications*, **2**(2): 265–273.

Mohr, J. and Li, X. (2005b). Wavetable interpolation of multiple instrument tones. In *Proceedings of the 2005 International Computer Music Conference*. Barcelona, Spain, pp. 741–744.

Moorer, J.A. (1976). The synthesis of complex audio by means of discrete summation formulas. *Journal of the Audio Engineering Society*, **24**(11): 717–727.

Moorer, J.A. (1977). Signal processing aspects of computer music—A survey. *Computer Music Journal*, **1**(1): 4–37.

Moorer, J.A., Grey, J. and Snell, J. (1977). "Lexicon of analyzed tones—Part I: A violin tone. *Computer Music Journal*, **1**(2): 39–45.

Moorer, J.A., Grey, J. and Strawn, J. (1977). "Lexicon of analyzed tones—Part II: Clarinet and Oboe tones. *Computer Music Journal*, **1**(3): 12–29.

Moorer, J.A., Grey, J. and Strawn, J. (1978). Lexicon of analyzed tones—Part III: The trumpet. *Computer Music Journal*, **2**(2): 23–31.

Moorer, J.A. (1979). The use of linear prediction of speech in computer music applications. *Journal of the Audio Engineering Society*, **27**(3): 134–140.

Morrill, D. (1977). Trumpet algorithms for computer composition. *Computer Music Journal*, **1**(1): 46–52.

Mrozek, E. and Wakefield, G. (1996). Perceptual matching of low order models to room transfer functions. In *Proceedings of the 1996 International Computer Music Conference*. Hong Kong, pp. 111–113.

Nagashima, Y. (1992). Real-time control system for pseudo granulation. In *Proceedings of the 1992 International Computer Music Conference*. San Jose, CA, pp. 404–405.

Ng, A. and Horner, A. (2000). Computation and memory tradeoffs in wavetable-filter matching of musical instrument tones. *Journal of the Audio Engineering Society*, **48**(10): 930–939.

Ng, A. and Horner, A. (2002). Iterative combinatorial basis spectra in wavetable-matching. *Journal of the Audio Engineering Society*, **50**(12): 1054–1063.

Oates, S. and Eaglestone, B. (1997). Analytic methods for group additive synthesis. *Computer Music Journal*, **21**(2): 21–39.

Orton, R., Hunt, A. and Kirk, R. (1991). Graphical control of granular synthesis. In *Proceedings of the 1991 International Computer Music Conference*. Montréal, Canada, pp. 416–418.

Partch, H. (1974). *Genesis of a Music*. Da Capo Press, NY.

Payne, R. (1987). A microcomputer based analysis/resynthesis scheme for processing sampled sounds using FM. In *Proceedings of the 1987 International Computer Music Conference*. Urbana, IL, pp. 282–289.

Polansky, L. (1987). Paratactical tuning: An agenda for the use of computer in experimental intonation. *Computer Music Journal*, **11**(1): 61–68.

Risset, J. and Mathews, M. (1969). Analysis of musical instrument tones. *Physics Today*, **22**(2): 23–30.

Roads, C. (1978). Automated granular synthesis of sound. *Computer Music Journal*, **2**(2): 61–62.

Roads, C. (1982). A conversation with James A. Moorer. *Computer Music Journal*, **6**(4): 10–21.

Roads, C. (1985). Granular synthesis of sound. In C. Roads and J. Strawn (Eds.), *Foundations of Computer Music*. MIT Press, Cambridge, MA, pp. 145–159.

Roads, C. (1991). Asynchronous granular synthesis. In G DePoli, A. Piccialli and C. Roads (Eds.), *Representations of Musical Signals*. MIT Press, Cambridge, MA, pp. 143–186.

Roads, C. (1996). *The Computer Music Tutorial*. MIT Press, Cambridge, MA.

Schatter, G., Züger, E. and Nitschke, C. (2005). A synaesthetic approach for synthesizer interface based on genetic algorithms and fuzzy sets. In *Proceedings of the 2005 International Computer Music Conference*. Barcelona, pp. 664–667.

Schottstaedt, B. (1977). The simulation of natural instrument tones using frequency modulation with a complex modulating wave. *Computer Music Journal*, **1**(4): 46–50.

Serra, M.-H., Rubine, D. and Dannenberg, R. (1990). Analysis and synthesis of tones by spectral interpolation. *Journal of the Audio Engineering Society*, **38**(3): 111–128.

Sethares, W. (1994). Adaptive tunings for musical scales. *Journal of the Acoustical Society of America*, **96**(1): 10–18.

Smith, J.O. (1983). *Techniques for Digital Filter Design and System Identification with Application to the Violin. Report No. STAN-M-14*. Ph.D. Dissertation. Stanford, CA: CCRMA, Dept. of Music, Stanford University.

So, K.F. and Horner, A. (2002). Wavetable matching of inharmonic string tones. *Journal of the Audio Engineering Society*, **50**(1/2): 46–56.

So, K.F. and A. Horner (2004). Wavetable matching of pitched inharmonic instrument tones. *Journal of the Audio Engineering Society*, **52**(5): 516–529.

Stapleton, J. and Bass, S. (1988). Synthesis of musical tones based on the Karhunen-Loüve transform. *IEEE Transactions on Acoustics, Speech, and Signal Processing*, **36**(3): 305–319.

Strawn, J. 1980. Approximation and syntactic analysis of amplitude and frequency functions for digital sound synthesis. *Computer Music Journal*, **4**(3): 3–24.

Takala, T., Hahn, J., Gritz, L., Greigel, J. and Lee, J.W. (1993). Using physically-based models and genetic algorithms for functional composition of sound signals, synchronized to animated motion. In *Proceedings of the 1993 International Computer Music Conference*. Tokyo, pp. 180–183.

Tan, B.T.G., Gan, S.L., Lim, S.M. and Tang, S.H. (1994). Real-time implementation of double frequency modulation (DFM) synthesis. *Journal of the Audio Engineering Society,* **42**(11): 918–926.

Tan, B.T.G. and Lim, S.M. (1996). Automated parameter optimization for double frequency modulation synthesis using the genetic annealing algorithm. *Journal of the Audio Engineering Society,* **44**(1/2): 3–15.

Tomisawa, N. (1981). *Tone production method for an electronic music instrument.* U.S. Patent 4,249,447.

Truax, B. (1988). Real-time granular synthesis with a digital processing computer. *Computer Music Journal,* **12**(2): 14–26.

Truax, B. (1989). Composing with real-time granular sound. *Perspectives of New Music,* **28**(2): 121–135.

Truax, B. (1993). Time-shifting and transposition of sampled sound with a real-time granulation technique. In *Proceedings of the 1993 International Computer Music Conference.* Tokyo, pp. 82–85.

Vuori, J. and Välimäki, V. (1993). Parameter estimation of non-linear physical models by simulated evolution—application to the flute model. In *Proceedings of the 1993 International Computer Music Conference.* Tokyo, pp. 402–405.

Waschka, R. and Ferreira, T. (1988). Rapid event deployment in a midi environment. *Interface,* **17**: 211–222.

Wun, C.W. and Horner, A. (2001). Perceptual wavetable matching synthesis of musical instrument tones. *Journal of the Audio Engineering Society,* **49**(4): 250–262.

Wun, C.W., Horner, A. and Ayers, L. (2003). Perceptual wavetable matching for synthesis of musical instrument tones. In *Proceedings of the 2003 International Computer Music Conference.* Singapore, pp. 251–258.

Wun, C.W., Horner, A. and Ayers, L. (2004). A comparison between local search and genetic algorithm methods for wavetable matching. In *Proceedings of the 2004 International Computer Music Conference.* Miami, pp. 386–389.

Wun, C.W. and Horner, A. (2005a). A comparison between local search and genetic algorithm methods for wavetable matching. *Journal of the Audio Engineering Society,* **53**(4): 314–325.

Wun, C.W. and Horner, A. (2005b). Evaluation of iterative methods for wavetable matching. *Journal of the Audio Engineering Society,* **53**(9): 826–835.

Xenakis, I. (1971). *Formalized Music.* Indiana University Press, Bloomington, IN.

Yuen, J., Chan S.K. and Horner, A. (1996). Discrete summation synthesis and hybrid sampling-wavetable matching with genetic algorithms. In *Proceedings of the 1996 International Computer Music Conference.* Hong Kong, pp. 49–51.

Yuen, J. and Horner, A. (1997). Hybrid sampling-wavetable synthesis with genetic algorithms. *Journal of the Audio Engineering Society,* **45**(5): 316–330.

4
Evolution in Creative Sound Design

PALLE DAHLSTEDT

4.1. Introduction

... But what if the synthesizer just 'grew' programs? If you pressed a 'randomize' button which then set any of the thousand 'black-box' parameters to various values and gave you sixteen variations. You listen to each of those and then press on one or two of them—your favourite choices. Immediately, the machine generates 16 more variations based on the 'parents' you've selected. You choose again. And so on. ... The attraction of this idea is that one could navigate through very large design spaces without necessarily having any idea at all of how any of these things were being made. ... (Eno 1996)

Many different synthesis techniques have been developed in the last few decades. They are widely available today in hardware or software synthesizers. Also, there are various music programming languages and tools available for the implementation of sound synthesis algorithms, e.g. Max/MSP, Pure Data (or PD), Csound and Nyquist.

Sound synthesis often involves a large number of parameters and the effective operation and implementation of a synthesizer often requires background in acoustics, signal processing and computer programming. This makes sound synthesis less accessible to non-technically oriented musicians. Even if one understands the effect of each isolated parameter, it is difficult to predict the action of the various parameters together because they often are mutually dependent. Also, the output space can sometimes be so large that it is often impossible to search it systematically and effectively. Musicians often end up using factory sounds (i.e. sounds from settings supplied by the manufacturers of the synthesizers), with occasional few minor modifications.

Clearly, there is a need for high-level interfaces to sound synthesis systems to help musicians to explore the possibilities of sound synthesis. This chapter discusses how interactive evolution can be used to implement such high-level interfaces.

The way in which sounds are represented is very important for interactive evolution of sounds. One good alternative is to represent sounds as arrays of synthesis parameters because interactive evolution of sounds allows for simultaneous control of a great number of parameters in a systematic and exploratory fashion. Also, synthesis parameters generally represent high-level perceptual properties of the sounds. The operators are applied to populations of such synthesis parameters to generate variations, which in turn are used to synthesize new sounds. Those sounds that are closer to the user's aesthetic preferences or goals are selected and the operators are applied once more to their respective synthesis parameters. This process continues until the user finds the target sound or sounds.

Sound synthesis parameters typically control the timbre of a sound, and also determine the gestural qualities through a variety of generators and processors, such as low-frequency oscillators (LFOs), envelopes, step sequencers and so on. The architecture of the synthesizer defines a space of possible output, which is navigated and explored by the sound designer through the interactive selection process. The efficiency of interactive evolution is greatly influenced by the representation of sounds, which may or may not include information about the synthesizer itself and the operators that produce the variations.

4.2. Interactive Evolution

Evolutionary algorithms have many interesting properties, rendering them suitable for work in computer-aided creativity. The notion of evolution resembles the notion of creativity in many respects. The creative process of an artist may involve keeping a number of ideas active, which are gradually elaborated and refined into artworks. Similarly, a group of improvizers may evolve a number of musical ideas together in jam sessions, constantly creating new variations, from which selected materials are further evolved and so on. These processes are largely related to the notion of memes (Dawkins 1976): Ideas or cultural elements that spread and evolve in a Darwinian-like fashion. Also, creativity may in many cases be regarded as a search for a solution to a problem, for a piece of material that fits a certain context or for something surprising but suitable for a developing work or design. Evolutionary algorithms are good at searching for solutions in a large space of possibilities, especially when the exact form of the solution is not entirely known at the outset.

The three basic properties of evolutionary algorithms are inheritance, random variation and selection. In most computer implementations of evolutionary algorithms, the latter is implemented by assigning a fitness score to every member of the population according to some evaluation criteria, technically referred to as *fitness criteria*. Those individuals with the highest score are selected to produce the next generation; those individuals that are not selected are removed from the population. This process is repeated until some halting condition is met (see Chapter 1 for an introduction to evolutionary algorithms).

The specification of fitness criteria is problematic for the evolution of aesthetic works. For example, how can one formally define what is a good sound for a specific musical context? Also, there is the problem that fitness criteria may differ from time to time. On certain occasions, the composer may be looking for an agreeable sound to fit smoothly within an existing musical setting. On other occasions, the composer may be looking for a contrasting sound to cause a negative emotional reaction. Moreover, the fitness criteria may well change during the evolutionary process. An initial musical idea may change when unexpected interesting variations are produced. To cut it short, the preferences of the creators themselves are the most effective fitness criteria for the evolution of pieces of arts and music.

By considering human aesthetic judgements as fitness criteria, the evolutionary process becomes an interactive process, requiring careful evaluation and active choices from the user in each generation. Hence the term *interactive evolution*.

The idea of interactive evolution has been advocated by scientists such as Richard Dawkins, who in the mid of the 1980s demonstrated the power and efficiency of evolution with his *Biomorph* software (Dawkins 1986). With *Biomorph*, simple recursive line-graphs could be evolved into intricate insect or plant shapes. In the early 1990s, Karl Sims (1991) proposed one of the first systems using interactive evolution to evolve art. In both systems, the user was presented with a grid of images showing the current population with the predecessors displayed at the top left-hand side corner. After browsing the images, the user selected one to be the predecessor for the next generation of the population and so on. Sims also included a reproduction method in his system, which crossed over two predecessors, allowing for aspects of conceptually different images to be combined to form new images.

As mentioned in Chapter 1, one of the first attempts at the design of a system using interactive evolution to synthesize sounds was proposed by Johnson (1999). Sounds pose different challenges than images because sounds are time-based. The human eye is capable to form an impression of a whole image in a fraction of a second, allowing for quick browsing of a large number of images. In contrast, it is difficult to evaluate a sound without hearing it entirely. Hence, the manual selection of sounds takes time, which jeopardizes the interactive evolutionary process. This problem is referred to as the *fitness bottleneck*. Visual representations of sounds, such as spectrograms, amplitude envelopes or pitch contours, may sometimes help but they cannot replace listening. Using a smaller population size can reduce the generation turnover time, but this has negative effects on the efficiency of the evolutionary process. Another remedy would be to evolve very short or repetitive sounds, but again, this is far from satisfactory.

When compared to evolutionary systems with formalized fitness criteria, where populations of thousands of individuals can be evolved automatically for thousands of generations, the fitness bottleneck of interactive evolution of sound can be very limiting.

Instead of considering interactive evolution as an optimization process, it might be better to think of it as a technique for the exploration of a parametric space defined by a sound synthesizer. The parameters of the synthesizer define a multi-dimensional space of possible sounds – the number of parameters corresponds to the dimension of the space. In addition to a space of possible sounds, a sound synthesizer also defines the topology of the space, that is, distances between sounds with relation to one another.

We can assume that a specific sound space contains some regions that are more interesting than others. The question is how to find them. As an example, consider a typical process of editing a sound in a synthesizer manually. In this case the

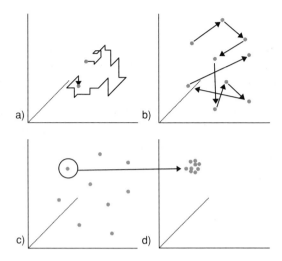

FIGURE 4.1. Different ways to navigate the parameter space of a synthesizer: (a) Traditional manual parameter editing, where one parameter is changed at a time. (b) Random search, where completely different random parameter sets are auditioned, until a suitable sound is found. (c) A random population is auditioned and the most promising candidate is used as a parent to produce the next generation. (d) With slight variations between the offspring.

starting point is either a predefined neutral sound, with all parameters set to their default values or a chosen factory sound. The space is explored by adjusting one parameter at a time while listening to the sound. This corresponds to a sequential stepwise navigation in the space, as shown in Fig. 4.1(a). In theory, all regions of the space could be reached by this method, but a prohibitive large number of steps would be required for doing so. Since the editing is driven by a search for better or more interesting sounds, each adjustment should lead to an improvement of some kind. Depending on the nature of the synthesizer, this may prevent certain regions from being reached, because the route to these regions may require passing through uninteresting regions. The probability of reaching the region near the departure point will be higher than the probability of reaching remote areas. An experienced sound designer, who may understand the role of each parameter, should be able to take shortcuts in order to target a certain sound directly. However, this would work satisfactorily only when the target is known, which may not always be the case.

Unknown regions of the space can be reached by sampling random points in the sound space as shown in Fig. 4.1(b), but this technique does not provide a way to refine the sounds once they are found.

Is it then possible to search a sound space systematically for interesting sounds? In general, the answer is no, because of the size of the space, which is often huge. A comprehensive search, even in large steps, would take an excessive long time. Even a simple synthesizer with a dozen parameters, with a range of 10 different values each, would require 10^{12} evaluations. Moreover, it is also difficult to form a mental image of the space because the synthesis parameters are highly interdependent.

Exploration using interactive evolution combines the exploratory ability of random search with the control of manual editing. Figs. 4.1(c) and 4.1(d) illustrate the case whereby one may start with a random population: A number of totally unrelated points in the space are used to survey the space for the first time. Since the sound space is very large, this random population will sample only a minute fraction of the space. Nevertheless, the random sounds will be dispersed in the space with equal probability, giving a fair preview of the possibilities of the synthesizer. If none of them sounds interesting, then a new random population is created and so on, until a promising starting point is found. Then, the region around that point can be searched for improvement, using mutations. Each mutated offspring corresponds to a randomly generated step in a random direction from the parent sound. The population is evaluated and if one child is considered better than the parent and the siblings, then this child is selected to produce new offspring. In order to allow for fine-tuning, the maximum size of the mutation steps can be gradually decreased as the outcomes approach a desired result.

With this method, the space is searched in shrinking steps, until an interesting target sound is found. If a dead end is reached, then fresh material can be introduced by means of a crossover operation with a different sound. Since the offspring from a two-parent crossover share parameter values with at least one of the parents, they have a high probability to appear in an interesting region in the sound space; that is, provided that at least one of the parents have interesting features to pass on to their children.

In order to be able to branch off the evolutionary process at various interesting points that may arise, it is important to have access to a temporary storage for potentially interesting sounds. It is useful to allow for promising but not so obvious candidate sounds to be stored for re-evaluation at a later stage. Also, if necessary, one should be able to feed back stored sounds from previous breeding sessions into the population. This provides a way to partially circumvent the sometimes too definitive one-child selection and the lack of genetic variation in a small population size. At the end of a run, the best sounds from the temporary storage can be finally selected for permanent storage. Typical workflows are shown in Figs. 4.2 and 4.3.

The aforementioned interactive search method may not be considered truly evolutionary in the classic sense of Darwinian evolutionary systems. It might be more sensible to consider it as a tool inspired by Darwinian evolution for exploration of an unknown sound space. Philosophical considerations aside, what is important here is that it allows for a fast workflow, with results enhanced by the computer-generated variations, while keeping control over the direction of the process.

A phenomenon that can have a serious impact on the evolutionary abilities of a synthesizer is the possibility of low-level chaotic behaviour, that is, the production of unpredictable outcomes at the signal level. This is a common issue with synthesis algorithms involving feedback signal connections, such as a network of oscillators modulating each other (Dahlstedt 2004). A chaotic sound is characterized by a continuous spectrum in some parts of the frequency range and they often sound very harsh, which may or may not be a desired quality. Musical taste is obviously a matter of opinion, but what really complicates the matter here is the effect of chaotic behaviour on the evolutionary process. In a region of the parameter space where the output is chaotic, many sounds are very similar. They may be structurally different at the micro level, but sound identical at the macro level. Hence, it is

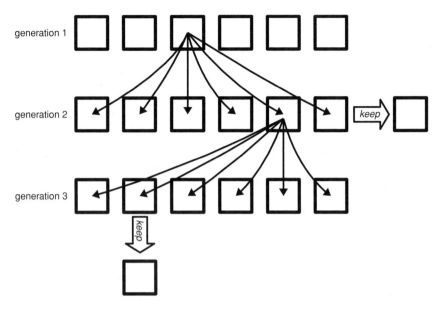

FIGURE 4.2. Typical workflow of interactive evolution based on one-parent reproduction. One sound from an initial random population (generation 1) is selected to create the next generation of sounds. In this case, each child is a mutated variation of the parent. From this generation, one sound is stored for future use and another one is selected to be a parent for the third generation, from which one sound is kept. Normally, this process continues over a large number of generations.

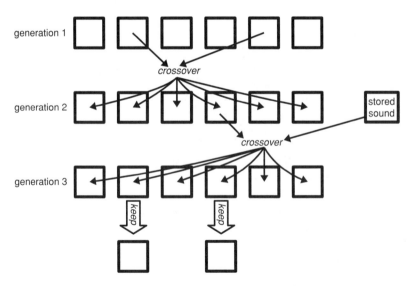

FIGURE 4.3. Typical workflow of interactive evolution using two-parent reproduction. From a random initial population (generation 1), two parents are selected. Then one child is selected from the second generation and mated with a previously stored sound to produce the third generation.

difficult to evaluate a population of such sounds, since the fitness landscape is essentially flat. Once the population enters such a region, it is very difficult to exit from it.

4.3. Genetic Representation

Interactive evolution of sound is based on random variation, selection and inheritance processes. This involves keeping a group of sounds, which are repeatedly modified, combined, evaluated and selected. The sounds must be represented by means of a suitable representation scheme for these processes to take place. Depending on the nature of the system, this representation may involve rather complex data structures or entire computer programs, such as composition algorithms (Thywissen 1999; Dahlstedt 2004) or functions that generate waveforms.

Using terminology inspired by biology, in interactive evolution a sound is referred to as a *phenotype* and its representation as its *genotype*. The phenotypes of a generation are evaluated and the genotypes that correspond to the most promising phenotypes are selected and used to produce the next generation. During the reproduction process, the genotypes of the parents are subject to random modifications and combinations by *genetic operators* (typically mutations and crossover) and the process is repeated again with the new group of sounds. For the sake of clarity, we shall refrain from using the term phenotype in this chapter.

The design of the genotype representation scheme and the genetic operators are crucial for the efficiency and the creative properties of the system: They define the space of possible results and the nature of the modifications that can be made. The genetic operators define the possible variations on the genotypes, that is, how to move from one point in the space to another. This affects how interesting regions of the search space can be reached and how attained properties and qualities are presented in the continued evolutionary process. For example, a small variation caused by a mutation should generally produce a small change in the sound. Otherwise, the offspring would be radically different and it would be hard to navigate the space because one would not be able to easily rely on attained properties to be presented or discarded. It would be difficult to ascertain if an interesting sound would have equally interesting neighbours.

One of the main issues concerning the design of a genetic representation scheme for evolving aesthetic objects is that it should be as generic as possible in order to allow for surprises and diversity beyond the artist's predictions or expectations. Also, the genetic operators should be meaningful in order to maximize the proportion of useful results. These two issues often conflict with each other. Generic representations tend to capture very low-level attributes rather than high-level ones. For example, in the case of a system for musical composition, a generic representation would represent musical sequences of notes rather than musical phrases or musical form. The more generic the representation is, the more likely it is for the system to produce useless results. In order to produce large proportions of useful musical materials and sensible variations, the representation should capture information about high-level musical structures. There are so many conceptually different ways to represent musical information that is very hard to design a representation scheme that can cover them all.

We distinguish between three different types of genetic representation: *basic*, *object-based* and *generative*. For example, when evolving images, the simplest representation data structure would be a bitmap array containing values corresponding to the colours of each pixel of an image. This is an example of *basic representation*. A bitmap array can represent any possible image where each image can be considered a point in the space of all possible images. But most of these images will be noise and the small fraction of all meaningful bitmap arrays will be scattered all over the huge space of possible images. The bitmap representation does not contain any structural information about the images.

A genetic operator could be defined to change a given pixel to a new colour according to some criterion, but the probability that the evolutionary process would converge to any meaningful image would be infinitely small. A bitmap array representation is computationally efficient, practical and generic, but the level of the description is excessively low to be any useful for an evolutionary system.

More complex genetic operators could be designed to process the image more intelligently. For example, using cellular automata, different types of filters, or an analysis and re-synthesis algorithm. Such a solution should be able to generate interesting variations on existing images, but it would be equally difficult to evolve images from scratch.

At a slightly higher level, images can be represented as vector graphics; that is, as lists of graphical objects such as lines, rectangles and arcs, each of which including information about shape, position and size. This is referred to as the *object-based representation*. In this case, the genetic operators would operate at the object level; e.g. mutations could modify, insert or remove objects from an image and/or two images could be combined by crossing over subsets of objects from each. But still, the representation would not hold any information about how the objects relate to each other to form an image. A dominant proportion of random configurations of objects would still be produced.

Finally, *generative representation* includes in the representation information about structural relationships between the objects. Two examples of systems using this approach are the aforementioned *Biomorph* software by Dawkins (1986) and Sims' system to evolve two-dimensional images (Sims 1991). In the first case, the objects are simple line drawings and the genotypes contain information about the number of lines and how they are connected to each other in a simple recursive configuration. The space is limited to a certain kind of line drawings, but on the other hand, the proportion of interesting points in the space is quite large. In the case of Sims' system, the range of diversity is enormous, but mutations produce very sensible variations, thanks to a well designed high-level representation.

4.4. Genetic Representation for Sound

The most basic genetic representation scheme for sounds is in the form of an array of numbers (or samples), representing air pressure at regular intervals in time. This representation contains only low-level information. With simple genetic operators, such as random changes of individual samples or cut and paste of fragments of the array, this basic representation is clearly inadequate for evolutionary applications. As with the case of bitmap arrays for representing images, the sample array representation scheme could be slightly improved by using more sophisticated genetic operators, such as time-varying filters, or analysis and re-synthesis-based operators, which could create interesting variations from carefully prepared initial material.

A suitable approach to create a genetic representation scheme for sounds is to represent synthesis parameters that control spectral properties of the sound (e.g. timbre, pitch, loudness) and gestural qualities (e.g. vibrato speed, filter sweep time, amplitude envelope), rather than the sounds per se.

The genetic operators for manipulating sound synthesis parameters can be very simple. For example, mutations could be implemented as random variations of parameter values and crossover as a merge of two parameter sets.

Depending on the choice of parameters included in the genetic representation, the random variations of the offspring may occur at a musically meaningful level. Such approach to representation could apply to a wide range of synthesis systems, from specifically designed synthesis algorithms to produce a specific class of sounds (e.g. organ sounds) to systems for producing almost complete electronic pieces, using various pattern and gesture generators combined with the synthesis parameters themselves.

A further extension of this idea would be to evolve the actual synthesizers, rather than to evolve only synthesis parameters. Some experiments at this front have been developed, using a modular synthesizer programming approach (When 1998; Garcia 2001) where synthesis algorithms are implemented by connecting various modules, each of which responsible for performing different signal processing functions, such as oscillators, filters, control functions and so on. However, it has proven very difficult to design a representation that prevents the large number of meaningless connections of modules.

Timbre is largely defined by the spectral content of a sound, but also how the spectrum of the sounds produced by a musical instrument varies over the instrument's range of pitches.

Different synthesis techniques have different ways to control the timbre; for an overview of various synthesis techniques see (Miranda 2002). For example, in simple subtractive synthesis, the timbre is defined by the filters and the nature of the source sound to be filtered. In this case, the selection of a waveform for a source oscillator and the type of filters to be used are parameters with very few discrete choices, while continuous variations of filter parameters over a wide range of values produce smooth changes in the timbre. This very simple example still covers a wide range of timbres and can easily be expanded to multiple sources and more complex filter arrangements.

The relationship between synthesis parameters and the sonic results is not straightforward in most standard synthesis techniques, such as synthesis by frequency modulation (FM). The timbre in FM depends on the ratios of the carrier to the modulation frequencies: Integer ratios, such as 4/1 or 3/2, produce harmonic spectra, while arbitrary non-integer ratios produce non-harmonic spectra. One of the main problems with FM is that harmonic sounds are not necessarily neighbours in the parametric space, but entwined with non-harmonic sounds.

The way in which the various properties of a sound change over time, forming musical textures and gestures, is an important issue in sound design. Amplitude, timbre and pitch normally change over the course of a sound. Most synthesis tools provide a range of gestural generators to modulate synthesis parameters, such as low frequency oscillators (LFOs), envelopes, step sequencers and triggers. These are often used not only to shape a musical note triggered by a keyboard in the traditional way, but also to form rhythmic or continuously changing patterns, textures, grooves and beats. It is therefore desirable to be able to evolve these gestural and textural qualities in the evolutionary process, which can be done by including parameters for gestural generators in the genotype.

Sound sequences can be represented in a variety of ways. A simple example is a short melody. The basic representation of a melody is a list of notes with no information about the internal relationships between the notes. For instance, if the melody contains a repeated motive, this information is not accounted for in the representation. If a genetic operation, such as mutation, changes a note in one of the repetitions, then it will no longer be a repetition; the character of the melody may be completely lost. It would have been more appropriate if the operation had changed all instances of the repetition. In order to make this possible, the melody would have to be represented in a different way; for example, as a sum of two synchronized LFOs. The LFOs provide periodic slow gestures, which are scaled and added together and then sampled at regular intervals and quantized to a diatonic scale. In this case, if the speed of one LFO is changed slightly, it will change the contour of the melody in a subtle way.

More complex genetic representations of melodic structure, rhythms and even of whole musical pieces are possible with grammar-based representations (Thywissen 1999; Dahlstedt 2004), but this is beyond the scope of this chapter.

It is worth noting that event-based structures are by no means the only way to organize sound. When confronted with the hyper-dimensional continuum of electronic music, it can be very limiting to think about music solely in terms of notes, events and rhythms. With all-purpose modular synthesis tools, any signal can be modulated by any other and the boundaries between timbre, gesture, rhythm and so on become blurred. All properties of a sound can change continuously in a periodic or non-periodic way, producing a diversity of musically interesting patterns.

The output from a synthesizer does not only depend on the parameter values. Many synthesizers have internal states, whose initial conditions may affect the sound. For example, the initial phases of oscillators and LFOs can lead to different result each time they run. This may affect the evolutionary process because the sounds that are being evaluated could have been different if the initial conditions were different. This can be avoided by including the initial conditions in the genotype.

4.5. MutaSynth

MutaSynth is a system for synthesising sounds with interactive evolution (Dahlstedt 2001b). The rationale behind the design of *MutaSynth* was to make a general tool that could be used with a wide variety of synthesizers, both implemented in software or hardware (Fig. 4.4). The initial motivation was to create an efficient and useful tool for the compositional work of this author, but then it ended up being generally available for other users in the form of *Patch Mutator* – a fully-fledged system that will be introduced in the next section.

MutaSynth's genetic representation was in terms of sound synthesis and sound patterning parameters, but it excluded information about the synthesis algorithms that it was supposed to control. Moreover, *MutaSynth's* breeding mechanism was generic in the sense that it did not know anything about the sounds it was supposed to evolve.

At the time of its development, *MutaSynth* was primarily intended to control hardware synthesizers, both standard fixed-configuration synthesizers and freely programmable hardware synthesizer. The Nord Modular served as the main platform for the development, but other synthesizers, such as the Yamaha TX 81Z and the Oberheim Matrix 6 were also used extensively to test the system.

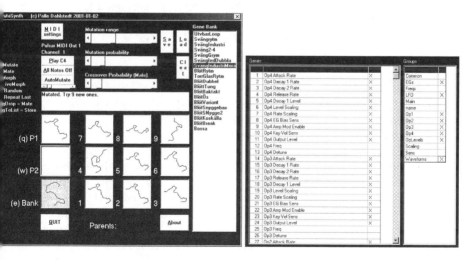

FIGURE 4.4. The user interface of *MutaSynth*. The main interface, on the left-hand side, shows a population of nine sounds represented by boxes with 'chromosome graphs', two parents and a gene bank. The parameter and group enable/disable dialog with a genome configuration for the Yamaha TX81Z hardware FM synthesizer is shown on the right-hand side.

MutaSynth was designed to meet a number of conditions that were established at the outset of its development. Firstly, the system was intended to be a general tool, usable with just about any MIDI-based sound synthesizer, in particular hardware synthesizers. Second, it was designed to be used in realistic music-making scenarios with fast and often unpredictable workflow. We wished for a tool that would be able to support creative situations where sudden surprises and unexpected turns are integral part of the sound design process. In such scenarios, the audition process and turnaround of generations must be fast.

MutaSynth was able to control any device capable of MIDI communication using control change or system exclusive messages. The genetic representation and the communication protocol for a specific synthesizer was defined in a text file and each parameter could belong to one or more parameter groups, which could be individually enabled or disabled during the breeding process. This made it possible to evolve the subsets of parameters for specific components of the synthesizer. For complex synthesizers (e.g. the Yamaha FS1R) or large modular synthesizer configurations, which could have hundreds of parameters, this turned out to be very useful. For example, the parameters for a single operator in a FM synthesizer could be evolved separately. An example of such parameter groups is shown on the right-hand side of Fig. 4.4.

The user interface was designed for easy navigation between sounds and provided keyboard shortcuts that allowed the user to keep one hand on the numerical keyboard of the computer and the other on the keyboard of the synthesizer to try out the sounds during the breeding process.

Each sound had a visual representation resembling biological chromosomes, to give a visual impression of the similarity between sounds. This was intended to aid the user to navigate the sound space. This visual representation was not a faithful representation of the actual sound. Rather, it was derived from the parameter values of the synthesizer, which were used as length and angle values for a multi-segment line, scaled to fit the window. A small change to a parameter value would cause a small change to the visual representation.

The generality of *MutaSynth* turned out to be both its strength and its weakness. It could be used to control almost any MIDI synthesizer but it required extensive manual configuration. Another disadvantage was the lack of direct communication between the synthesizer and *MutaSynth*.

There are often cases in evolutionary sound design where the user may identify the weakness of a promising but not yet ideal sound, which could be fixed manually; i.e. outside the evolutionary process. MutaSynth had a primitive mechanism for such manual off-line adjustments, where a received parameter change would be integrated into the genotype and be inherited in the breeding process. However, it would have been useful to be able to start with a few manually tuned sounds in order to reduce the initial random search for good starting points and this was not facilitated by *MutaSynth*.

MutaSynth was used to compose a number of works, using a variety of different synthesis algorithm and devices (Dahlstedt 2004). A special version of *MutaSynth* was developed in 2001 for an interactive music installation. This version featured a built-in synthesis algorithm and a simplified user interface (Dahlstedt 2001a).

4.6. Patch Mutator

A co-operation between this author and Clavia, a synthesizer manufacturer based in Sweden, was initiated in 2004 to integrate *MutaSynth's* breeding engine into the Nord Modular G2 (NMG2) series of synthesizers. The NMG2 are general-purpose virtual modular synthesizers and effects processors based on digital signal processing (DSP) hardware with a freely configurable performance interface. The collaboration resulted in *Patch Mutator*, whose first version was released in January 2006. As far as this author is aware of, it is the first time that a professional sound synthesis tool is provided with an interactive evolution mechanism. It is available both as a tool integrated into the modular synthesis editor environment for Clavia's hardware synthesizers and as a free stand alone software synthesizer downloadable from the Internet: http://www.clavia.se/products/nordmodular/demo.htm (Accessed on 17 April 2006).

4.6.1. Integration into an Existing Architecture

The task of integrating *MutaSynth* into the NMG2 was not without complications. There are about 160 types of modules in the NMG2, most of which inspired by the architecture of vintage analogue modular synthesizers, including oscillators, filters, envelopes, mixers and effects. The available DSP resources can be allocated to any combination of modules. A synthesis algorithm or a *synthesis patch*, consists of a number of modules connected with virtual cables, created using NMG2's own editor software running on a generic computer connected to the synthesizer. When a synthesis patch is finished, it can be saved onto the hardware synthesizer and the computer is no longer needed to play the synthesizer.

Each synthesis patch can store eight variations of itself. These are groups of parameter settings that can be used to create slight variation to a patch, which can produce completely different results. The environment encourages more active patching than tweaking of synthesis parameter values. Users tend to produce new patches all the time, in spite of the fact that a single patch can be rather complex, some of which would require months to explore its full potential. The interactive evolution tool is therefore an ideal aid for musicians in this very flexible environment.

Patch Mutator lives as a floating window on top of the NMG2 patch editor (Fig. 4.5). It is always available and active and it can be used at anytime.

4.6.2. The Interface

Patch Mutator's window is divided into five different sections (Fig. 4.6). At the upper part of the window are buttons for tuning the different genetic operators

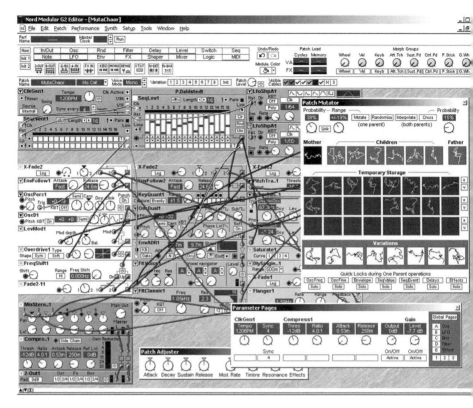

FIGURE 4.5. The Nord Modular editor, with the *Patch Mutator* on the right-hand side. *Patch Mutator* is available at all times as a floating window.

and a few knobs to control their behaviour. Below these buttons are the current offspring (six children) and on the sides are their parents. Then, there are a number of slots, which serve as temporary storage for keeping promising sounds. Below these slots is a row representing the eight variations of the NMG2 patch. This row holds the sounds that would actually be stored with the patch.

The lowest part of the window contains buttons to define which synthesis parameter categories will be included in the breeding process and which ones will be kept unchanged through the breeding process.

Patch Mutator uses the same visualization technique of *MutaSynth* in order to help the user to keep track of the different sounds. A wiggly line derived from the values of the synthesis parameters serves to visualize the differences between sounds; that is, between the values of the synthesis parameters that produced them (Fig. 4.7).

In order to allow for quick and efficient evolution, all operations can be controlled with either the mouse or through key combination shortcuts on the computer keyboard. For example, a sound is auditioned with a simple mouse-click and

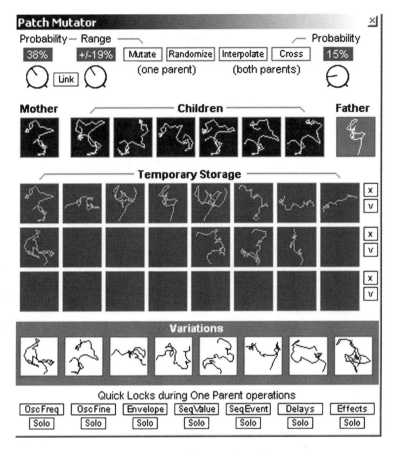

FIGURE 4.6. *Patch Mutator's* window.

a double mouse-click produces a new population of mutated children with the chosen sound as parent.

The fact that *Patch Mutator* is a floating window allows for quick modification of the patch; for example, a manual correction of a promising sound or the addition or deletion of modules. Such changes have immediate effect on the genotype and will be inherited by the offspring.

4.6.3. Genetic Representation and Parameter Selection

In contrast to *MutaSynth*, where the breeding engine was generic, the breeding engine of *Patch Mutator* is integrated into the synthesis environment of the NMG2 synthesizer. This makes it possible for the breeding engine to make fairly intelligent choices about which parameters should be included in the genotype. For various technical reasons, however, it was not possible to allow for complete flexibility of parameter selection. This was implemented as a per-module selection scheme

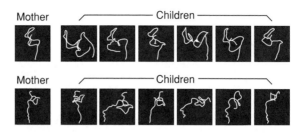

FIGURE 4.7. *Patch Mutator* uses the same visualisation technique of *MutaSynth* in order to help the user to keep track of the different sounds: A wiggly line derived from the parameter values.

instead of as a per-parameter selection scheme. Each module can be assigned for inclusion or exclusion in the breeding process and the user can change this assignment at anytime. The parameters of those modules that are excluded from the breeding process are not altered by mutations or other random alterations. Some modules are excluded from mutation by default. However, they can be included again if the user wishes to do so.

In order to circumvent the partial inflexibility of the per-module assignment scheme, each module type has a predefined list of parameters to be included in the breeding process. Those parameters that we felt that were not very useful to be included in the breeding process were excluded permanently from the system, such as sequencer loop length, signal polarity and options to bypass sound effects, to cite but three of them. In many cases, the per-module limitation can be circumvented by careful patch design. For example, if one wishes to evolve the oscillator's pitch but not the waveform, then one can choose to exclude the oscillator module (or 'quick lock' the oscillator, see below) from the genotype and include a constant module that modulates the pitch instead.

Patch Mutator is equipped with a number of quick lock buttons for different parameter categories. For example, it is possible to evolve everything but the oscillator tunings, or only the step sequencer levels and gate parameters. In this way, it is possible to focus on specific aspects of the sound at a time and avoid affecting parameters that should not be altered.

In *Patch Mutator*, all parameters are assigned a certain probability distribution, which controls values given by the randomization process and the results of mutations. For example, the fine-tune parameter of an oscillator ($+/-$ 50 cent) has a higher probability to fall in the middle range, while the attack time of an envelope tends towards the low range. Extreme values are still possible, but with a lower probability.

4.6.4. Selection and Population Size

As discussed in Chapter 1, the selection of individuals to be reproduced can be done in different ways in artificial evolution. In cases involving a large population and automated fitness evaluations, it is important to keep genetic variations within the population, where the norm is to select a larger number of individuals from each generation. They are often paired randomly to produce offspring, based on a probability proportional to their fitness scores. However, the size of the populations in *Patch Mutator* is rather small. The small population size is compensated by active use of the temporary storage, which is essential for interactive evolutionary systems to work. Temporary storage is useful because there may be two or more good offspring sounds in a population. Only one will be selected to be a parent for the next generation, while one or more can be saved in the temporary storage. These are available for re-introduction into the breeding process at any time thereafter. Moreover, the individuals of the current population are not only compared to each other or to the current parent or parents, but also to the sounds in the temporary storage. Previously stored sounds can be brought in from the temporary storage if the current population does not improve for a number of generations.

In practice, the temporary storage scheme is akin to the elitism technique that is often used in genetic algorithms, which retains some of the best individuals from each generation unaltered in order to avoid loosing attained fitness in the next generation.

4.6.5. Genetic Operators

Patch Mutator provides four operators: Mutation, crossover, randomize and inter- polate.

Mutation introduces random changes to individual parts of the genotype and crossover is a way to combine information from the genotype of parents to generate a child. In most implementations of genetic algorithms, both are normally applied together to pairs of parents. In *Patch Mutator*, however, only one operator is applied at a time: The offspring is produced either by mutation of one parent or by crossover of two parents.

In a standard genetic algorithm with automated selection and large populations, there will typically be a large number of similar individuals in the population. Those with the highest fitness are crossbred to produce the child. Crossover of very similar individuals produces small variations, since parts of only slightly different genotypes are combined. Conversely, crossover of radically different individuals produces large variations, which can help a sub-population to escape a local optimum. Only a larger jump can help in situations where the mutations produce worse results. A crossover operation provides such a jump, while keeping the genetic information in known parts of the space. It is assumed that the result might improve because part of the genome is inherited from one of the parents who have survived this far.

However, it is not affordable to apply large genetic variations to a small pop- ulation. In this case, the user should take the role of the fitness function and be able to adjust the algorithm in midstream to fit the current situation. For example, if mutations no longer produce interesting variations, the mutation range could be temporarily increased or a new population could be produced by crossover with a previously stored sound in order to introduce some genetic variation in the pool.

When new offspring are produced by mutation, all parameters are copied from a single selected parent, with a certain probability of taking place. The mutation range is manually set in terms of a percentage of the parameter range. A mutation with low probability of taking place but with a high range produces few but significant changes. Conversely, a mutation with high probability but with a low range produces more subtle changes. These two extremes give very different sonic results. The probability and range can be linked in an inversely proportional way or they can be set individually.

If the mutation range is very narrow, one mutation will seldom be enough to jump from one value to the next. In order to alleviate this problem, *Patch Mutator* allows for small mutations to accumulate and the genotype is stored as a string of floating-point numbers. When they are sent to the synthesis patch, they are rounded to the nearest integer. When a synthesis patch is loaded, all parameter values are dithered to floating point numbers by addition of a random value between zero and one. This allows for mutations with noticeable changes on parameters whose ranges are too narrow. Otherwise, a large number of small mutations would be required before any noticeable change takes place.

Crossover merges two genotypes by copying consecutive chunks of the genotype from each parent. The information from the genotype of one parent will have a certain probability of being crossed with information represented at different position in the genotype of the other parent in a zigzag manner. The crossover probability can be adjusted from 1% to 100%. With a low probability setting, large chunks of information are copied unchanged from each parent. In other words, this means that the offspring will bear close resemblance to the parents. If the crossover probability is high, the copying will jump back and forth between the parents. Even though every parameter will come from one of the parents, they will be combined in new ways, which may result in rather different sounds.

The randomize operator creates a new random set of offspring. Random values are generated for all parameters that are included in the genotype, excluding those parameter categories that are affected by the quick lock buttons. All unaffected parameters are copied from the current sound. In this way it is possible to have a great deal of control over which synthesis parameters should be randomized. The randomize operator can be used to search for good starting points for a breeding session or to get a feeling for the potential of a synthesis patch by sampling the space randomly.

The interpolate operator generates a series of sounds whose synthesis parameters are interpolated linearly between the two parent sounds. Interpolation is useful for creating transitions between sounds or to explore the region between two existing sounds.

4.7. Concluding Discussion and Further Work

This chapter demonstrated the potential of interactive evolution for sound synthesis. The developments of *MutaSynth* and *Patch Mutator*, started with the desire to make synthesis programming more widely accessible to musicians who may not necessarily have technical expertise in sound synthesis. We had hoped that by leaving the detailed level of synthesis parameter values transparent to the users, they could free themselves from low-level technicalities and concentrate on the sonic result. The rationale is that musicians should be given the means to concentrate on the high-level perceptual characteristics of the sound (such as intensity, brightness or rhythmic feel) rather than confronting themselves with the technical idiosyncrasies of the various different synthesis techniques.

Patch Mutator provides a set of exploratory tools, tightly integrated into the NMG2 synthesizer, comprising a powerful new way to create and explore the sonic possibilities of a professional synthesis and sound processing system.

Any tool for aiding creativity will in some way or another affect the result. Either because the tool favours certain kinds of solutions to posed problems or because certain kinds of problems are more likely to be solved by the given tool. *Patch Mutator* supports the creation of sounds by focusing on the aural relationship between the sounds rather than focusing on the role of the various synthesis parameters needed to produce the sounds. Considering this fact alone, *Path Mutator* clearly affects the creative process. For example, one user reported that he has been using the *Patch Mutator* '*when the patch I'm working with is too complex for me to make a direct association with tweaking multiple variables and getting a 'good' sound'*.

Furthermore, interactive evolution allows for more efficient navigation into different parts of the sound space given by a synthesis patch than manual editing. Chance and unpredictability are well-known devices for reaching uncharted territory in art and in the breeding process this can be done while keeping some kind of control over the output. Another user referred to it as '*a means to find inspiration for sounds that I wouldn't think of naturally'*. Yet another user expressed that the breeding process '*allows me to discover some sounds from a patch that I normally wouldn't have thought of making by customizing all the parameters myself'*.

Besides breeding sound synthesis parameters, *Patch Mutator* also facilitates the design of new synthesis patches, especially for people who are not so familiar with modular synthesis. Although a certain level of knowledge about sound synthesis is required, users can now concentrate on the configuration of the major components of the synthesis patch and leave the breeding engine to take care of the adjustment of the parameters. A user reported that: '*I hardly made any patches of my own before. It was too tedious to get nice sounds with it. Now I make a patch in a way that I know will have possibilities to make good sounds and have the mutator bring these to me... It gave me the opportunity to make my own patches where I did not have the guts before.*' On the same vein, yet another user expressed that *Patch Mutator* '*makes a modular architecture more accessible to people like me who have a pretty rudimentary knowledge of synthesis.*'

The way in which *Patch Mutator* can influence the creative process of composers who are not experts in sound synthesis is well illustrated by this comment from a professional composer: '*...Patch Mutator allows me to stay more in focus with creating music for the project rather than designing patches. Once I establish my* *core group of sounds I use the mutator to find gems, often some very unexpected delightful gems. I think of the process as walking on the beach and finding a special shell or sharks tooth. You always stay in the creative space—the sounds come to you.'*

There are some aspects of *Path Mutator* that could certainly be improved. Some features were never implemented due to time constraints.

It is important to have detailed control over the genetic representation of a synthesis patch in order to fine-tune it for efficient breeding. One major limitation with this respect is the module-based exclusion of parameters where either all parameters of a module are included in the genetic representation or none. As described above, some shortcuts are available to compensate for this and it is possible to create workarounds at the cost of more modules. Still, it can be difficult to achieve some configurations of parameters to evolve. Also, the preset choices for parameter probability distributions may not fit all synthesis patches. It would be desirable to have individual control over the probability distribution for each parameter in order to optimize different synthesis patches for breeding sounds more efficiently.

A potentially interesting improvement would be to allow for some form of pre-selection mechanism to alleviate the fitness bottleneck problem. A larger population of offspring could be generated internally and some automated fitness criteria could either select the most promising children or rule out the complete failures, which are sometimes easier to define formally. A similar approach was applied to autonomous evolution of piano scores in the music installation *Ossia* (Dahlstedt 2004), which could probably be applied to sounds. In manual evaluation, many sounds are ruled out because of disqualifying properties, such as being noisy, un-ordered, harsh or simply too quiet, and some of these properties could be evaluated automatically.

Another useful feature would be to have the ability to specify beforehand what kind of sound one is looking for, either by providing an example sound or some general characteristic, such as frequency range, spectral centre of gravity or spectral shape. One problem of using an example sound as target for the evolution is the measurement of sound similarity, which is not trivial to formalise.

The selection process currently moves in discrete steps. Sometimes a child sound is in the right direction, but a little too far or not far enough from the parent. In those cases it would be very useful to be able to interpolate continuously between the parent and the child or between promising children in order to search for a suitable sound for further breeding.

Another promising development would be to represent parameter changes over time in the genotype. Simpler periodic gestures can already be used in synthesis patches, but a more sophisticated representation scheme is needed to allow for structurally more complex gestures and greater formal diversity. Some experiments have been made using the recursive hierarchical score representation developed for the music installation *Ossia* to produce parameter changes over time (Dahlstedt 2004). The results were promising, but much work still needs to be done in order to enable the generation of various different kinds of idiomatic parametric gestures.

To conclude, interactive evolution has proven to be a valuable tool in creative sound design, regardless of synthesis techniques and musical styles. Its implications for music-making are twofold. Firstly, it simplifies the sound design process for the technically uninitiated. Secondly, it provides new ways of working for the more advanced user, who can design custom sound engines specifically for evolutionary exploration, concentrating on the desired potential musical elements. Thanks to the ability to control a large number of parameters simultaneously by ear, these sound engines can be large and complex, beyond those that would be feasible for conventional manual sound design. Altogether, this technique provides a fruitful combination of chance and control, two essential ingredients for musical creativity.

References

Dahlstedt, P. (2001a). A MutaSynth in parameter space: Interactive composition through evolution. *Organised Sound,* **6**(2): 121–124.

Dahlstedt, P. (2001b). Creating and exploring huge parameter spaces: Interactive evolution as a tool for sound generation. In *Proceedings of the International Computer Music Conference 2001.* Habana, Cuba, pp. 235–242.

Dahlstedt, P. (2004). *Sounds Unheard of – Evolutionary Algorithms as Creative Tools for the Contemporary Composer.* Doctoral Dissertation. Chalmers University of Technology, Göteborg.

Dawkins, R. (1976). *The Selfish Gene.* Oxford University Press, Oxford.

Dawkins, R. (1986). *The Blind Watchmaker.* Longman, Harlow.

Eno, B. (1996). *A Year with Swollen Appendices.* Faber and Faber, London, Boston.

Garcia, R.A. (2001). Growing sound synthesizers using evolutionary methods. In *Proceedings of the Sixth European Conference on Artificial Life. Workshop on Artificial Life Models for Musical Applications.* Editoriale Bios, Prague.

Johnson, C.B. (1999). Exploring the sound-space of synthesis algorithms using interactive genetic algorithms. In A. Patrizio, G.A. Wiggins and P. Pain (Eds.), *Proceedings of the AISB'99 Symposium on Musical Creativity.* Brighton, UK, Society for the Study of Artificial Intelligence and Simulation of Behaviour, pp. 20–27.

Miranda, E.R. (2002). *Computer Sound Design: Synthesis Techniques and Programming.* 2nd ed. Elsevier/Focal Press, Oxford, UK.

Sims, K. (1991). Artificial evolution for computer graphics. *Computer Graphics,* **25**:319–328.

Thywissen, K. (1999). GeNotator: An environment for exploring the application of evolutionary techniques. *Organised Sound,* **4**(2): 127–133.

Wehn, K. (1998). Using ideas from natural selection to evolve synthesized sounds. In *Proceedings of the Digital Audio Effects DAFX98 workshop*, Barcelona.

5
Experiments in Generative Musical Performance with a Genetic Algorithm

QIJUN ZHANG AND EDUARDO R. MIRANDA

5.1. Introduction

It is commonly agreed in the context of Western tonal music that expression is conveyed by delicate deviations of the notated musical score, through shaping physical parameters of performance, such as timing, loudness, tempo and articulation. Expressive music performance research is aimed at establishing why, where and how these deviations take place in a piece of music. Interestingly, even though there are many commonalities in performance practices, these deviations can vary substantially from performance to performance, even when a performer plays the same piece of music more than once.

Different approaches and techniques have been employed in research into expressive performance of music in order to capture common performance principles or the differences, including analysis-by-measurement, analysis-by-synthesis, machine learning and so on (see Gabrielsson (2003), Palmer (1997), Poli (2004) and Widmer and Goebl (2004) for reviews about these works). One of the major caveats of the great majority of these works is that they do not consider the role of social factors in musical performance. By social factors we mean the influence of historical practices and the interactions between performers and audience, which play an important role in musical performance (Davidson and North 1999).

We propose an evolutionary computing approach to building systems for generative musical performance; that is, we aim at systems that are able to evolve their own strategies, or *performance profiles*, to perform pieces of music. This evolutionary approach offers the possibility of taking into account social factors in these systems by simulating interactions between virtual performers and listeners (agent-performers and agent-listeners), through which expressive music performance profiles may emerge as a result of musical constraints combined with social pressure.

The focus of the chapter is, however, on the design of the agent-performer. More specifically, it focuses on the development of the system that will eventually be embedded into these agents to evolve their performance profiles. We devised a prototype using genetic algorithms (GA), which evolves performance profiles with fitness rules informed by musical constraints derived automatically from the structure of the pieces to be performed. More precisely, the system evolves suitable performance profiles from randomly initiated ones using genetic algorithms (GA) combined with generative rules of expressive musical performance (Clarke 1988). Performance profiles are represented as hierarchical pulse sets, which define deviations for the duration and amplitude values of the notes of a piece of music represented in MIDI format. The fitness of a pulse set is calculated according to rules derived from the research into perception of musical structure (Temperly 2004). Rather than directly constructing a rigid performance profile with these rules, our GA-based approach gives the agents flexibility as to how they will perform the piece. This flexibility is desirable because musical performance varies substantially from performance to performance, even when a performer plays the same piece of music more than once. Moreover, this flexibility will allow for taking into consideration the role of social pressure when it comes to the forthcoming implementation of the agent-based model. This will allow for negotiations between the agents in order to decide upon best practices when performance rules conflict with one another or allow for multiple choices.

5.2. Musical Performance with Hierarchical Pulse Set

In this section we introduce the notion of pulse sets and how we use them as performance profiles to perform musical pieces.

5.2.1. Notion of Pulse Set

Fig. 5.1(a) shows a pulse represented as a curve of measurements of finger pressure on a pressure sensor pad. The information in a pulse is a wrap of temporal patterns with amplitude patterns, which can be quantified as real numbers: Width and height correspond to duration and amplitude, respectively (Fig. 5.1(b)). A pulse can operate at different levels of temporal organization and can be grouped into a hierarchical structure. Manfred Clynes (1986) proposed the representation of a hierarchical pulse set as a matrix of duration and amplitude values (Fig. 5.1(c)), which defines the deviations of the physical attributes of musical notes. This makes it possible to generate computer performances for pieces of music by modulating the physical attributes of musical notes according to these deviations.

5.2.2. Pulse Sets as Performance Profiles

The rationale for adopting the notion of hierarchical pulse sets to represent performance profiles is twofold. Firstly, assignment of duration and amplitude values for notes significantly influence the expressive quality of a musical performance, albeit not fully. Secondly, the hierarchical nature of pulse sets matches important features of most music genres; for example, the notions of grouping and hierarchical structures are important for almost all genres of Western music.

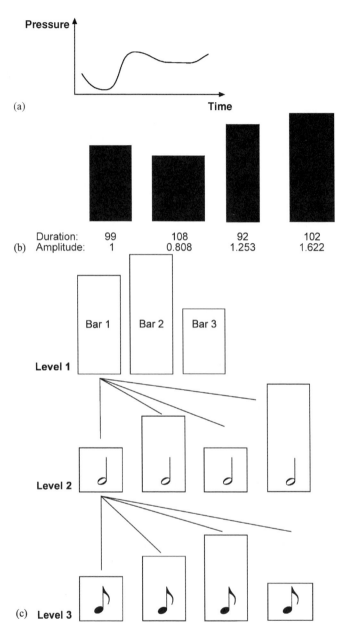

FIGURE 5.1. Illustration of a pulse and the notion of hierarchical pulse sets (after Clynes (1995)). (a) A pulse represented as finger pressure measurements in time. (b) A representation of pulse as a wrap of real numbers (duration versus amplitude). (c) A hierarchical pulse set derived from grouping pulses.

TABLE 5.1. Representation of pulse set and explanation.

Pulse set example	Meaning
8	The length of note at the lowest level
4 4 3	Number of elements in three levels (from the lowest level to the highest)
0.339 0.762 0.953 0.319	Level 3 amplitude (lowest level)
73 93 66 124	Level 3 duration
0.453 0.798 0.498 1.333	Level 2 amplitude
62 103 114 118	Level 2 duration
1.398 1.476 1.864	Level 1 amplitude
73 121 120	Level 1 duration

Table 5.1 shows an example of a hierarchical pulse set and the meaning of its components. This example is the quantification of the pulse set drawn in Fig. 5.1(c). In the first line, the number 8 defines the smallest unit of the piece, which in this case is the eighth note. In the present version of the system, the other possible values could be 32, 16 or 4. That is, the shortest note can be a thirty-second note, a sixteenth note, an eighth note or a quarter note.

In this example, there are four, four and three elements in each level, from level 3 (lowest) to level 1 (highest). All elements of a given level characterize each element of the level immediately above. Therefore, as depicted in Fig. 5.1(c), the length of an element in level 2 is equal to the total length of all elements of level 3, that is $4 \times$ 8th notes $=$ a half note. Similarly, the length of one element of level 1 is equal to the total length of all elements in level 2. Assuming that there are four beats in each bar, then this pulse set defines three groups lasting for two bars each. In the present version of the system, the number of elements in one level is valid if it is an integer higher than two and lower than nine (two and nine are inclusive).

Since a hierarchical pulse set informs the deviation of durations and amplitudes of notes, this information is given from the third to the last line of the representation of a pulse set. The duration value can be any integer between 75 and 125 and the amplitude value can vary from 0 to 1.5.

5.2.2.1. Calculating a Deviation Pattern from a Pulse Set

As explained earlier, the pulse set example in Table 5.1 defines a performance profile for a musical segment lasting for six bars. There are 48 ($4 \times 4 \times 3$) hierarchically organized pulse elements that together compose the segment. The duration and amplitude values for each element are calculated in a top–down manner, by multiplying the parameters of the corresponding elements of different hierarchical levels. For instance, the 1st and the 40th pulse element (represented as e1, e40) are defined as follows:

e_1: the 1st in Level 1, the 1st in Level 2, the 1st in Level 3
e_{40}: the 3rd in Level 1, the 2nd in Level 2, the 4th in Level 3

TABLE 5.2. Calculation for a pulse element in a pulse set.

Note	Duration	Amplitude
e_1	$(73 \times 62 \times 73)/100^3$	$1.398 \times 0.453 \times 0.339$
e_{40}	$(120 \times 103 \times 124)/100^3$	$1.864 \times 0.798 \times 0.319$

Considering the parameters of the pulse set given in Table 5.1, the algorithm calculates the duration and amplitude values for these two pulse elements (see Table 5.2). With this method, we can draw deviation patterns, for both duration and amplitude values. Once started, these patterns are repeated until the piece finishes. For the sake of clarity, Fig. 5.2 shows only the first half of a deviation pattern based on the example pulse set. The index of the beat in the piece is given by the abscissa, while the ordinate corresponds to the calculated percentage deviation of duration or amplitude.

5.2.2.2. Implementation Issues

The musical pieces that were used to test our system were represented as flat MIDI files; that is, they have no timing deviation (the duration of the notes is exactly as written on the score) and all notes have equal loudness (MIDI velocity values are even for all notes).

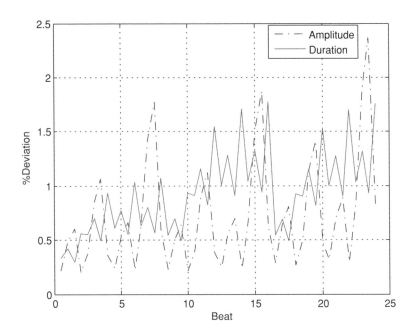

FIGURE 5.2. Deviation pattern for the pulse set in Table 5.1.

The performance of a piece proceeds as follows: For each note the system looks up its start time with respect to the aforementioned deviation list in order to infer its position in the sequence, along with its duration and amplitude values. Inspired by a method proposed by Clynes (1995), the playing time of a note is given by adding all the durations of the pulse components, while the amplitude is defined by the amplitude information of its first pulse component. When the system modifies the duration of a note it changes the play back tempo of the MIDI file at the required position. When the system modifies the amplitude, it changes the 'note-on velocity' MIDI code of the note. The system produces a new MIDI file with added expressions, which is subsequently evaluated according to the fitness criteria introduced below.

5.3. Fitness Function Based on Musical Structure

It is commonly agreed that there is a strong relation between expression in musical performance and musical structure (Repp 1992; Sundberg 1999; Todd 1985). This may explain the existence of commonalities in different performances of a piece and thus a necessary hypothesis for modeling expressive musical performance. Those using the analysis-by-synthesis approach have built models loaded with comprehensive rules. However, a critical problem of these rule-based systems is the way in which they combine these rules (Oostem 1993). They can be combined in many different ways and most combinations can generate conflicting situations with no objective solution. Although commonalities in performance do exist, differences abound. The reality is that there are different ways to perform a piece of music, which makes it very difficult to fully formalize musical performance with rules.

In this research we are not interested in the compilation of a comprehensive collection of fixed performance rules manually. Rather, we are interested in a system that can evolve these rules dynamically. Nevertheless, we undoubtedly need guidance from musically meaningful rules in order to evaluate whether an evolved pulse set constitutes an acceptable performance for a given piece. For this purpose, our approach is to design descriptive performance principles without quantified regulations. Then we employ GA, whose fitness function is informed by these principles, to select and evolve suitable pulse sets, starting from randomly generated ones. In this sense, the usage of GA is ideal here because otherwise it would be hard to design a decent performance profile based on such descriptive principles manually. Furthermore, GA can evolve different and suitable pulse sets for the same piece. This diversity is a noticeable phenomenon in real performances and also a pre-requisite for the next stage of our research, which will involve the role of social pressure, as briefly discussed at the introduction of this chapter.

5.3.1. Structure Analysis

In order to use structural principles for calculating fitness values, we need to analyse the structure of the piece in question. The system currently uses David

Temperley's software *Melism* to perform several structural analysis, such as metrical analysis, group analysis, harmony analysis and key analysis (Temperly 2004).

5.3.2. Selected Performance Principles

The current version of the system takes into account descriptive performance principles inspired by Eric Clarke's generative rules for expressive performance (Clarke 1988). The system associates expressions in performance with the piece's structure features of grouping, accentuation and cadence. The fitness value of a pulse set consists of three parts: *FitGrouper*, *FitAccent* and *FitCadence*.

5.3.2.1. FitGrouper

FitGrouper is obtained by considering the fitness of a pulse set in relation to two rules, mainly concerning the duration of the notes at group boundaries:

Rule 1—The time deviation of the last note of a group has either larger or smaller timing deviation than the preceding and succeeding notes.

Rule 2—The last note of a group is always lengthened in order to delay the following note and indicate the starting of a new group.

The value of *FitGrouper* takes into account the violation of the above two rules. A parameter *numVio* (initialized equal to 0) increases whenever the pulse set breaks either Rule 1 or Rule 2. Considering that the number of groups in the piece is N_{group}, then we define

$$FitGrouper = 1 - \frac{numVio}{N_{group}}$$

The maximum value of *FitGrouper* is equal to 1.

5.3.2.2. FitAccent

FitAccent is an assessment of how well the loudness contour of the notes of a 'performed' piece (i.e. after the flat MIDI file is modulated by a given pulse set) fits the metrical analysis. The rule is as follows:

Rule 3—Preference should be given to loudness contours whose shape is close to the accentuation analysis of the piece.

Given two successive notes N_0 and N_1, *FitAccent* is produced by calculating

(i) the accentuation information (b_0, b_1) from the structure analysis and
(ii) the velocity information (v_0, v_1) from the 'performed' MIDI file.

Because the accent value b_i varies from 0 to 4, the system firstly normalizes the velocity difference ($v_1 - v_0$) to integers in the range of $[-4, 4]$. Then it assigns a reward value between 0 and 1 to parameter x based on the difference between ($v_1 - v_0$) and ($b_1 - b_0$). The closer they are to each other, the larger the value assigned to x. Considering that the number of notes in the piece is N_{note}, then *FitAccent* is defined as follows:

$$FitAccent = \frac{\sum_1^{N_{\text{note}}-1} x_i}{N_{\text{note}} - 1} \quad (0 \leq x_i \leq 1).$$

As with *Fit Grouper*, the maximum value of *FitAccent* is equal to 1.

5.3.2.3. FitCadence

FitCadence takes into account chord progressions, which also can indicate group boundaries. While both *FitGrouper* and *FitAccent* operate at the lower level of musical notes, *FitCadence* operates at the higher level of groups of musical notes. The rule for calculating *FitCadence* is as follows:

Rule 4—Both segments corresponding to two chords in a cadence (e.g. V→I, IV→ I or Dominant→Tonic, Subdominant→Tonic, respectively) should be lengthened. Different weights are set for different categories of cadences because they have varying importance for the structure of a piece.

As with *FitGrouper*, the value of *FitCadence* is also decided by the violation of a rule: in this case Rule 4. The pulse set will receive more penalties if it breaks the rule when stronger cadences are involved. Considering that the number of cadences in a piece is N_{cadence} and that we assign a weight w_i to the ith cadence, then *FitCadence* is calculated as follows:

$$FitCadence = 1 - \frac{\sum_1^{N_{\text{cadence}}} w_i}{N_{\text{cadence}}}$$

As with the previous two fitness measures, the maximum value of *FitCadence* is equal to 1.

In the present version of our system, we define the total fitness of a pulse set to be the sum of *FitGrouper*, *FitAccent* and *FitCadence*, i.e., *Fitness = FitGrouper + FitAccent + FitCadence*, with maximum value equal to three.

5.4. Evolution Procedure

5.4.1. Genome Representation of a Pulse Set

A pulse set is represented by a long string of real numbers in the same order as shown in Table 5.1. Technically, lines are separated with ';' and elements of the same line are separated by ','. This makes it convenient to access and operate on parameters of different hierarchical levels. An additional number, either 0 or 1, is added at the end of an individual pulse set. This is used to indicate one of the possible two ways of applying a crossover operation, which will be clarified later.

As an example, the pulse set in Table 5.1 is represented as follows (for the sake of clarity, we omitted level 2 and level 1); in this case the additional number at the end of the string is equal to 0:

8; 4, 4, 3; 0.339, 0.762, 0.953, 0.319; 73, 93, 66, 124; ... ; 0

5.4.2. Initialization of the First Generation

The individual pulse sets of the first generation are randomly generated. For the moment, we have established that all pulse sets have three levels. All pulse set values are randomly generated, including

(1) the length of the quickest note;
(2) the number of elements in each hierarchical level;
(3) the amplitude and duration values for each element in every level;
(4) the additional number at the end of the string (for selecting the crossover operation).

5.4.3. Evolution Algorithm

For every generation, each pulse set is used to modulate the flat MIDI file of the piece in question, as described in Section 5.2, and a fitness value is calculated according to the definition of the fitness functions introduced in Section 3. The result is given in the form of an array of values $Fit0 = f_1, f_2, \ldots, f_n$, where f_i is the fitness value of the ith individual pulse set. The offspring pulse sets for the next generation are created on the basis of this fitness array. The procedure is as follows:

(1) Calculate the fitness values of the current generation $P0$.
(2) Select parent candidates to compose the population $P0_1$.
(3) Operate mutation on $P0_1$ in order to obtain population $P0_2$.
(4) Operate crossover on pairs of pulse sets in $P0_2$ in order to obtain population $P0_3$.
(5) Rank the fitness values of Generation $P0$ and $P0_3$ and the best half become generation $P1$.
(6) Repeat the steps from (1) to (5) until completing a preset number of generations.

5.4.4. Genetic Operations

In this section we explain the three genetic operations used in the evolution procedure: Selection, mutation and crossover, respectively.

5.4.4.1. Selection

Based on Blickle's comparative study (Blickle 1995) of various widely used selection operators in GA (such as, tournament, linear and exponential rankings and proportional), we opted for using exponential ranking. This is because we wish to keep a certain degree of diversity in the evolutionary process and exponential ranking has proved to work well for this purpose. The algorithm of our exponential ranking selection is as follows:

Exponential-ranking(c, J_1, ... , J_n)
J ← sort population J according to fitness (first is the worst)
$S0$ ← 0
For I ← 1 to N do
    s_i ← $s_{i-1} + p_i$
    For I ← 1 to N do
        r ← random$[0, s_N]$
        J_i ← J_k such that $s_{i-1} \leq r < s_k$
Return

Here, the value of c is randomly generated for every generation from 0.75 to 1:

$$p_i = \frac{c^x(N-i)}{\sum_{j-1}^{N} c^{N-j}} \qquad i \in 1, \ldots, N.$$

5.4.4.2. Mutation

Considering the hierarchical property of a pulse set, we defined four different mutation schemes to be applied selectively on a single pulse set. Given a pulse set, Fig. 5.3 shows examples of how each of the following mutation schemes work, referred to as Ma, Mb, Mc and Md, respectively.

Mutation scheme Ma: Randomly modify every duration or amplitude values in the pulse set. The range of changes for the amplitude is $[-0.1, 0.1]$ and the range of changes for the duration is $[-5, 5]$.

Mutation scheme Mb: Append new duration and amplitude wraps or delete existing wraps from the end of the string. The number of added or removed elements is defined randomly, with the condition that the resulting pulse set is a valid pulse set. New added elements also are generated randomly. Note that the length of the shortest note in the pulse set may be changed in this mutation.

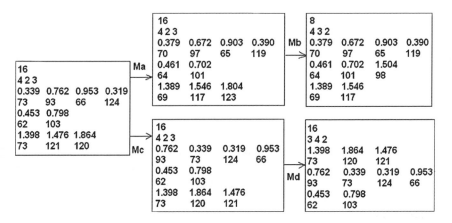

FIGURE 5.3. Examples of mutation schemes.

TABLE 5.3. Possible crossover schemes.

	$y = 0$	$y = 1$
$x = 0$	$X1Y2X3x$	$X1X2Y3y$
	$Y1X2Y3y$	$Y1Y2X3x$
$x = 1$	$X1Y2Y3y$	$X1Y2X3x$
	$Y1X2X3x$	$Y1X2Y3y$

Mutation scheme Mc: Swap the order of the elements of the same level of the pulse set randomly, but do not change the duration and amplitude wraps.

Mutation scheme Md: Swap the order of the hierarchical levels in the pulse set randomly.

An integer between 1 and 4 is generated randomly in each generation in order to define which mutation schemes will be used. For example, if the random number is equal to 2, then only the first two mutation schemes (Ma and Mb) will applied to the respective generation; in this case, the decision as to whether to perform Ma or Mb to an individual pulse set is also decided randomly.

5.4.4.3. Crossover

In order to maintain the hierarchical structure of the evolved parameters, the system performs crossover only within a given level of the hierarchy. For example, let us consider the crossing over of two pulse sets: X and Y. They can be respectively represented as $X_1X_2X_3x$ and $Y_1Y_2Y_3y$, where X_n or Y_n refers to the nth level of pulse set X or Y, including duration and amplitude parameters. The variables x and y are the numbers at the end of X and Y respectively, which can value either 0 or 1. The system uses the value of $x - y$ (which can be 0, 1, or -1) to decide how the crossover between X and Y will operate. This includes the choice between a one-point crossover or a two-point crossover, as well as which levels of the parent pulse sets the crossover will operate on. Possible crossovers are shown in Table 5.3. If x equals to y, then X and Y exchange their middle level, keeping all other information unchanged. If $x = 0$ and $y = 1$, then X and Y exchange their lowest level including the last number. Otherwise, if $x = 1$ and $y = 0$, then the highest level of X and Y are crossed over.

5.5. Demonstration

As a demonstration of the system, let us consider the melody of Robert Schumann's *Träumerei* shown in Fig. 5.4. The figure also shows the structural analysis used for calculating the fitness value, including grouping structure, metrical analysis and harmonic progression. Group boundaries are indicated by 'xx', vertically positioned under the staves at segmenting positions. The numbers at the bottom of the notes correspond to accent information (from metrical analysis). The chord names above the staves indicate chord progressions.

FIGURE 5.4. A melody from Schumann's *Träumerei* and its structural analysis.

The system ran 35 times. In each run, 100 individual pulse sets were randomly generated for the first generation and then we let them evolve for 100 generations.

For each generation of every run we recorded

a) the pulse set's fitness values including *FitGrouper*, *FitAccent*, *FitCadence* and the total fitness (i.e. the sum of the three) and
b) the best pulse set.

Fig. 5.5 depicts the final best fitness values that were recorded from all runs. These are the best fitness values of the generation number 100 for each of the 35 runs. As shown in Fig. 5.5, 'excellent' pulse sets whose fitness values reached 3.0 have evolved in the 4th, 6th, 15th, 23rd and 28th runs. This does not necessarily mean that each of these runs produced only one 'excellent' pulse set each; in fact each run has produced more than one 'excellent' pulse set. Although most of these 'excellent' pulse sets may share identical configurations (which is a pulse set's basic structure given by the first two lines of its representation), they always have

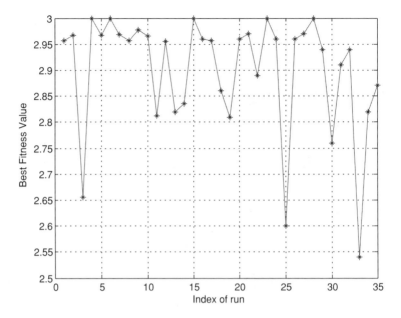

FIGURE 5.5. The best fitness values produced in 35 runs.

different duration and amplitude parameters, resulting in different performance profiles. A few examples are given in Table 5.4: Two pulse sets evolved in the 4th run and two evolved in the 15th run.

From Table 5.4, we can infer that both pulse sets evolved in run 4 have a repeated deviation pattern that consists of: 8th note $\times$ 8 $\times$ 2 $\times$ 2 = 16 beats, which

TABLE 5.4. Example of 'excellent' pulse set.

Run4_1	Run15_1
8	16
8 2 2	4 4 2
1.464 0.767 0.925 0.15 1.262 0.622 1.025 0.388	1.382 0.573 0.676 0.109
97 86 116 107 123 106 60 113	125 116 100 80
1.046 1.004	1.369 0.875 1.107 0.883
95 115	116 115 109 80
1.282 1.331	1.133 1.116
118 121	115 122

Run4_2	Run15_2
8	16
8 2 2	4 4 3
1.478 0.582 1.036 0.344 1.301 0.305 1.022 0.606	1.418 0.598 0.525 0.232
101 84 121 101 123 113 54 101	122 120 102 90
1.057 1.05	1.336 0.853 1.087 0.87
100 115	116 123 111 88
1.393 1.348	1.154 1.113 1.096
124 121	118 122 110

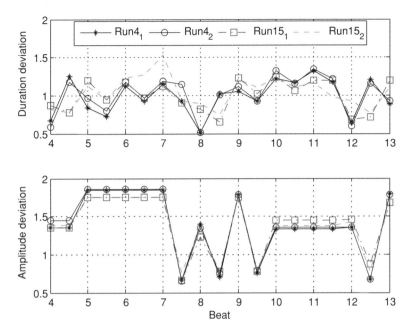

FIGURE 5.6. Two examples of deviation patterns by evolved pulse sets. It starts from the fourth beat because the piece actually begins with an upbeat at the fourth beat.

corresponds to the length of four bars. The other two pulse sets evolved in Run 15 have different configurations: Run 15_1 is for a two bar period (16th note × 4 × 4 × 2 = 8 beats) and Run 15_2 is for a three-bar period (16th note × 4 × 4 × 3 = 12 beats). Fig. 5.6 depicts their deviation pattern in eight beats (two bars).

At present, the system assesses whether or not a pulse set is suitable for the piece mostly based on how well it fulfills the devised rules for the fitness function. This is done by checking whether the important deviations of the notes correspond to those described by the rules. As an example, let us briefly consider the patterns shown in Fig. 5.6. Firstly, we can list the group boundaries in the piece based on the score in Fig. 5.4. They are the notes at the 10th, 18th, 26th, 37th beat and so on, always taking more than one beat. The graph at the top of Fig. 5.6 shows that each of these durations (adding all the beats occupied by each note) deviates mostly compared with its two neighbour notes. In this way, it is fair to say that both Rule 1 and Rule 2 have been satisfied because all notes were lengthened accordingly. As for Rule 3, it is the only rule affecting the amplitude of the notes. The graph at the bottom of Fig. 5.6 shows that all those 'excellent' pulse sets follow identical amplitude deviation patterns, which match the accentuation information shown in the score. Finally, in terms of Rule 4, there are several cadences such as V→I, IV→ I in this piece. In most of the cases, both groups of notes composing the two chords of a cadence were lengthened. Other violations might have occurred because the concurrent effect inflicted by Rules 1 and 2.

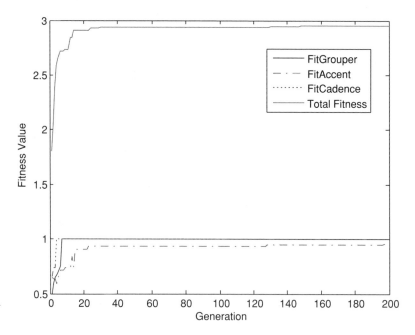

Fig. 5.7 shows four curves corresponding for the values of *FitGoruper*, *FitAccent*, *FitCadence* and the total fitness, in order to follow the development of fitness values through 100 generations for the 35 runs; it plots the geometric mean of these 35 groups of curves. These fitness curves show how the best pulse sets changed through the generations. We can observe that *FitGrouper* and *FitCadence*, which are fitness components defined as penalties for breaking the rules, have invariably played a dominant role in the beginning of the evolution. It is also possible to observe that after both of them have reached the maximum value 1, the configuration of the best pulse set in the following generations had hardly changed. During this steady period, the best pulse set gradually extended over the population. This indicates convergence, even though modifications of the duration or amplitude parameters continued to occur. Although this is a dominant development, it is not an absolute one because there still is the possibility that some exceptionally good configuration had emerged; a good example of this are the pulse sets in the 15th run.

We also have performed other experiments to observe the effects of mutation on the best fitness value that pulse sets can have. For example, by adding the step to randomly generate a new value for the quickest note of every mutation scheme, we found that it is hard to evolve pulse sets with fitness value as high as 3.

The mutation scheme Ma is always performed in the present version of the system. Although this has been decided on purpose, it would be interesting to observe what would happen if one changes the order of the mutation schemes.

5.6. Concluding Discussion

This chapter introduced a GA-based system to evolve performance profiles to play a piece of music. It evolves suitable pulse sets for musical performance using fitness rules derived from the structure of the piece to be performed. Furthermore, the 'excellent' pulse sets evolved by the GA, no matter whether they were from the same run or not, have shown diversity and also commonality. This could be observed both objectively (by comparing the figures of deviation patterns by different pulse sets) and subjectively (by listening to the 'interpreted' MIDI files).

When listening to pieces performed with the evolved pulse sets, we can perceive the expressive dynamics of the piece, mainly due to lengthening or shortening of related notes. However, we acknowledge that such subjective assessment of the results does not hold much scientific value. We are currently developing methodology to validate the evolved pulse sets against human performances (Repp 1992).

At the time of writing, the system is being tested on multiple interactive agents. A group of agents negotiate best practices amongst themselves when performance rules conflict with one another or allow for multiple choices. Other ongoing work includes the implementation of a mechanism to vary the number of hierarchical levels in order to render the model more robust when it encounters more complex music structures. We feel that the system would benefit from being able to cope with more hierarchical levels when evolving pulse sets for pieces of higher complexity than the pieces we have tested so far. Also, we are devising a new way to compute the fitness function, as a weighted sum of the fitness values for different performance principles. We are interested in letting these weights to evolve with the pulse sets.

The natural future progression for this research is to use actual sound recordings rather than MIDI representation of the pieces of music. Although the system still is in development, this chapter demonstrated the potential of yet another application of evolutionary computation in music. Should research in evolutionary generative music performance continue to make progress, we would witness in a not so distant future the appearance of musical devices that will be able to actually perform pieces of music in different ways, rather than simply playback recordings of performed music.

References

Blickle, T. (1995). *A Comparison of Selection Schemes Used in Genetic Algorithms*. Technical report. Computer Engineering and Communication Networks Lab (TIK), Swiss Federal Institute of Technology (ETH), Zurich.

Clarke, E.F. (1988). Generative principles in music performance. In J. Sloboda (Ed.), *Generative Processes in Music. The Psychology of Performance, Improvisation, and Composition*. Oxford Science Publications.

Clynes, M. (1986). Generative principles of musical thought integration of microstructure with structure. *CCAI, Journal for the Integrated Study of Artificial Intelligence, Cognitive Science and Applied Epistemology*, **3**: 185–223.

Clynes, M. (1995). Microstructural musical linguistics: Composers' pulses are liked most by the best musicians. *COGNITION. International Journal of Cognitive Science*, **55**: 269–310.

Davidson, J.W. and North, A.C. (1997). *The Social Psychology of Music*. Oxford University Press.

Gabrielsson, A. (2003). Music performance research at the millennium. *Psychology of Music*, **31**(3): 221–272.

Oosten, P. van (1993). Critical study of Sundberg's rules for expression in the performance of melodies. *Contemporary Music Review*, 9: 267–274.

Palmer, C. (1997). Music performance. *Annual Review of Psychology*. **48**: 115–138.

Poli, G.D. (2004). Methodologies for expressiveness modelling of and for music performance. *Journal Of New Music Research*, 33 :189–202.

Repp, B.H. (1992). Diversity and commonality in music performance: An analysis of timing microstructure in Schumann's Traumerei. *Journal of the Acoustical Society of America*, 2546–2568.

Sundberg, J. (1999). Grouping and differentiation two main principles of music. In T. Nakada (Ed), *Integrated Human Brain Science: Theory, Method, Application (Music)*.

Temperly, D. (2004). *The Cognition of Basic Musical Structures*. The MIT Press.

Todd, N.P.M. (1985). A model of expressive timing in tonal music. *Music Perception*, **3**(1): 33–58.

Widmer, G. and Goebl, W. (2004). Computational models of expressive music performance: The state of the art. *Journal of New Music Research*, **33**: 203–216.

6
Composing with Genetic Algorithms: *GenDash*

RODNEY WASCHKA II

6.1. Introduction

This chapter describes the author's ongoing work with evolutionary computation in the composing of 'art' or 'concert' music. Over the course of many years, the author has written and rewritten a computer program called *GenDash* that employs evolutionary computation. *GenDash* has been used to help compose pieces ranging from works scored for solo human speaker to string quartets to orchestral works to pieces for instrumentalist and electronic computer music to operas.

Only the author has used this particular program and over time *GenDash* has undergone a number of significant revisions. Since the author never entertained any idea of distributing the program in any form, changes and additions were made to the program and those accretions were bent, stretched, and sometimes, hammered into shapes useful to the author. For some pieces, *GenDash* provided the total algorithmic support for the composition of a particular work. For other pieces, the author might have used *GenDash* for one aspect of the work, such as the instrumental part of a composition, while employing a different program and algorithm for the electronic portion. Some people might characterize the structure, revisions and uses of *GenDash* as 'idiosyncratic,' while others might find 'eccentric' a better term. In any event, aside from some initial testing to help the author figure out what might be possible, the program always had to serve the creation of the music, with pieces often made on a deadline for a performance already scheduled. The very name of the program, inspired by Al Biles' *GenJam* program, indicates the author's frequent need for quick results.

After providing brief background information, this chapter describes in general terms the *GenDash* program and the thinking behind its various attributes and incarnations. Different requirements for each commission meant small or even large changes in the program. Additionally, changes in the author's thinking about how to use evolutionary computation resulted in other changes to the program. Some of this explanation may seem wayward, but if one wishes to understand the working method of a particular composer, one is forced to follow the composer's particular thought patterns no matter how nonlinear or even silly. Following that discussion, a list of the author's pieces made with evolutionary computation appears and finally some specific examples from those pieces are described. Small sections of this chapter are based on short articles the author published previously (Waschka 1999, 2001).

6.2. Background

In the 1990s, some composers and/or engineers attempted to make use of evolutionary computational models of different types to create various kinds of music or musical sounds. The range of these musical projects from before, during and after the creation of *GenDash* extended from harmonizing chorale melodies in the style of Johann Sebastian Bach (Horner and Ayers 1995; Maddox and Otten 2000) to timbre development (Horner et al. 1992; Horner and Goldberg 1993; Horner et al. 1993; Fujinaga and Vantomme 1994; Horner et al. 1995), to attempts to find efficient synthesis techniques that produce sounds that mimic acoustic instruments (Horner et al. 1992; Vuori and Valimaki 1993; Horner et al. 1996), to the creation of a musically intelligent soloist for jazz standards (Biles 1994; Biles and Eign 1995; Biles 1998), to attempts to utilize these artificial life models for the making of new music (Waschka 1999; Thywissen 1996). While the list above represents only a sampling of the work done, it does give an indication of the type and breadth of those efforts. Some of this work has been summarized in more recent writings, most notably this volume.

Al Biles with his program *GenJam* accomplished compositional work within a well-understood format. *GenJam* composed solos for jazz standards. Intrigued by a presentation Biles made about his research in 1994 at the International Computer Music Conference in Aarhus, Denmark, the author immediately set to work on a program that would help compose new works for traditional 'art/concert' music ensembles as well as works involving electronic computer music. A solo work, *Solo Song*, was completed in 1995 (Waschka 1996a) and a work for orchestra, *Empty Frames*, in 1996 (Waschka 1996b).

6.3. First Thoughts

One of the conditions often cited for the ideal use of evolutionary computation is that of a 'well-defined problem space.' When an architect or designer or engineer or computer programmer sets out to create a building or a faucet or a fork or an inventory database, they find the project burdened with various limitations. Often these limitations help determine whether the project will be considered a success. The bridge must span a certain length and carry a certain weight. The fork must be easy to use by adults and children, the arthritic and the handicapped. The building must contain a certain number of square meters or feet, have a certain volume, remain standing and require little maintenance. The inventory program must allow novice and occasional users, who generally drive forklifts and trucks, to find specific items in a matter of moments. All of these projects come with budget constraints. These limitations together with the many known aspects of the materials available: The density and carrying capacity of metals, stone, wood, concrete, etc., combine to define the problem space with a clear minimum level of success. A building or bridge that falls down is a failure. A fork that an average, healthy 20-year-old human cannot keep food upon is a failure. An inventory program that requires the designer to spend 5 min clicking buttons to find out if widget type 'D' is in stock is a failure.

Music remains free from many of the physical constraints common in other art forms. Because its material can be made indistinguishable from its form, Walter Pater claimed that 'All art constantly aspires towards the condition of music' (Pater 1873). Music may be the most ephemeral, ghostly and useless of the arts. Dance, like music, is here and gone in an instant, but choreographers must cope with the abilities and disabilities of human bodies. In the documentary film, *The Collaborators: Cage, Cunningham, Rauschenberg (1987)*, about the collaborative work of composer John Cage, choreographer Merce Cunningham and visual artist and costume and set designer Robert Rauschenberg, an interview segment illustrates the point. Both Cunningham and Rauschenberg complain that because Cage's work was the least corporeal, he always had the most freedom. Rauschenberg comments on the limitations of size, weight, material, etc., that constantly constrained the visual art of his set and costume design. Cunningham notes that he was not free in his use of chance techniques in choreography because such techniques could lead to dancers running into each other, 'but if John's sounds ran into each other, no one got hurt'.

The problem of composing new works of art music is, at least in the author's view, far from a well-defined problem. The obvious question is what makes for good new music? What is meant by 'new' here is both currently made and different, non-formulaic, perhaps experimental and/or avant-garde. Most composers, upon hearing a piece, even for the first time, feel confident of their ability to judge its quality and believe they will be able to point out what things about the piece worked well and what did not. However, such estimations differ significantly from knowing, *a priori*, what will make a good, non-formulaic, experimental, or avant-garde piece. Many composers do not have this *a priori* knowledge and, if they did, could easily find that composing no longer interested them. To paraphrase Morton Feldman paraphrasing someone else: When we get to the point where we do not know what we are doing, that's when we have truly started to compose. This is not true for all composers – those who wish to write in a well-understood style from a previous time period, may, in fact, have very detailed ideas about the rules for making a piece, as might, for example, an integral serialist. For those who do not have a very specific idea of the end result as they begin composing, developing evolutionary priorities as defined by a fitness function could easily prove impossible. One could begin by thinking about the limitations of the human ear as a basis for marking the boundaries of music making, which still leaves an infinity of possibilities, but then, what to do about 'conceptual music' or pieces of music that cannot be heard by human ears?

In many instances, of course, a commission gives the composer some limitations. For example, the work must be for string quartet and must last between 15 and

20 min. Other commissions constitute even fewer boundaries. A composer might be asked to 'make an electronic piece without performers for our next festival with a maximum of eight channels of sound'. Regarding cost, another usual limitation, there are clear expense differences between erecting a building or bridge and making and presenting a piece of electronic computer music. Even computer music for traditional performers is much less costly than many other kinds of projects (artistic or otherwise) to which evolutionary computation models might be applied. Once a certain relatively low expense standard is reached, a composer can present a piece that will last at least as long as the typical audience is willing to sit still to hear it. In the case of electronic music, the composer can easily make pieces that last much longer than that for only tiny increases in cost. Once a piece is scheduled to be on a regular concert series, meaning the hall has been rented and the performers have been paid to play something at that time and place, then the real budget factor is the amount and cost of rehearsal time. This factor can act as a limitation for the composer.

6.4. First Attempts

With something akin to these thoughts in mind, in 1995 the author attempted to create an evolutionary computational program that would help compose a piece for the simplest and handiest performance situation: The composer as solo human speaker (*Summer Song* 1996). The process and the two small pieces made in this way interested the composer sufficiently to warrant a continued exploration of the possibilities and to risk attempting to use evolutionary computation as a method for making a piece for orchestra. This exploration eventually resulted in the chamber orchestra piece (*Empty Frames* 1996), but along the way, the author's use of evolutionary computation in composition crystallized in the development of *GenDash*. The making of this orchestral piece, then, traces the development of *GenDash*.

After working on the orchestra piece for some time, a number of problems pushed the author to make radical changes in the approach to the algorithm. Working with what seemed like an elaborate program that would select musical material from the initial population, then breed and after many generations assign offspring to different instruments, the author immediately began struggling with general philosophical questions and practical procedures, some of which have been mentioned already. Attempts at 'composing' or at least writing a vast, diverse and complicated initial population of gestures, themes, motives, harmonies, etc., provided material that never seemed to organize itself into anything the author considered musically intelligible and sufficiently sophisticated for this piece. Repeated changes in the fitness function seemed to produce entirely unexpected changes in the musical result. In addition, practical problems arose. After the program had run the designated number of generations, the resultant musical material was assigned to the instruments of the orchestra. Sometimes that material could not be performed on the instrument indicated. A problem of the 'fitness function bottleneck' described by Al Biles (1995) also existed.

Obviously, the metaphor for evolutionary computation involves biology and genetics, with the idea of creating a situation in which one, or a very, very small number of best solutions for a particular problem or environment are determined after many iterations. If, however, as might be the case in music, the 'problem' is poorly defined and a correct 'solution' may not be obvious even when the composer literally has it in hand, then another way of looking at evolutionary computation could be used. Thinking about the writings of John Cage, Felix Salten and Kurt Vonnegut suggested another way of working.

6.5. Cage, Bambi and Vonnegut

The author remembered Cage saying that he believed nature operated by chance procedures. The intervention of man into some of nature's processes seemed not to remove the chance element. If thinking of evolutionary computation while reading the book *Bambi* by Salten (1928), one is struck by a couple of instances. First, Bambi's mother is a magnificent specimen. She has been brought to a high level of ruminant perfection through ages of evolution. Still, little in the evolutionary process has prepared her for the advent of gunpowder, rifled barrels and sighting lenses. Nor is she capable of dealing with the sheer dumb bad luck of being in the wrong place at the wrong time when hunters who do not follow the rule of killing only males come into the forest. Second, Bambi's father, another magnificent result of evolution, nearly dies in a forest fire. Imagine a fire starts, through natural processes, on one side of a chasm and not the other. A spectacular deer happens to be grazing on the same side of the chasm that begins burning. With its highly developed (through evolutionary processes) sense of smell and instincts we may not yet understand, the buck quickly realizes the danger and flees. Trapped by the precipitous canyon and the fire, it dies. On the other side of the chasm a not-very-bright and somewhat scraggly deer watches the death in silence then continues foraging. It lives long enough to breed and give birth to a fawn. The same kinds of things apply with humans. An evil, stupid and ugly man buys a lottery ticket. He wins. As the saying goes, 'No man who can afford a luxury car, no matter how ugly, ever had a problem passing on his genes'.

Next the author considered that unlike material objects, including some works of art, music is based in time. The changes heard in a piece over its duration and how those changes are handled can be the most important aspect of a work. This thought was combined with something Vonnegut wrote to the effect that mostly humans are trained to work hard and succeed; unfortunately, mostly what humans do is fail. Most humans experience a great deal of failure in their lives. Often, things do not work out, no matter how much effort the human expends. We usually do not receive training that helps us deal with failure. The author thought that reconsidering evolutionary computation in that context might be helpful. Could it be that many of nature's evolutionary experiments playing out over millennia fail also? These ideas resulted in major changes to the program and the creation of the basic *GenDash* program.

6.6. *GenDash*

GenDash has the following attributes: (1) An 'individual' consists of a measure of music; (2) all individuals that are 'born' in any generation are performed; (3) the fitness function is random, which leads to random selection; (4) only one crossover point is used for each breeding, but its placement varies with each generation; (5) space is set aside for individuals that are unheard in the current generation but may appear and/or breed in a later generation; (6) space is set aside for an intact individual that may breed in the current generation and in a succeeding generation; (7) individuals within a single generation can mate with more than one other individual and/or mate with the same individual more than once; (8) mutations can occur and finally, (9) a two parent model is used, but without regard to sex; (10) the composer chooses the initial population. The most unusual things about *GenDash* can be seen in the first three aspects of the program.

The first attribute, that a measure of music constitutes an individual, appeared to be the simplest way to deal with the problem of defining an individual for traditionally notated music. Of course, for other types of work, such as working with recorded sound, the composer would need a different procedure. Since, at some point, a digital representation of an individual is needed and since these pieces of music were to include traditional notation, it seemed to make sense simply to use the measure number in the initial population and in the final piece to indicate a particular individual. In other words, as individuals are generated, their birth order determines their position in the final piece, which takes advantage of *GenDash*'s second attribute.

The second attribute, that all individuals created as a result of the breeding segment of the algorithm would be heard, meant that the evolutionary process itself, not the result of a particular number of iterations, constituted the music. The pieces made with the program mirror the changes that take place over the generations. The author gained a number of advantages because the evolutionary process, rather than the result, creates the piece. The listener, whether cognizant of the process or not, will hear chunks of clearly related material succeeding one another whether the listeners consciously note the 'individuals' as related or not. As with other evolutionary computation programs, in *GenDash* there is a clear diminution of diversity in the succeeding generations and a tendency towards replication of one or a few individuals. In a typical problem-solving situation, this narrowing means a closing in on a possible solution. In this situation, where each individual in each generation is performed, it means an increasing repetition of musical material. If the stage of simply replicating one or a few individuals were to be reached, the music would soon become devoid of interest. In the natural world, such a group might be headed for trouble or extinction: the problems of incest or the disaster of a narrowly evolved species unable to cope with a change in the environment. In music, however, short of simple and potentially endless repetition, this narrowing of the diversity of the material can provide a sense of form. As the piece proceeds, the repetition of certain elements or whole individuals allows the listener to make connections with other parts of the work. Finally, the increased similarity of the musical material and the repetitions of motives or measures can provide for both the composer and the audience a sense of closure and help to bring the piece or section to a 'natural' and 'satisfying' end.

If the composer finds that the succeeding generations converge too quickly to be successful in the piece she or he is working on, there are a number of simple solutions. A situation in which this might arise could be the case of a composer with a commission for a 15-min work, but a convergence that prompts an end to the piece occurs at around 10 min. Potentially, the easiest solution is to re-initialize the population and run the generations again; the time required to do this is literally seconds. Another easy solution might be to increase the size of the initial population. Depending on the desired final length of the piece, the style of music and the predilections of the composer, the size of the initial population could be adjusted before any runs of the program created the needed generations. A certain amount of experience working with *GenDash* has enabled the author to estimate beforehand the necessary size of the initial population. Other composers using similar programs would probably quickly achieve similar estimating abilities.

When a new generation is called for, the program randomly selects which individuals will breed, how many times and with which other individuals. This third attribute, related to the discussion above regarding the role of chance in nature, meant that problems with the fitness function bottleneck were immediately solved: there effectively is no fitness. When using a completely random fitness function, the author thrust the program into its most extreme position, which raised at least two questions. First, how could the composer exert some kind of control over the piece if the fitness function is random? Secondly, did it make sense to employ evolutionary computation under such circumstances? In order to answer those questions, we continue the story of the making of the orchestra piece.

6.7. *Empty Frames* and Beethoven

As the author worked on this piece, a very important factor soon became apparent. A random selection fitness function places considerably more importance on the initial population. It became clear that if a composer wanted to exert some kind of control over the shape of the piece, the chief method would be through careful organization of the initial population. Secondly, even if the composer did not care about exerting any control, the quality of the resultant piece definitely rested in a very significant way on the quality or appropriateness of the initial population. In this case the author struggled, writing initial population after initial population with unacceptable results. Eventually, the author decided to try utilizing a high-quality piece of music as the initial population: The second movement from Ludwig van Beethoven's *Symphony Number Seven*. At the same time the author determined to use the *GenDash* program in a linear or layered approach. This meant, for example, that the flute part would be composed in a series of generations with the initial population consisting of only the flute part from Ludwig van Beethoven's *Symphony Number Seven*. Then the oboe part could be composed using only the oboe part from the *Symphony* and continuing on with each part until the whole was completed with the completion of the string bass part. Of course, this procedure solved the problem of generating parts for an instrument that were unplayable on that instrument. With this procedure, almost nothing could come out of an initial population of violin music by Beethoven that would be unplayable on a violin.

Empty Frames has a duration of 10 min. As it turned out in a kind of pleasant surprise, the piece seemed to converge 'naturally' to an ending as a result of the decreasing diversity of material. In addition to the use of the *GenDash*-produced material, the composer added a couple of other elements. These were a short introduction and the inclusion of a couple of simple presentations of two previously composed melodies. *Empty Frames* was premiered by the Raleigh Civic Chamber Orchestra on 23 April 1998.

The results of this work provided answers to the questions posed above. The first question concerned the ability of the composer to exert some control over the work despite the random fitness function. Now it could be seen that despite the random selection, the composer could maintain some capacity to shape a work by maintaining particularly careful oversight of the initial population. In addition, this work suggested that a fitness function based on random selection together with a very minimal rule or preference could also succeed. In other words, faced with multitude of potentially successful (and potentially fruitless) musical results, a random or minimally limiting fitness function might be best. Beyond that, other attributes of the program mentioned above and discussed below also play important roles in shaping the music. The second question concerned whether or not it made sense to use evolutionary computation under such circumstances. The answer here was 'yes,' because it seemed to work well not only as a way of searching a well-defined problem space, but when the composer used each generation to translate the process into music, it appeared to display an otherwise unexpected effectiveness.

Finally, it should be noted that this also led the composer to explore the use of minimal fitness functions. These fitness functions would have one and only one requirement. For example, the individual (measure) that contained the highest pitch could breed only once and produce only one offspring. In effect, a minimal fitness function implements a single, very specific constraint but provides little 'guidance' for the evolutionary process. Occasionally, that small amount of 'guidance' can have a significant impact over time.

6.8. Other Attributes: Johnny Carson, Late Bloomers and Elizabeth Taylor

The other seven attributes of the *GenDash* program were developed after hearing about aspects of evolutionary strategies in nature and after simple reflection by the author on aspects of human and non-human behaviour.

A television program (now forgotten by the author and possibly part of the NOVA series) about behaviour and genetics pointed out that some human males monopolize most, if not all, of the potential child bearing years of a number of women. The example given, Johnny Carson (a now-deceased American television entertainer) stuck in the author's mind. Carson, like some other men, married several times, with each succeeding bride appearing very similar to the preceding wife, as well as to his first wife. This action of repeatedly 'trading in for a newer model' or 'serial polygamy' meant that whether he intended to or not and he probably did not, Carson achieved a situation in which, generally, he had access to these women during a significant portion of the fertile period of their lives. If the women were faithful in their marriage to him, this reduced the number of their potential mates and, therefore, the genetic opportunities for other men.

Attribute six, which set aside space for an intact individual that may breed in the current generation and in a succeeding generation, resulted from thinking about this particular human behaviour. In *GenDash*, therefore, it is possible for an individual to appear in one generation (and be heard), breed in that generation and then find itself held over intact into the next generation, where it breeds and is heard again. In the program there is an ever-decreasing chance that this could continue indefinitely. The actions of Carson and other wealthy or powerful men in this regard, exert relatively little impact within the context of a nation of 200 million people – if one is thinking only of the United States in the last 40 years of the twentieth century, for example. However, within in the context of a small, relatively or thoroughly isolated tribal group, such actions by a rich or powerful human male could produce noticeable effects. For most of the pieces composed with *GenDash*, the initial population has been small, as few as 10 individuals for very short pieces and often 26 individuals. In such cases, the selection of an individual to breed in more than generation can have a notable effect.

The fifth attribute of the program, that space is set aside for an individual or individuals that are unheard in the current generation, but may appear and/or breed in a later generation, takes into account the classic late-bloomer. Imagine human individuals who are not successful in the early part of their lives. As a result, they have trouble attracting a mate. For example, a human male who drops out of college and starts his own business in a generally not well-known field of endeavour might have trouble finding a mate from among the females of his generation and producing offspring. If, as the years go by, however, that business makes him rich, many members of the succeeding generation of females will find this male attractive. Outside the human species, similar events occur also. An older dominant male of an African lion pride successfully fights off two rivals. A year passes and one of the two rivals has weakened and died, but the other, younger one has grown stronger and manages to chase off the older male and become the dominant male of the pride. There are many other such scenarios, for instance, a male bird that fails to mate in one year figures out how to build a nest and attracts a female in the following year. These kinds of scenarios happen often enough that it seemed worthwhile to incorporate a technique to mimic this behaviour.

Within *GenDash*, the likelihood of this kind of event transpiring is relatively high.

Although the author does not know whether the actress Elizabeth Taylor bore children by more than one husband, the author seems to recall that she married quite a number of men and that she married one of those men twice. Whether any of this is true or not, these thoughts suggested the seventh attribute listed above: An individual can breed more than once within its generation, including more than once with the same individual. In other words, it is possible that individual 34 might mate with individual 27, producing two offspring, then mate with individual 46, producing two offspring, then mate with individual 27 again, producing two more offspring. It is also possible that individual 34 could simply mate with individual 27 twice, producing in all four offspring. In *GenDash*, the chances of an individual breeding more than once within a generation are relatively high. The chances of an individual breeding three times: once with one individual, then with a different individual and finally with the initial individual again are relatively low, but not zero. An exception to this attribute might come when a 'minimal fitness function' (discussed above) was used. In that case, the fitness function might stipulate that individual number 17, which contains the longest note duration in a given generation, could breed a maximum of one time.

The eighth attribute listed above states that, as is the case with most evolutionary computation programs, random mutations occur in *GenDash*. The rate of occurrence, although low, remains, as in some other programs, much higher than the rates normally seen in earth's biology. Typically, the program allowed for two types of mutation. In the first case, when the program determined a mutation took place with the breeding of a particular individual, *GenDash* called upon a list of mutations, intuitively decided upon by the composer. For example, the first mutation on the list could be 'change the first pitch in this individual to the nearest 'E' pitch.' The second mutation on the list might be, 'halve the duration value of the second note in this individual and replace the other half with a rest.' The program would simply move down the list as needed in order to modify the offspring with a mutation. The second type of mutation was a 'wild card' in which anything could happen because *GenDash* simply alerted the composer that the program needed a mutation in a particular individual. The author would supply the variation based on a sense of how the piece had progressed and whether the piece seemed to need some kind of major or minor new element at that moment in its development.

GenDash uses a typical two-parent model. A single crossover point is used, but where the crossover will be varies with each individual instance of breeding (*GenDash*'s fourth attribute). Individuals are not 'sexed' and can breed with any other individual (the ninth attribute). In other words, 'individual 9', for example, could mate with any other individual. There is no set of 'males' and set of 'females'. Of course, many other behaviours could suggest other modifications that could be instituted.

Finally, when using *GenDash*, the composer chooses the initial population. While this attribute may seem trivial in some ways, this appears to be a crucial aspect in the process, emphasized as it is by the random nature of the fitness function. And there are alternatives too. For example, another programmer might have made the initial population large and always the same in order more easily to observe the effects of the fitness function. Another person might believe that a random initial population is more in keeping with the other ideas embodied in the program.

6.9. A Brief Example

The resultant determinations by the *GenDash* program for a particular generation might be summarized by the information presented in Table 6.1. The table shows the creation of a first generation of 10 offspring from the initial population of 10 parents. The 'birth order' indicates what the measure number of the particular offspring will be. In this case, the first 10 individuals, created or chosen by the composer, constitute measures 1 through 10 in the piece. The individual indicated by birth order 11 will constitute measure 11 and so forth. Assuming a 4–4 metre, individual 11 will have the first three beats of measure 10 and the last one beat of measure 9. In this example, individual 10 has mated four times, twice with individual 7 producing 'twins' and once each with individuals 4 and 9. Individuals 1 and 3 have 'mated for life' producing two offspring and not mating with other individuals. Individuals 6 and 8 have mated only with each other and have also produced two offspring. Individual 6, however, is being held over to the next generation intact, meaning it has survived its mate and might or might not mate again. This mirrors the situation of a widow or widower. Note that individual 5 did not mate. Therefore, its material will not be heard again in the piece, unless the composer employs a 'wild card' mutation to reconstruct individual 5. Likewise, the first three beats of measure 2 and the last beat of measure 7 have been removed from the potential genetic material. Fig. 6.1 shows the musical result, given a sample initial population of measures. Finally, measure 20 has been mutated. In this case, the second parent, measure 4 has been altered. As expected, beats 3 and

TABLE 6.1. Example of *GenDash* determinations,
(crossover point at beat 3, one offspring per mating).

"Birth order"	Parent 1	Parent 2	Notes
11	10	9	
12	1	3	
13	7	10	
14	6*	8	
15	3	1	
16	4	9	
17	9	2	
18	8	6	
19	7	10	
20	10	4	Mutation

*Holdover: 6.

FIGURE 6.1. Musical result of Table 6.1.

4 of measure 4 are used; however, the accidentals have been removed and the 'E' has been lowered to an 'A'.

6.10. Individual Pieces

The author has created 10 pieces using some form of evolutionary computation program. These works include two relatively small-scale pieces: *Summer Song* (1996) for solo vocal performer and *Six Folksongs from an Imaginary Country* (2003) for viola alone. There is a medium-scale piece, *Singing in Traffic* (1997) for solo instrumentalist and recorded electronic computer music. However, large-scale works dominate the list: *Empty Frames* (1996) for orchestra; *String Quartet: Laredo* (1998) with a version for string orchestra (2000); *Saint Ambrose* (1999–2001) and *Sappho's Breath* (2001–2002), both chamber operas; *String Quartet: Ha! Fortune* (2003); *Eclogues for Woodwind Quintet* (2003); and another opera begun in 2002 and still in progress at the time of this writing. The appendix provides complete information on forces required, duration, premieres and recordings of these pieces.

The making of *Empty Frames* has already been described above. Comments on other individual pieces and some detail on how they were put together follow in this section. The works discussed are *Singing in Traffic* (1997), *Saint Ambrose* (1999–2001), *Sappho's Breath* (2001–2002), *Six Folksongs from and Imaginary Country* (2003) and *String Quartet: Ha! Fortune* (2003). In some cases, the author used *GenDash* to help in composing every aspect of the piece. For other works, the program helped generate the overwhelming majority but not all of the music. In still other instances evolutionary computation output from *GenDash* provided the instrumental portion of a piece while the electronic portions were composed with other algorithms or intuitively. While a purist might decry some of these working methods, the author believes that in the long run the music should matter and that algorithmic techniques should be interesting, useful and serve the composer – not the other way around.

6.10.1. Singing in Traffic

Singing in Traffic was composed for Jonathan Kramer, cellist, ethnomusicologist and haegum player. He had learned to play the haegum while on a fellowship in Korea and wanted to have something new to play on the instrument. The haegum is a Korean two-stringed fiddle of Mongolian origin that typically plays single line melodies. The bow is entwined within the strings and, therefore, cannot fall away from the instrument. Such an arrangement has its advantages for nomadic peoples—one less thing to forget. Figuring that relatively few people played the haegum and that an even smaller subset would take an interest in contemporary American music, the author decided to make a piece based on haegum music that could also be played by other instrumentalists.

Kramer kindly loaned the author some haegum music and taught the author how to read traditional Korean music notation. The author transcribed the pieces into Western notation and then created an initial population based on this music. *GenDash* then produced several generations that became the instrumental part. The initial population and subsequent generations contained only 8 individuals. The original structure of the initial population was retained in that it and each subsequent generation featured 7 three–four-time measures followed by a bar of four–four. Fig. 6.2 shows the first population that appears in the piece (the first eight measures) followed by a segment five generations later (measures 40–47).

In order to provide an improvizational aspect, after every generation, there is a repeat sign with the instruction to embellish the material during the repetition. Performers who have played the piece have taken this to mean everything from small changes in pitch and rhythm with a subtle nuance in the phrasing, to a wide ranging, jazz-like improvization based on the original melody.

The author employed a different algorithm in the making of the electronic part for *Singing in Traffic*. Referred to as a 'mosaic' technique by the composer, it is

FIGURE 6.2. Beginning of the soloist's part for *Singing in Traffic* by Rodney Waschka II (initial population) and a section of five generations later (measures 40–47). Copyright Borik Press 1997. All rights reserved. Used by permission.

based on the theory of centonization from medieval chant (Hoppin 1978). The raw material for the electronic part consists of a single digital recording; the author recorded the sound of a single car passing his house at approximately three in the morning while a bird sang. The piece has a duration of 8 min and 21 s.

Kramer gave the premiere performance of *Singing in Traffic* on his haegum on 7 October 1997 in Raleigh, North Carolina. The piece has been performed on haegum, cello and soprano, alto and baritone saxophones. Saxophonists Steve Duke, Phil Barham and Harry Bulow have played the piece, as well as cellist Jonathan Kramer and others. Subsequent performances have been in given in Chicago, Denton, at the Third Practice Festival in Richmond and elsewhere.

6.10.2. Saint Ambrose

Commissioned by saxophonist Steve Duke, *Saint Ambrose* is a chamber opera for soprano saxophonist, recorded electronic computer music and visual projections. Duke gave the premiere performance of the work in Chicago and he has recorded the piece for Capstone Records (CPS 8708). The opera, in 12 scenes, has a duration of slightly more than 40 min. Based on the life and writings of Ambrose Bierce, the title comes from his definition of a saint: 'n., a dead sinner, revised and edited'. Bierce fought in the United States Civil War. After the war, as a journalist, he took on some of the most famous 'robber-barons' of his day including Stanford, Crocker and Huntington. He wrote short stories and essays about his experiences in the Civil War. He also wrote a book of definitions, *The Devil's Dictionary*, which contains witticisms sufficiently brilliant that they have become part of the English language. For example, 'Love, n., a temporary insanity curable by marriage'. At the age of 71, in 1913 or 1914, Bierce disappeared in Mexico during the Mexican Revolution. Some believe he was killed and his body burned at the battle of Ojinaga. Some believe he left Mexico for Europe, while others contend he returned to the Grand Canyon in the United States where he committed suicide. The opera takes as its conceit that Bierce is still alive and has come to the concert hall to deliver a lecture. The structure of the opera is as follows:

Scene 1:   Overture: Nothing matters
Scene 2:   Good evening
Scene 3:   Interlude #1
Scene 4:   Unlike William
Scene 5:   Interlude #2
Scene 6:   After the war
Scene 7:   Interlude #3
Scene 8:   In 1913
Scene 9:   The definitions aria
Scene 10: Interlude #4: Clementine variations
Scene 11: Now, as promised
Scene 12: Saintly jam

Scene 1, the overture, consists of electronic music. While it plays, the performer walks out on stage. During scenes 2, 4, 6, 8 and 11, the performer acts and speaks

FIGURE 6.3. First five measures of *Interlude 3* of *Saint Ambrose* by Rodney Waschka II. Copyright Borik Press 2001. All rights reserved. Used by permission.

(but does not sing) while electronic music is heard. During scenes 3, 5, 7 and 12, the performer plays the saxophone together with electronic music. In scene 9, *The Definitions Aria*, the performer must alternate between playing the saxophone and speaking, while recorded electronic computer music plays. *The Definitions Aria* was created in such a way that it would also stand alone as a concert work. In this it has succeeded; John Sampen has performed *The Definitions Aria* many times across the United States over the course of a number of years.

The author created the saxophone parts for the opera using *GenDash*. In *Interlude 3*, the author wished to create a saxophone part that invoked the bugle sounds and motives of the American military piece known as 'Taps' without using that work as the initial population. Fig. 6.3 shows the first part of the resultant piece.

6.10.3. Sappho's Breath

Sappho's Breath is a chamber opera for soprano (singing and playing hand-held percussion instruments) and recorded electronic computer music. The work was commissioned by soprano Beth Griffith, who gave the premiere performance in New York City and has recorded the opera for future release. The opera, in 12 scenes and an overture, has a duration of approximately 30 min and is based on the life and writings of the ancient Greek poetess, Sappho. The opera takes as its conceit the idea that Sappho, called forth by the composer from Hades, is briefly allowed to return to the land of the living. She talks and sings about her life touching on the nature of gossip, lesbianism and art.

In this work, the author attempted to provide an extremely simple yet elegant musical and textual setting in keeping with the plain speaking of the poetry. To that end, the arias contain no sung text. The performer chooses syllables to sing with the notes and speaks the text. In addition, no electronic music plays with the arias; the performer accompanies herself with the hand-held percussion instruments. Recorded electronic computer music is heard in the overture and in those scenes where the performer speaks but does not sing. Fig. 6.4 shows part of an aria from this opera.

FIGURE 6.4. Excert from *Aria 1: Tell Everyone* from the opera *Sappho's Breath* by Rodney Waschka II. Copyright Borik Press 2002. All rights reserved. Used by permission.

6.10.4. Six Folksongs from an Imaginary Country

Six Folksongs from an Imaginary Country was written for violist Vladimir Bistritsky. He gave the premiere performance of the work at the Composer's Center in St. Petersburg, Russia in 2003 and has recorded the work for future release. The six movements as follows:

1. Night song
2. Walking song
3. Dance
4. Children's song
5. Drinking song
6. Horse song

No folksong material appears in the work. The six short pieces were created using an initial population of 10 individuals (10 measures). The pieces vary in difficulty, but, partly because of the medium, maintain a sense of simplicity. The imaginary country of these 'folksongs' contains many horses, good food and drink, and children that can sight read complex atonal melodies. These pieces represent some of the author's most straightforward use of evolutionary computation. Fig. 6.5 shows a portion of 'Horse Song.'

6.10.5. String Quartet: Ha! Fortune

String Quartet: Ha! Fortune was written for the Nevsky String Quartet. The quartet gave the premiere performance of the work at the Composer's Center in St. Petersburg, Russia in 2003. The piece has been recorded for future commercial release.

The Quartet is in five movements. The piece uses two older works as initial population material, primarily, the isorhythmic motet *Qui es promesses-Ha! Fortune-Et non est qui adjuvat* by Guillaume de Machaut (c.1300–1377) and the last movement of the Frederik Chopin (1810–1849) Piano *Sonata* in B-flat minor, opus 35. These initial populations are particularly noticeable in the fourth movement, which employs the Machaut motet as an initial population and in the fifth movement, which employs the Chopin *Sonata* movement. Quotations from the motet also turn up in the other movements. Other structural notes on the Quartet include an abrupt end to the first movement, while the third movement takes up where the first movement ended. Fig. 6.6 shows six measures from the fifth movement.

6.11. Conclusion and Future Work

Using the computer program *GenDash*, the author has been able to create a significant body of new art music based on evolutionary computation. The works have achieved many of the usual hallmarks of success: Numerous performances in various countries, financial support, recordings, broadcasts and positive reviews

FIGURE 6.5. First 20 measures of *Horse Song*, the sixth of the *Six Folksongs from an Imaginary Country* by Rodney Waschka II. Copyright, Borik Press. All rights reserved. Used by permission.

(Lambert 2004; Gooud 2002; Sharyshkin 2003; Link 2005). The *GenDash* program presupposes that the process of evolutionary change might be more interesting than any one particular 'solution' for a given musical segment. The program does not rely on fitness functions based on older, well-understood musical styles, nor on the particular preferences of the author or user (which have always been the same person). However, the program's structure does incorporate specific approaches to the modelling of evolutionary behaviour.

FIGURE 6.6. Measures 11–16 of *Movement 5* from *String Quartet: Ha! Fortune* by Rodney Waschka II. Copyright Boric Press 2003. All rights reserved. Used by permission.

A combination of commissions received and the ideas and influences of other researchers working with evolutionary computation will drive future work with *GenDash*. The program will continue to be a practical tool for work on the continuing and ultimate problem for a composer: To make large-scale musical works of art that audiences (who, for the most part, are not interested in the technique of its creation) will find beautiful, enriching, worthwhile and enjoyable.

Appendix: Compositions Created by the Author Using Evolutionary Computation

1. *Summer Song* (1996) for solo performer: Speaking voice, hand-held percussion and optional electronic processing. Duration: 4 min. Premiere Longwood College, 27 February 1997.
2. *Empty Frames* (1996) for orchestra. Duration: 10 min. Premiere: Raleigh, Raleigh Civic Chamber Orchestra, 23 April 1998. Randolph Foy, conductor.
3. *Singing in Traffic* (1997) for solo instrument and recorded computer music. Duration: 8 min. Premiere: Jonathan Kramer, Stewart Theatre, Raleigh, 7 October 1997.
4. *String Quartet: Laredo* (1998). Duration: 20 min. Premiere: Nevsky String Quartet, Sheremetev Palace, St. Petersburg, Russia, 2 June 2002.

4a. *String Symphony: Laredo* (string orchestra version of item 4, 2002) Premiere: University of Georgia String Orchestra, Southeastern Composers League Forum, University of Georgia, 6 March 2003.

5. *Saint Ambrose* (1999–2001) chamber opera for saxophonist/actor, recorded electronic computer music, visuals. Duration: 40 min. Commissioned and premiered by Steve Duke, HotHouse, Chicago, 17 November 2002. Recorded on Capstone Record.

5a. *Clementine Variations.* Premiere: International Computer Music Conference, Beijing, China, 27 October 1999.

5b. *The Definitions Aria.* Premiere: World Saxophone Congress, Montreal, 7 July 2000.

5c. *Overture: Nothing Matters.* Premiere: Montego Bay, Jamaica, 21 December 2000.

6. *Sappho's Breath* (2001–2002) chamber opera for soprano and recorded electronic computer music. Duration: 30 min. Premiere: Beth Griffith, Christ and St. Stephen's Church, New York City, 2 April 2002.

7. *String Quartet: Ha! Fortune* (2003). Duration: 20 min. Commissioned and Premiered by the Nevsky String Quartet, Composer's Center, St. Petersburg, Russia, 12 October 2003.

8. *Six Folksongs from an Imaginary Country* (2003) for viola alone. Duration: 8 min. Commissioned and premiered by Vladimir Bistritsky, Composer's Center, St. Petersburg, Russia, 12 October 2003.

9. *Eclogues for Woodwind Quintet* (2003). Duration: 32 min. Commissioned and premiered by the Louisville Woodwind Quintet, University of Louisville, 6 November 2003.

10. *II* (working title) in progress. Chamber opera for clarinetist/actor, recorded electronic computer music, projected visuals. Duration: 40 min.

References

Biles, J. (1994). GenJam: A genetic algorithm for generating jazz solos. *Proceedings of the 1994 ICMC.* ICMA, San Francisco, pp. 131–137.

Biles, J. (1998). Interactive GenJam: Integrating real-time performance with a genetic algorithm. *Proceedings of the 1998 ICMC.* ICMA, San Francisco, pp. 232–235.

Biles, J. and Eign, W. (1995). GenJam Populi: Training an IGA via audience-mediated performance. *Proceedings of the 1995 ICMC.* ICMA, San Francisco, pp. 347–348.

Fujinaga, I. and Vantomme, J. (1994). Genetic algorithms as a method for granular synthesis regulation. *Proceedings of the 1994 ICMC.* ICMA, San Francisco, pp. 138–141.

Gooud, J. (2002). Broadening Horizons-Sappho's breath. *The Daily Dispatch* (South Africa). Arts. 3. On-line version: http://www.dispatch.co.za/2002/07/02/features/ART3.HTM.

Hoppin, R. (1978). *Medieval Music.* Norton, NY.

Horner, A. and Ayers, L. (1995). Harmonization of musical progressions with genetic algorithms. *Proceedings of the 1995 ICMC.* ICMA, San Francisco, pp. 483–484.

Horner, A., Beauchamp, J. and Cheung, N.M. (1995). Genetic algorithm optimization of additive synthesis envelope breakpoints and group synthesis parameters. *Proceedings of the 1995 ICMC.* ICMA, San Francisco, pp. 215–222.

Horner, A., Beauchamp, J. and Haken, L. (1992). Wavetable and FM matching synthesis of musical instrument tones. *Proceedings of the 1992 ICMC*. ICMA, San Francisco, pp. 18–21.

Horner, A., Beauchamp, J. and Packard, N. (1993). Timbre breeding. *Proceedings of the 1993 ICMC*. ICMA, San Francisco, pp. 396–398.

Horner, A., Chan, S. and Yuen, J. (1996). Discrete summation synthesis of acoustic instruments with genetic algorithms. *Proceedings of the 1996 ICMC*. ICMA, San Francisco, pp. 49–51.

Horner, A. and Goldberg, D. (1991). Genetic algorithms and computer-assisted music composition. *Proceedings of the 4th International Conference on Genetic Algorithms*. San Mateo, Morgan Kauffman.

Horner, A. and Goldberg, D. (1993). Machine tongues XVI: Genetic algorithms and their application to FM matching synthesis. *Computer Music Journal*, **17**(4): 17–29.

Lambert, J. (2004). http://www.CVNC.org/reviews/cd_dvd_book/cd/RodneyWaschka.

Link, S. (2005). Saint Ambrose. *Journal Seamus*, **18**(1): 19–21.

Maddox, T. and Otten, J. (2000). Using an evolutionary algorithm to generate four-part 18th-century harmony. *Mathematics and Computers in Modern Science: Acoustics and Music, Biology and Chemistry, Business and Economics*. World Science and Engineering Society, Athens, pp. 83–89.

Pater, W. (1873). The school of Giorgione. *The Renaissance: Studies in Art and Poetry*. Oxford University Press, Oxford, 1998.

Salten, F. (1928). *Bambi; a Life in the Woods*. Simon and Schuster, NY.

Sharyshkin, N. (2003). Saint Ambrose. http://www.paristransatlantic.com/magazine/monthly2003/07jul_text.htm.

Thywissen, K. (1996). GeNotator: An environment for investigation the application of genetic algorithms in computer assisted composition. *Proceedings of the 1996 ICMC*. ICMA, San Francisco, pp. 274–277.

Vaughn, D. (1987). Merce Cunningham Dance Foundation. *The Collaborators: Cage, Cunningham, Rauschenberg*. KETC Public Television, St. Louis, MO.

Vouri, J. and Välimäki, V. (1993). Parameter estimation of non-linear physical models by simulated evolution—application to the flute model. *Proceedings of the 1993 ICMC*. ICMA, San Francisco, pp. 402–404.

Waschka, II R. (1996a). *Summer Song*. Borik Press, Raleigh.

Waschka, II R. (1996b). *Empty Frames*. Borik Press, Raleigh.

Waschka, II R. (1997). *Singing in Traffic*. Borik Press, Raleigh.

Waschka, II R. (1998). *String Quartet: Laredo*. Borik Press, Raleigh.

Waschka, II R. (1999–2000). *Saint Ambrose*. Borik Press, Raleigh.

Waschka, II R. (1999). Avoiding the fitness 'bottleneck': Using genetic algorithms to compose orchestral music. *Proceedings of the 1999 ICMC*. ICMA, San Francisco, pp. 201–203.

Waschka, II R. (2001). Theories of evolutionary algorithms and a 'new simplicity' opera: Making *Sappho's Breath*. *Artificial Life Models for Musical Applications*. Cosenza, Italy: Editoriale Bios, pp. 79–86.

Waschka, II R. (2003). *String Quartet: Ha! Fortune*. Borik Press, Raleigh.

Waschka, II R. (2003). *Six Folksongs from an Imaginary Country*. Borik Press, Raleigh.

Waschka, II R. (2002). *Saint Ambrose*. Brooklyn: Capstone Records (CPS 8708). Steve Duke, performer.

Waschka, II R. (2001–2002). *Sappho's Breath*. Borik Press, Raleigh.

7
Improvizing with Genetic Algorithms: *GenJam*

JOHN A. BILES

7.1. Introduction

Imagine you are walking down the street past a coffeehouse that features live jazz. From inside the coffeehouse you hear a jazz quartet begin to play a tune. As you pause outside to listen, it sounds like a tenor sax player backed up by a standard jazz trio of piano, bass and drums. You recognize the tune as John Coltrane's *Giant Steps* as the tenor player plays the song's original melody in the first chorus of the tune. Once this 'head' chorus is complete, everyone continues playing in the second chorus, but the tenor player plays a melody that is decidedly not the original melody of the song, switching from the half note rhythm of the original melody to a more active eighth-note-based rhythm. The piano, bass, and drums seem to be playing things that are similar to what they played on the first chorus, except that the bass player is playing a note on every beat instead of roughly every other beat, and the drummer is more active and assertive. This continues for four more improvized choruses, at which point the tenor player begins playing the original melody of the tune again. After this reprise of the tune's head, there is a brief coda and the tune ends.

This little vignette, which could be experienced with live musicians by anyone who patronizes jazz clubs, is actually a description of the tune the author uses for sound checks when he sets up to perform, and the tenor player is actually *GenJam*, the author's EC-based improvization agent. *Giant Steps*, whose difficult chord progression is a right of passage for most budding improvizers, is not a problem for *GenJam*, and while its improvization is certainly not in Coltrane's class, it is definitely competent.

This chapter focuses on applying evolutionary computation (EC) to improvization, using *GenJam* as an in-depth case study. After briefly discussing improvization as a musical task, the focus will shift to *GenJam* – its design and implementation, its evolution and development, and its impact, both musically and technically. This will lead to a broader discussion of how *GenJam* demonstrates the mutual influence of technology and application domains on one another.

7.2. Improvization

Improvization is in some sense the purist of musical activities because it integrates aspects of just about every musical task. Improvizers compose melodic material; they spontaneously arrange and perform their compositions; they develop harmonic and rhythmic structures, and even entire musical forms; and they listen to and interact with other players in the performing group. All of these tasks are performed concurrently, in real time, with little if any rehearsal. In other words, improvization happens in the present – an improvizer cannot edit the composition after it has been performed and cannot wait for inspiration to strike; everything has to happen *now*. This immediacy is one reason improvization can be very exciting, and, as the defining aspect of jazz, it is the main reason jazz is a uniquely stimulating art form (Berliner 1994).

Improvization is interactive and collaborative – improvizers play off of one another and hopefully inspire one another. The level of interaction can range from a soloist playing over a fairly standard rhythmic backing that adheres to a specific rhythmic style and set of chord changes, as was described in our little vignette above, to free-wheeling, no-holds-barred collective improvizations where the form of the tune emerges serendipitously as the conversation (or shouting match) between players unfolds.

To provide a perspective on this broad range of musical experiences, we can categorize improvization along several dimensions, each of which allows setting a level of constraint over some musical aspect. Some of these dimensions are mutually independent, and others overlap, providing different ways of thinking about improvization.

One set of dimensions pertains to how much a source tune is altered in adapting it to become a vehicle for improvization. The way the rhythm section and improvizer handle chord changes suggests a harmonic dimension. Many jazz performances begin with a 'standard' tune, often coming from the American popular songbook. For instance, there have been literally thousands of tunes written to the chord progression of George Gershwin's *I Got Rhythm*. One approach would be to use Gershwin's original chords without alteration as the harmonic foundation for improvization, which would represent the most constrained end of this harmonic dimension. Much more common would be to substitute specific chords in the progression to make it more amenable to improvization or in response to the harmonic direction in which an improvizer seems to be heading. Even less constrained would be to use the original progression as a jumping off point or inspiration for a new, but still related progression. The least constrained end of this dimension would be to ignore the original changes altogether and play whatever seems appropriate at the time.

Similarly, a source tune's rhythm might remain unaltered, or it could be modified to a different style (like playing *Rhythm* changes as a Bossa Nova instead of the standard swing style), or played in a different metre (7/4 instead of Gershwin's 4/4 conception), or played arrhythmically with no defined pulse. At the extreme end of this dimension, the resulting tune may bear no discernable resemblance to the source tune, except possibly in the minds of the performers.

Another dimension rests on timbres, which can range from traditional instruments played in traditional ways, through extended instrumental techniques like multiphonics, to approaches where the timbre itself is evolved in real time, as in Tim Blackwell's *Swarm Granulator* system (see Chapter 9).

A classic pair of dimensions identified by George Russell (1959) is inside versus outside and vertical versus horizontal. The vertical versus horizontal dimension refers to how closely the improvizer follows the chord changes. A vertical player will 'hit every change', which means that the choices of which pitches to play are governed by each specific chord in the progression. One way of thinking about this is that a vertical player tends to select or bend melodic ideas to fit specific chords, which can lead to solos that track the underlying tune very well but may be less flowing. A horizontal player, on the other hand, will choose a set of pitches that are suggested by several successive chords, typically the key suggested by a tune or a section of a tune. This can lead to melodic lines that are more flowing but which may not match the underlying progression as exactly. One way to think about this is that a horizontal player will focus on longer melodic lines and will not 'sweat the small stuff' harmonically.

Russell's conception of an inside player is one who chooses pitches that are closely related to the harmonic progression or the keys it suggests. An outside player will choose pitches that might be unrelated to the underlying progression. Harmonically, this dimension runs from diatonic players, who stick to the notes in a diatonic scale, to chromatic players, who insert more dissonant notes but still at least respect the underlying progression, to 'free' players, who ignore any progression.

Russell's dimensions are independent, a point driven home by his characterization of four contrasting jazz greats. Coleman Hawkins is an inside-vertical player, Lester Young is inside-horizontal, John Coltrane is outside-vertical (at least in his sheets-of-sound period, during which he wrote *Giant Steps*) and Ornette Colemen is outside-horizontal (Russell 1959). As we shall see in Section 7.4, *GenJam* is definitely an inside-vertical player.

One final dimension is simply how many improvizers will be playing at one time. This can range from a single soloist, to pairs of soloists trading fours or eights, to pairs of soloists improvizing collectively (simultaneously) to the entire group improvizing collectively. Obviously with more players improvizing at the same time, there is more chance for chaos. In the case of traditional New Orleans jazz, which tends to be pretty 'inside', each collectively improvizing instrument (trombone, clarinet, trumpet, tuba, etc.) plays a specific role, which results in almost guaranteeing the integrated counterpoint that is characteristic of that style. In the case of an avant garde performance group, which usually pegs the meter at 'outside', chaos is often the goal.

Clearly, improvization is a rich and varied domain that presents lots of interesting problems for evolutionary computation. Let us now turn our attention on one project that has used the evolutionary paradigm to improvize jazz in real time: *GenJam*.

7.3. *GenJam* Overview

GenJam, which stands for *Genetic Jammer*, is a real-time, interactive performance system that uses evolutionary computation to model a jazz improvizer. The *GenJam* project dates back to the fall of 1993, and its first public performance occurred in the spring of 1994. Since that time it has evolved from a proof-of-concept demonstration to a viable improvization agent that maintains a regular performance schedule as a soloist in the author's virtual quintet. The current incarnation of *GenJam* can improvize in several time signatures – 4/4, 3/4, 12/8, 5/4, 7/4 and 16/8 (double time), and its current repertoire numbers over 250 tunes in a variety of jazz-influenced styles. *GenJam* is capable of taking full chorus solos; trading fours, eights, 12s or 16s with a human improvizer; and improvizing collectively with a human. It can interactively evolve original musical ideas (licks) under the guidance of a human mentor, can autonomously evolve new ideas from a database of style-specific licks and can autonomously interbreed its own licks with those of a human performer in real time during the performance of a tune.

Fig. 7.1 shows *GenJam*'s architecture in performance situations. When *GenJam* is executed, it performs a single tune and then terminates. When performing a tune, *GenJam* first reads several files that provide information about the tune it is playing, along with the musical ideas it will use for improvizing on that tune. The *Chord Progression* file tells *GenJam* what octave to play in, the tempo of the tune and the quantization for eight notes (swing, even, or bop) in the first line of the file.

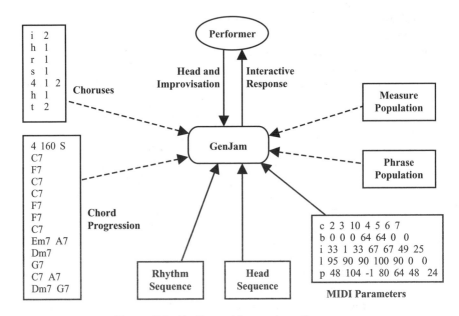

FIGURE 7.1. *GenJam* architecture in performance.

The remaining lines give the chord progression of the tune, one line per measure and up to two chords per measure. In Fig. 7.1 we have a 12-bar blues in C major played around octave 4 (good for tenor sax), at 160 beats per minute, using swing eighth notes.

The *Choruses* file tells *GenJam* what it should do for each succeeding repetition (chorus) of the form defined in the chord progression. In Fig. 7.1 *GenJam* will mark time through a two-measure introduction, play the tune's head for the first full chorus, rest for the next chorus (presumably while the human soloist improvizes), take a full-chorus solo, trade 4's for two choruses with *GenJam* taking the first four in each chorus, play the head for the final full chorus, and then mark time for a two-measure tag before ending the tune and terminating execution of the program.

The *Rhythm Sequence* is a canned MIDI file that supplies the rhythm section background for the tune. The author uses *Band in a Box* (Gannon 1991–2006) to generate these files for the tunes he performs with *GenJam*. Consequently, *GenJam* expects to see a MIDI sequence file with up to five channels (bass, piano, drums, strings and guitar). The author's repertoire features tunes that use as few as one channel (solo piano or bass accompaniment).

The *Head Sequence* is a second MIDI file, which supplies harmony parts for the heads and other specifically scored parts for the tune. This can include riffs for shout choruses, distinctive bass lines, and strategic drum hits that supplement what *Band in a Box* generates.

The *MIDI Parameters* file configures the tone generator for up to 35 different parameters for each of seven MIDI channels that *GenJam* can address. The parameters include obvious ones like channel numbers, program patches, loudness and stereo pan, as well as synthesizer-specific parameters like pitch envelope generator attack, decay and release times.

The *Measure* and *Phrase Populations* are actually data structures that represent hierarchically interrelated populations of melodic fragments (licks) that *GenJam* uses to construct its improvizations. The Measure Population contains 64 individuals, each of which represents one measure of eighth-note-length events. The Phrase Population consists of 48 individuals, each of which contains a sequence of four indices of members of the measure population. An example phrase will illustrate this representation in the next section.

These data structures can be populated in two different ways, interactively and autonomously, which reflect two different evolutionary modes. In interactive mode, *GenJam* maintains fitness values for each individual in both populations, which are derived from feedback provided by a human mentor as the populations evolve during training. A full discussion of this training process will follow in Section 7.5, but a brief explanation is needed here to explain the fitness values used in the example. When training a soloist, a human mentor listens to *GenJam* improvize full-chorus solos and types either 'g' or 'b' (good or bad) whenever so moved. When a 'g' is typed, the fitness values for the currently playing measure and phrase are incremented by 1, and when a 'b' is typed, those fitness values are decremented by 1. Fitness values are initialized to 0 when new individuals in both populations are created.

In autonomous mode, as we shall see in Section 7.8, fitness is unnecessary. Either way, the resulting populations are treated the same in performance, and full chorus solos are constructed by randomly selecting enough phrases to fill out the form of the tune.

During performance *GenJam* interacts with its human partner using a pitch-to-MIDI converter, which allows it to interact in three different ways: (1) trading fours or eights, (2) performing collective improvization and (3) interbreeding human measures from the head and the human's solo chorus with measures in the measure population. These interactive modes will be detailed in Section 7.7.

7.4. Representation – Genotype to Phenotype Mapping with GJNF

Fig. 7.2 shows an example phrase and its constituent measures represented schematically as part of their respective populations. This particular example was created by the author to illustrate features of the representation scheme, which he calls *GenJam normal form* (GJNF), so it was not evolved by *GenJam*. The total phrase population numbers 48 individuals, indexed 0 through 47. Our example arbitrarily focuses on phrase 11. Phrase 11 has a fitness of −5, which means that a mentor has judged it as a slightly 'bad' phrase overall. Newly generated phrase and measure individuals receive an initial fitness of 0, which is considered neutral.

The 64 measures in the measure population are indexed 0-63, which can be represented with a six-bit string. This means that a phrase chromosome is 24 bits, and any 24-bit string will map to a 'legal' phrase. Phrase 11 in our example is made up of measure 34, followed by measure 34 again, followed by measure 55, followed by measure 13.

The measures that are included in phrase 11 are shown schematically in the measure population in Fig. 7.2. Measure 34 has a fitness of 21, which means that the mentor has regarded it as a 'good' measure. It may seem odd that a phrase can

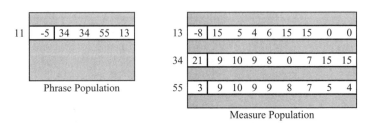

FIGURE 7.2. Example phrase individual and its constituent measure individuals.

have a low fitness while one of its measures has a high fitness, but with 48 phrases, each containing four measures, and only 64 actual measures to assign to those 192 measure slots, each measure will appear an average of three times in the phrase population. In interactive mode, as both populations evolve, some measures will earn higher fitness values and tend to end up appearing more frequently in the phrase population, and others will earn lower fitness values and will tend to appear less often. This phenomenon will be discussed further in the context of *GenJam*'s genetic operators in Section 7.6.

Getting back to our example, measure 34 has eight events, each of which is coded by a 4-bit string. Each event maps to an eighth note of time, which means that in 4/4 time, there are 8 eighth-note-length events, leading to a chromosome of 32 bits. In 3/4 time the chromosome would be 24 bits to accommodate three beats to a measure with two eighth notes to a beat. Other time signatures lead to different chromosome lengths.

The four bits that represent an event provide 16 possible event values, two of which are used to encode note lengths and rhythm. An event value of 0 decodes to a *rest event*, which *GenJam* performs by generating a MIDI note-off event. An event value of 15 decodes to a *hold event*, which *GenJam* performs by doing nothing or holding the previous event through that eighth-note window in the measure. Event values of 1-14 are *new-note events* and decode to pitches in roughly two octaves of the scale suggested by the chord for the current half measure of the tune, as given in the chord progression file and as adjusted to fit the range of the instrument *GenJam* is playing for the tune. When *GenJam* performs a new-note event, it generates a MIDI note-off event, followed immediately by a MIDI note-on event using the decoded pitch. Like the phrase chromosome, this representation is highly robust, in that any 32-bit string will decode to a playable measure in 4/4 time. One constraint is that *GenJam* can play only eighth-note multiples, which is not a severe limitation at medium and fast tempos. Actually, the 12/8 and double time versions of *GenJam* break a 4/4 measure up into 12 eight-note triplets and 16 sixteenth notes, respectively.

Returning to our example, Fig. 7.3 shows phrase 11 as it would be played against the first four measures of the chord progression shown in Fig. 7.1, which is a 12-bar blues in C. Since measure 34 was repeated as the first two measures of our phrase, it generated both of the first two measures of Fig. 7.3. First, notice the 0 in the fifth position of measure 34. This rest event maps to the eighth-note rest in the first and second measures of Fig. 7.3. The two 15s that end measure 34 hold the 7 in the sixth position to produce the C dotted quarter note that ends both measures.

FIGURE 7.3. Phrase from Fig. 7.2 played against first four bars of progression in Fig. 7.1.

TABLE 7.1. Scales used for mapping C7 and F7 chords to actual pitches.

Chord	1	2	3	4	5	6	7	8	9	10	11	12	13	14
C7	C	D	E	G	A	Bb	C	D	E	G	A	Bb	C	D
F7	C	D	Eb	F	G	A	C	D	Eb	F	G	A	C	D

The remaining events in measure 34 are all new-note events whose specific pitches come from the scales suggested by the chords in the chord progression. Because measure 34 is played against a C7 chord in the first measure and an F7 chord in the second measure, the specific pitches are slightly different. Table 7.1 shows the actual scales used to map new-note events for those two measures, assuming an instrument range centered an octave above middle C.

Notice that the scale used for a dominant seventh chord is a hexatonic scale that avoids the fourth. This is because a major fourth (F for a C7) may sound dissonant in some contexts, and a Lydian fourth (F# for a C7) may sound dissonant in other contexts. In fact, the jazz theory literature is divided over the major fourth (Coker 1964) versus Lydian fourth (Russell 1959) for dominant seventh chords, so in a spirit of consensus, *GenJam* simply avoids playing any fourths at all on dominant seventh chords (Haerle 1980, 1989). Similarly, hexatonic scales are used for major sixth and seventh, minor seventh, half-diminished, and a few other chord types (Sabatella 1992, Levine 1995). Table 7.2 shows the complete list of chord types *GenJam* recognizes, along with the name of the corresponding scale and one octave of the notes in that scale, assuming a root of C.

This list grew over time as the author worked up tunes that included chord types that *GenJam* had not encountered before and so the list in Table 7.2 is essentially chronological. The author feels he has come full circle by adding a blues scale a few years ago, which happened to be the only scale in the original proto-version of *GenJam*, which could only play the blues in a specified key.

Once more returning to our example, notice that measure 13 begins with a hold event, which results in the last note of the third measure of Fig. 7.3 being held into the first note of the fourth measure. If the chord for the new measure would have suggested a scale that did not include the held note, then there would likely be a momentary dissonance, but that would tend to 'resolve' once the first new-note event in the new measure is performed. If a measure began with several hold events, then the possibility for a more pronounced dissonance would result, and that measure individual would more likely curry disfavour with the mentor and be less likely to survive.

Also notice the Eb in the third measure of Fig. 7.3. Since measure 55 is played over a C7 chord to generate that measure, we can use the same C7 scale from Table 7.1 to map to actual pitches. An examination of measure 55's chromosome indicates that instead of the Eb, *GenJam* should have played another E natural for the fourth eighth note. Instead, *GenJam* played a chromatic passing tone, using a heuristic that tries to replace repeated eighth notes with chromatic passing tones or chromatic neighbour tones instead of repeating the note in the actual scale.

TABLE 7.2. Chord-scale mappings used to map new-note events to pitches.

Chord	Scale	Notes (root = C)
Cmaj7	Major (avoid 4th)	C D E G A B
C7	Mixolydian (avoid 4th)	C D E G A Bb
Cm7	Minor (avoid 6th)	C D Eb F G Bb
Cm7b5	Locrian (avoid 2nd)	C Eb F Gb Ab Bb
Cdim	W/H Diminished	C D Eb F Gb G# A B
C+	Lydian Augmented	C D E F# G# A B
C7+	Whole Tone	C D E F# G# Bb
C7#11	Lydian Dominant	C D E F# G A Bb
C7alt	Altered Scale	C Db D# E Gb G# Bb
C7#9	Mixolydian #2 (avoid 4th)	C Eb E G A Bb
C7b9	Harm Minor V (avoid 6th)	C Db E F G Bb
CmMaj7	Melodic Minor	C D Eb F G A B
Cm6	Dorian (avoid 7th)	C D Eb F G A
Cm7b9	Melodic Minor II mode	C Db Eb F G A Bb
Cmaj7#11	Lydian	C D E F# G A B
C7sus	Mixolydian	C D E F G A Bb
Cmaj7sus	Major	C D E F G A B
C7Bl	Blues	C Eb F Gb G Bb

Except for these special cases, then, *GenJam* will always play notes in the 'theoretically correct' scale, which means that *GenJam* cannot play a theoretically wrong note, unlike the author. The author can break the harmonic rules and 'play outside', if so moved, to add harmonic tension, and the author can also get lost in the chord changes and play notes he did not intend. *GenJam* can do neither. The initial design decision was that *GenJam* should always sound at least competent and never 'wrong', which has resulted in a highly robust system.

7.5. Evolving a Soloist

The measure and phrase populations can be evolved in two different ways, depending on which evolutionary mode is used. The original version of *GenJam* used an interactive genetic algorithm (IGA) to perform generational evolution under the guidance of a human mentor (Biles 1994). This process is shown in Fig. 7.4.

To prepare for training, the mentor sets up a collection of tunes that *GenJam* will perform during the training process. While the mentor could evolve a new soloist for just a single tune, the author tends to evolve a soloist for a style of tune and sets up a handful of representative tunes from which to select during training. Training on a single tune runs the risk of over-specializing the resulting soloist and also causes fatigue for the mentor, who would have to listen to the same tune

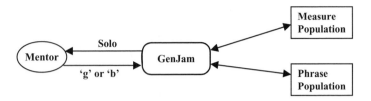

FIGURE 7.4. Interactive *GenJam* training process.

over and over (Biles 1999). Each training tune will consist of three or so choruses, with *GenJam* taking a full-chorus solo for all choruses.

Each tune in training mode evolves a new generation of the soloist. *GenJam* first reads the measure and phrase populations from text files. It then runs its genetic algorithm on each population independently to generate a new generation of the soloist. After it evolves the next generation, it performs its solo choruses for the mentor, who listens and types 'g' for good or 'b' for bad whenever so moved. The mentor's interface is as simple as possible to allow the mentor to focus on the listening task. Every time the mentor types 'g', *GenJam* increments the fitness values for the currently playing measure and phrase individuals, offset by empirically derived delays to give the mentor a chance to hear, process and respond to *GenJam*'s improvization. The delay for measures is two beats, and the delay for phrases is one measure (Biles 1998).

Fig. 7.5 shows how *GenJam* evolves a new generation of a soloist. Half of each population is replaced with new children in each generation, which is 50% elitism. The tournament selection scheme tends to select and preserve the better measures and phrases, and their children tend to replace the worse ones.

The specific implementations of crossover, mutation and the other genetic operators will be presented in Section 7.6, but it should be noted that mutations are repeatedly applied to the children created by their parents' crossover until they are unique with respect to the individuals in their target population. This ensures there are no individuals that are exact copies of one another in either population, which is motivated by the need to insure diversity and minimize convergence. This issue will be discussed more fully in Section 7.6.1.2.

As *GenJam* improvizes using its new-generation soloist, it first selects the new child phrases to construct its solo choruses. With 48 phrases in the phrase population and 50% elitism, this means that *GenJam* evolves 24 new child phrases per

Repeat
    Select 4 individuals at random to form a family (*tournament selectiion*)
    Select 2 family members with the greatest fitness to be parents
    Perform *crossover* on the 2 parents to generate 2 chidren
    Mutate the resulting 2 children until they are unique in the population
    Assign 0 as fitness for both children
    Replace the two non-parent family members with the new children
Until half the population has been replaced with new children

FIGURE 7.5. Genetic algorithm for evolving a new measure or phrase generation.

generation, which in turn means that the mentor should hear at least 24 phrases in *GenJam*'s solo to insure that the mentor will hear all the new children and have a chance to provide feedback. 24 four-bar phrases adds up to 96 measures, which happens to be three choruses of a 32-bar tune, which happens to be the most common form in jazz. When training on a blues progression, the mentor should set up a tune with eight 12-bar (3-phrase) choruses to get the required 24 phrases.

Early in *GenJam*'s development, the author found that three choruses of a standard tune was about the upper limit on his attention span for the intense level of listening required to perform the mentoring task effectively. Assuming 50% elitism, those 24 phrases then, had to be 50% of the phrase population, which explains the choice of 48 as the size of the phrase population (Biles 1994). This somewhat convoluted line of reasoning exemplifies how EC has to adapt to the music domain. This recurring theme becomes more interesting when those adaptations challenge the definitions of EC, as we shall see.

7.6. Genetic Operators

GenJam's genetic operators are an even more pronounced example of how music as an application domain led the author to bend EC in developing *GenJam*. In short, *GenJam*'s initialization, selection, crossover, mutation, and replacement operators have become intelligent, which is in sharp contrast to these operators in traditional EC-based systems.

We'll start with *GenJam*'s mutation operators, which are used when training soloists, trading fours and eights, and improvizing full-chorus solos in performance. *GenJam*'s crossover operators are used to train soloists interactively, evolve soloists autonomously, and interbreed human melodic ideas with those of a soloist in real time during performance. *GenJam*'s selection and replacement operators are fairly traditional in the original, interactive version of *GenJam*, but they, too, have acquired some intelligence in the autonomous version. Finally, *GenJam*'s initialization operators have literally evolved from a uniform random number generator to style-specific generators that guarantee musically promising individuals.

7.6.1. Mutations

In most evolutionary computation-based systems, mutation is implemented by occasionally flipping a random bit. Over the course of hundreds or thousands of generations of large populations, these tiny alterations provide enough novelty to explore the search space and keep a population from converging on suboptimal peaks (Goldberg 1989). However, this approach would be essentially useless with *GenJam* for several reasons. First, the mentor is not going to listen to hundreds of solos in order to train a new soloist. Second, occasional random bit flips will

Original measure	9	10	9	8	0	7	15	15
Transpose down 2	7	8	7	6	0	5	15	15
Reverse	15	15	7	0	8	9	10	9
Rotate left 3	8	0	7	15	15	9	10	9
Sort new notes up	7	8	9	9	0	10	15	15
Sort new notes down	10	9	9	8	0	7	15	15
Invert (15 – loci)	6	5	6	7	15	8	0	0
Range-corrected invert	8	7	8	9	15	10	0	0
Invert reverse	0	0	8	15	7	6	5	6

FIGURE 7.6. Musically meaningful mutations on measures.

make little difference in how a measure sounds, although a bit change in a phrase individual will replace one of the four measures with a different measure. Third, while random changes will make measures and phrases different, they are unlikely to make them sound better. Fourth, when trading a four, which will be described in Section 7.7.1, *GenJam* has to evolve a musically stimulating response in a few milliseconds without the benefit of generational search or even fitness. In other words, it has to sound good in one try.

The overwhelming requirement, then, is that mutated measures and phrases must at least sound no worse than their predecessors, and, when evolving a new soloist, the mutated descendants should tend to sound better. Consequently, *GenJam*'s mutation operators cannot be the traditional low-probability, 'dumb' bit flip and are, instead, *musically meaningful mutations*. We will first look at mutations that operate only on measures, then those that operate only on phrases, and finally on some comprehensive mutations that manipulate an entire phrase and its constituent measures.

7.6.1.1. Measure Mutations

Fig. 7.6 lists several of *GenJam*'s measure-level mutation operators. These mutations are drawn from the toolbox of simple melodic development devices familiar to any composer. However, because they operate on a measure's genotype (its event chromosome) instead of its phenotype (the actual notes and rests that result when the chromosome is played over one or two chords), the effect is subtly different from traditional retrograde, inversion, reversion, etc. (Reti 1951).

For instance, applying the reverse operator to a quarter note, which in GJNF is encoded as a new-note event followed by a hold event, results in holding a different note. In the case of the Reverse mutation example in Fig. 7.6, the result is to begin the measure with a tied quarter note, whose pitch is determined by the pitch established at the end of the previous measure, whatever that may be. In Fig. 7.7, which shows the measures in Fig. 7.6 played consecutively against a sustained C7 chord, we can see that the result is a $2\frac{1}{2}$-beat A-natural that spans the second and third measures. There was no A-natural in the original measure and so the reverse did more than simply play the notes in reverse.

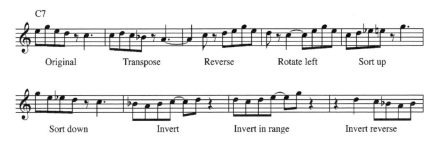

FIGURE 7.7. Mutations from Fig. 7.4 played over a C7 chord.

Another subtlety stems from the invert mutation, which is neither true inversion of intervals nor contrary motion (Reti 1951), but instead inverts the rough melodic contour by subtracting each event locus from 15. In addition to making low notes high and high notes low, it changes the rhythm by exchanging hold and rest events, as can be seen in the invert and range-corrected invert in Figs 7.6 and 7.7. The range-corrected invert transposes the inverted measure to retain the pitch range of the original measure, which is especially useful when trading fours.

Finally, notice the chromatic passing tones in measures 5 and 6 of Fig. 7.7, which came about from the repeated 9s in the sorted measures. This again highlights the fact that the mutated genotype is an abstraction of a melodic fragment whose mapping to actual notes is context dependent.

7.6.1.2. Phrase Mutations

The phrase-level mutations *GenJam* can use are summarized in Fig. 7.8, using the phrase from Fig. 7.2 as an example. The reverse and rotate operators simply alter the order of the measures in the phrase. The sequence phrase mutation repeats a randomly selected measure, which results in a 'sequence' (Berliner 1994).

The Genetic Repair and Super Phrase mutations attempt to promote measures with higher fitness and thin out measures with lower fitness. The genetic repair mutation replaces that measure with the lowest fitness in the phrase with a randomly selected measure. In Fig. 7.8 the randomly selected measure, 61 in this example, is underlined to denote that it was not in the original phrase. The super phrase mutation generates an entirely new phrase consisting of the winners of four

Original Phrase	34	34	55	13
Reverse	13	55	34	34
Rotate Left (1)	34	55	13	34
Sequence Phrase	34	34	55	55
Genetic Repair	34	34	55	61
Super Phrase	17	43	8	27
Lick Thinner	47	34	55	13
Orphan Phrase	5	60	23	40

FIGURE 7.8. Musically meaningful mutations on phrases.

fitness tournaments. This provides an opportunity to collect high-fitness measures in a single phrase and is an extreme mutation in that the original child is totally discarded.

The last two mutations in Fig. 7.8 try to address the convergence problem, which has been a conspicuous issue in *GenJam*'s development from the beginning and which once again illustrates how improvization bends the EC paradigm. Unlike traditional EC systems, which treat the population of candidate solutions as competitors for the single 'best' solution, the individuals in *GenJam*'s measure and phrase populations must work together to provide a rich and varied idea base from which *GenJam* can generate its improvizations. The tendency of the EC machinery to converge on a few highly fit individuals would result in *GenJam* playing minor variations of a small set of melodic ideas. The author has characterized this lack of originality as 'the lick that ate my solo'. While the author has certainly encountered human soloists at jam sessions who played minor variations of the same small set of licks over and over and over and over, he tried to set the bar higher for *GenJam*.

This led to phrase-level mutations and other mechanisms to encourage, and in some cases guarantee, diversity in the measure and phrase populations. The Lick Thinner mutation in Fig. 7.8 replaces the measure in the phrase that occurs most frequently in all the phrases in the phrase population with a measure that occurs infrequently in the phrase population. This thins out over-represented measures and promotes under-represented measures in the phrase population. One specific goal is to eliminate 'orphan' measures, which exist in the measure population but are not included in any phrase in the phrase population. Such measures can never be heard by the mentor, and if their fitness is high enough, they will not likely be replaced and therefore so they effectively use up population space unproductively.

A more extreme version of this mutation is the orphan phrase mutation, which generates an entirely new phrase consisting of the losers of four frequency tournaments. This tends to bundle rarely heard measures together to give the mentor a chance to hear and evaluate them.

7.6.1.3. Comprehensive Mutations

Some of *GenJam*'s mutations operate on phrases but also mutate the measure individuals referenced by the phrase to perform a more comprehensive mutation. In essence, these mutations treat the concatenated measures in a phrase as one long measure. Because these operators mutate measure individuals in the context of a phrase-level mutation, they are used only when trading fours and eights.

GenJam can perform mutations that approach phrase-level retrograde, inversion, and retrograde inversion. The basic idea for the phrase-level retrograde is to apply the phrase-level reverse mutation to the phrase chromosome and then apply measure-level reverse mutations to each of the measure chromosomes. While this does not lead to a true retrograde because of the way reversals cause hold events to extend a different new-note event, as discussed in Section 7.6.1.1, the resulting phrase will sound good if the original phrase did.

The phrase-level inversion leaves the phrase chromosome unaltered and inverts the constituent measure chromosomes using the measure-level inversion operator. To ensure that the resulting phrase ends up in the same range as the original phrase and that the measure boundaries retain the original horizontal intervals, all four inverted measures are transposed the same amount as part of a phrase-level, range-corrected inversion.

The phrase-level retrograde inversion simply does both the phrase-level retrograde and the phrase-level, range-corrected inversion on the same phrase. This is probably the most extreme mutation performed by *GenJam* and is, in fact, something no human could perform in a real-time performance setting when trading fours. This is one reason *GenJam* is such a formidable opponent when trading fours. Not only does it hear the human's four more accurately than a human could hear it, even taking pitch-tracking mistakes into account, it can develop the human's four in ways that no human could in real time.

The final comprehensive mutation is a hemiola operator, which extends the notion of sequencing across measure boundaries by creating a sequence that is shorter than the length of a measure. A hemiola is a repeating melodic pattern that is shorter than the length of a measure and has the effect of temporarily imposing a new time signature. The traditional example is a three-beat melodic figure repeated in 4/4 time (Slonimsky 1998).

GenJam's hemiola operator identifies a likely melodic 'seed' that is shorter than the measure length and occurs early enough in the four-bar phrase to allow it to be repeated a total of three times. For a melodic fragment to be selected as a seed, it must start with a new-note event, must contain a minimum number of rest and/or hold events and must have a minimum number of new-note events. After a suitable seed has been selected, it is simply repeated twice more, immediately after its original occurrence, replacing the events that were in the original measures. When the repetitions run out, the original events take over to complete the phrase.

The specific timing for a hemiola is not critical, except that the seed must occur early enough in the phrase to be repeated twice more. Whether the seed begins on or off the beat and which beat in a measure it starts near simply do not matter, because as long as there is the perception of repetition, the listener will interpret it in the context of the improvization.

7.6.2. Crossover

GenJam's crossover operators have evolved from a traditional, single-point, random crossover operating at the bit level, to an intelligent crossover operating at the note level. *GenJam*'s original crossover operated at the bit level and was identical for both the measure and phrase populations. The chromosomes from the

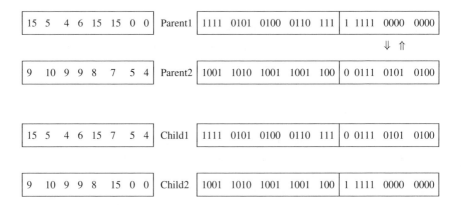

FIGURE 7.9. Random bit-level measure crossover at an unfortunate crossover point.

two parents were treated as flat bit strings, and the crossover point was chosen at random. Fig. 7.9 illustrates this process with an example using measures 13 and 55 from Fig. 7.2.

This example shows the problem with traditional random crossover. The crossover point selected, between the 19th and 20th bits in this case, falls between bits 3 and 4 within a four-bit event substring, which facilitates the generation of new events in the children. Specifically, the events being split by crossover in our example are a hold event (1111) in Parent 1 and a new-note event (1000) in Parent 2. The result in Child 2 is a third 1001 new-note event in a row. In the current version of *GenJam*, the chromatic neighbour heuristic produces the Eb in Child 2, which makes for a relatively pleasing note (see Fig. 7.10).

The result in Child 1, however, is a new-note event (1110) that is not only absent in either of the parents, but also yields horizontal intervals greater than an octave (the high D in the fifth note position in Child 1). This note is 'unfortunate' in that most mentors, or at least the author, will find it unappealing and will likely sit on the 'b' key upon hearing it. This may be acceptable when training a soloist over the course of several generations, but it is unacceptable when performing a crossover between a measure from the measure population and a measure that the human just played during the head or a full-chorus solo, because in that context there is no opportunity for a mentor to provide negative fitness and weed out the measure.

FIGURE 7.10. Parents and children from Fig. 7.9 played against a sustained C7 chord.

At each of the seven potential crossover points (in 4/4 time)
    Compute horizontal intervals that would result in both children
    Return the smaller interval as "fitness" for that point
If more than one crossover point has the same fitness
    If breeding two of *GenJam*'s measures
        Select crossover point closest to the centre of the measure
    If breeding a *GenJam* measure with a human measure
        Select corssover point that maximizes the human's contribution
Perform crossover at selected point

FIGURE 7.11. Intelligent note-level measure crossover algorithm.

7.6.2.1. Intelligent Measure-Level Crossover

The intelligent measure-level crossover in the current version of *GenJam* addresses this problem, first by selecting crossover points only at event boundaries, which preserves the parents' events in the children, and then by choosing the specific crossover point intelligently. Fig. 7.11 gives the intelligent measure crossover algorithm.

The heuristic being applied is to minimize the horizontal interval at the crossover point, which tends to generate smooth measures. If more than one crossover point would yield the same horizontal interval, the tie is broken by heuristics that depend on the context in which the crossover is occurring. Specifically, the crossover point is biased towards the middle of the measure when breeding two of *GenJam*'s measures, in order to break up *GenJam*'s stored licks. When breeding a human measure with a *GenJam* measure, which will be described in Section 7.7.3, the crossover point is biased to include as much of the human's measure as possible, in order to tilt *GenJam*'s material towards the immediate performance.

Fig. 7.12 shows the application of the algorithm in Fig. 7.11 to the two measure chromosomes from Fig. 7.9. In this case the smoothest crossover point occurs between the fifth and sixth events, which leads to a horizontal interval of one step

| 15 | 5 | 4 | 6 | 15 | 15 | 0 | 0 | Parent1 | 1111 | 0101 | 0100 | 0110 | 1111 | 1111 | 0000 | 0000 |

⇓   ⇑   ⇓ ⇑

| 9 | 10 | 9 | 9 | 8 | 7 | 5 | 4 | Parent2 | 1001 | 1010 | 1001 | 1001 | 1000 | 0111 | 0101 | 0100 |

| 15 | 5 | 4 | 6 | 15 | 7 | 5 | 4 | Child1 | 1111 | 0101 | 0100 | 0110 | 1111 | 0111 | 0101 | 0100 |

| 9 | 10 | 9 | 9 | 8 | 15 | 0 | 0 | Child2 | 1001 | 1010 | 1001 | 1001 | 1000 | 1111 | 0000 | 0000 |

FIGURE 7.12. Intelligent note-level measure crossover at a smooth crossover point.

| Parent 1 | Parent 2 | Child 1 | Child 2 |

FIGURE 7.13. Parent and child chromosomes from Fig. 7.12 played against C7 chord.

in child 1 (the 6 in position 4 held through position 5, followed by the 7 in position 6) and a horizontal interval of zero in child 2 (the 8 in position 5 is held in position 6, followed by rest events to finish the measure). Fig. 7.13 shows the parent and child chromosomes from Fig. 7.12 played against a C7 chord.

7.6.2.2. Intelligent Phrase-Level Crossover

Crossover at the phrase level only occurs when evolving a new soloist and is not used for trading fours or interbreeding what the human plays with *GenJam*'s ideas. However, the issues with performing crossover on phrases are similar to those for measure crossover, in that introducing brand new measures into the mix via a bit-level crossover point that happens to fall within a measure index can lead to unfortunate horizontal intervals at the boundaries between the 'new' measure and those that come immediately before and after it.

Therefore, the intelligent phrase crossover operates at measure-index boundaries, which means that there are only three potential crossover points in the four-measure phrase representation of GJNF. By prohibiting crossover points within measure indices, the parents' measures are guaranteed to survive in the children, which limits the introduction of new measures into the mix but insures that the horizontal intervals at measure boundaries will be preserved, except for the actual crossover point(s). Preserving the parents' horizontal intervals at the crossover points, in fact, is the primary goal of this operator, as shown in Fig. 7.14.

Notice that the number of crossover points is not fixed. This allows the creation of phrases that could hop back and forth between the parent measures. By trying to preserve the parent's horizontal intervals at the crossover points, the measures in the new phrases will hopefully fit together well, and since the measures themselves can be expected to sound good, the resulting phrase should blend the material from the measures indexed by the parents in the 'smoothest' way possible. As is the case for the musically meaningful mutations, the goal for intelligent crossover operators is to 'guarantee' that the children of good-sounding measures and phrases sound good themselves.

At each of the three potential crossover points at measure boundaries
    Compute horizontal intervals in both parents
    Compute horizontal intervals in both children
    Compute interval differences for both combinations of parent and child interval
    Return the smaller differences as "fitness" for that point
Select crossover point(s) with smallest differences (could be 1, 2, or all 3, if there is a tie)
Perform crossover(s) at selected point(s)

FIGURE 7.14. Intelligent measure-level phrase crossover algorithm.

7.6.3. Initialization

Initialization in most EC-based systems is random, which typically is important for conducting an unbiased search for an optimal solution. With *GenJam*, however, random musical phrases sound, well, random. Nonetheless, the original version of *GenJam* used a uniform random number generator to initialize the chromosomes in the measure and phrase populations for generation zero. This led to a flat, uniform distribution of new-notes events in the measure individuals and an average horizontal interval of about a seventh, which made the initial generation pretty unappealing to most mentors.

Training a soloist initialized this way was a fairly boring task in the early generations. Typically, four or five generations would go by with the mentor mostly tapping absently on the 'b' key, with an occasional flurry of 'g's when something remotely musical occurred. Usually, a 'golden generation' would occur around five generations in, after which the mentor could begin shifting to a more musically discriminating mindset.

The musically meaningful mutations were largely responsible for the emergence of musically meritorious individuals, and it occurred to the author that it was possible that the mutations might be powerful enough by themselves to improve a soloist without fitness. To test this, he built several soloists without providing any feedback at all, which kept the fitness values for all individuals at their initial value of zero and led to random selection. The result was a series of soloists who were a bit smoother than an untrained soloist, but not nearly as musical as a trained soloist, even after four to five times as many generations of training. Fitness, then, is important, at least when the initial generation is maximally random.

However, what if the initial population is random in a more musical way? In 1998 the author began using a simple fractal generator patterned after Martin Gardner (1978) to initialize generation zero. This guaranteed that the initial generation would have a distribution of new-note events very similar to that of a mature, trained soloist. Specifically, the average horizontal interval came out to about a third, and the distribution of new-note events was roughly bell-shaped with the peak near the middle of the instrument's range. The result was that generation zero sounded significantly less bad than when the uniform generator had been used, which led to more rapid training.

Taking it one step further, in 2001, the author began using a Markov chain initialization procedure that performed even better and generated generation-zero soloists that allowed the user to be musically discriminating from the outset. The Markov chain procedure was a byproduct of making *GenJam* autonomous, which will be discussed in Section 7.8.

7.7. Interactivity

GenJam's ability to interact effectively in real time with a human performer in live performance situations is arguably its greatest strength as an improvizer, and it certainly is the author's favourite feature when playing gigs with *GenJam*. Interaction requires that both parties be able to hear what each other is playing and use what they hear in what they play. The most obvious way this is done is the tradition of trading fours, where soloists take turns improvizing over successive four-bar sections of the tune. Trading fours is often regarded as a competition between soloists, something of a musical dual, where each combatant tries to 'one-up' the other by quoting from their opponent's four and then extending it. This mutual pursuit explains the use of the term 'chase chorus' to refer to a chorus in which soloists trade fours.

7.7.1. Trading Fours

By 1997, the author had been performing with *GenJam* for about three years. A well-trained soloist could play competent full chorus solos, and *GenJam* could trades fours, but when it traded fours, it did so in a vacuum, essentially playing a phrase individual from its population without regard to what the human soloist did. The human could play off of what *GenJam* played, but *GenJam* couldn't return the favour. This made playing gigs a bit tiring for the author because he didn't get much creative energy from what *GenJam* played.

To address this issue, the author purchased a Roland GI-10 pitch-to-MIDI converter, which was designed to plug into Roland's guitar-MIDI interface. However, the Roland engineers also included a $1/4$-inch microphone input, apparently hoping folks would plug in acoustic instruments or try to sing into it. When the product was discontinued at about this time, the author purchased one at a fraction of the original list price in the spring of 1997 and extended *GenJam* to really trade fours.

The basic strategy was to use the GI-10 to listen to what the author was playing on trumpet for four bars, reverse the scale-index-to-pitch mapping to generate new-note events in four measure chromosomes, quit listening in the last instant of the human's four to give *GenJam* time to mutate those measure chromosomes and the trivial phrase chromosome that joined them to make a phrase, and then play the mutated phrase as *GenJam*'s response in the next four bars.

The measure and phrase chromosomes used for trading fours employed the same GJNF representation described above for the measure and phrase populations, but they are not actually in those populations. Because GJNF is so robust, as described above, *GenJam*'s fours are guaranteed to be playable and theoretically correct, which is important, because the GI-10 makes a lot of mistakes.

A test of the GI-10 in a performance setting demonstrated that it generated roughly twice as many note-on/note-off pairs as the author actually played notes (Biles 2001a). In fact the author tweaked the GI-10 to generate as many note-on/note-off pairs as possible by turning off pitch-bend and setting the 'touch' to a hair trigger. The algorithm for mapping MIDI events to event loci in a measure chromosome is summarized in Fig. 7.15.

This algorithm is surprisingly effective, mainly because the target representation is GJNF, which is highly robust. Multiple note-on events occurring in the same time window are resolved by simply keeping the last one to occur that was loud enough.

Initialize all loci in the measure chromosome to hold events
While walking through the event windows in the measure in time with the tempo
    As MIDI events occur in a given event window
      If a MIDI note-on event occurs
        If the event's velocity (loudless) is too low
          Ignore the event
        Else
          Find the nearest pitch in the scale for the current chord
          Assign the scale offset of that pitch as the value for the locus
      Else If a MIDI note-off events occurs
        If the current locus is still a hold event
          Assign a rest event to the locus
        Else
          Leave the locus alone (stays a new-note event)
      Else no event occurs in the window, so the locus stays a hold event
    End As
End While

FIGURE 7.15. Algorithm for listening to human measure when trading fours.

The loudness threshold helps filter out ambient noise in the room, including sound from the speakers playing the rest of the band, so that *GenJam* only pays attention to the close-miked trumpet. Mistakes in timing are irrelevant because when the phrase is played back, it will always sound in time. Mistakes in pitch, made either by the GI-10 or by the human, are not a problem because the target is an offset into the scale that the measure will be played against when it is performed. The measures are likely to be mutated anyway, so precision really doesn't matter. In fact, the author views mistakes made by the GI-10 as 'melodic development', not errors. In short, mapping to GJNF as a target makes the system highly fault-tolerant (Biles 1998).

7.7.2. Collective Improvization

In 2002, the author added an interactive collective improvization feature, where *GenJam* and the human improvize simultaneously. In effect, this is implemented as an intelligent delay line, where *GenJam* listens to the human and maps what it hears to measure chromosomes, as it does when trading fours. However, it plays back the chromosome material from 'a while ago' as it is filling up the current chromosome with what it is hearing.

For instance, if the delay is set to one full measure, then *GenJam* toggles between two measure chromosomes, playing back what it heard the human play in the previous measure while it is listening to the current measure. It does not mutate the measures in this mode because the human's task is to play harmony or counterpoint against what he played 'a while ago', which is hard enough to do when *GenJam* simply tries to echo what the human played. The delay can be set to four measures, one measure, or a part of a measure (some number of events less than the length of a measure). The author seldom uses a delay of four measures because he usually can't remember that long ago, but uses delays of a full measure or a half measure frequently. Half measure delays are interesting in odd time signatures like 5/4 (delay of five events) or 7/4 (delay of seven events).

This intelligent delay is something of a tribute to the late Don Ellis, who pioneered using live electronics for jazz trumpet, including loop delays, beginning in about 1967 (Ellis 1967). Most of Ellis's loop-delay solos were in static harmonic settings or were unaccompanied cadenzas, because a simple loop delay echoes whatever audio the mic picks up after a fixed delay. In Ellis's case, this precluded any but the simplest harmonic and rhythmic forms. Since Ellis's time, of course, the repeating loop concept has become a compositional paradigm that underlies entire musical genres and provides the fundamental paradigm for music software like *GarageBand* (Apple 2006). *GenJam*'s collective improvization feature attempts to apply loops in an improvizationally agile manner to return to and extend Ellis's conception. Whether this has much to do with evolutionary computation is an interesting question, but that discussion will follow.

7.7.3. Interbreeding GenJam's Ideas with a Live Human's

The final mode of real-time interactivity that *GenJam* supports is a feature where *GenJam* listens to human measures both during the human's solo and during the head chorus that typically begins a tune and states its original melody. As the human plays, *GenJam* listens to each measure and maps it to a measure chromosome as described in Section 7.7.1. After a measure is complete, *GenJam* searches the measure population for that measure whose first and last new-note events are closest to the first and last new-note events of the human's measure. The measure it selects is then bred with the human's measure, using an intelligent crossover operator that selects a crossover point that generates the smallest horizontal interval at the crossover point, as described in Section 7.6.2.1. Of the two resulting children, the one whose first and last new-note events are closest to the first and last new-note events of the parent that came from the measure population then replaces that parent in the measure population. The result is a subtle evolution of the soloist toward the tune's original melody and the human's solo.

The selection method for this feature has to cope with two issues. First, a given human measure may not make a good parent. This is particularly true on the heads of tunes, where the human might be playing a simple background harmony part or might be resting. To handle this, the selection algorithm only selects measures in which the human played a minimum number of new-note events and in which there are no silences longer than a certain threshold; otherwise the human's measure will be ignored. In other words, a parent measure needs to be busy enough to insure interest. While a measure with a long silence and/or only one or two notes can be effective in a solo, that artful use of space is not easy to pull off. *GenJam*, then, does what most intermediate-level improvizers do and prefers to play too many notes rather than risk not playing enough.

The second selection issue stems from the fact that the heads of most tunes will include repeated phrases, whose measures could be over sampled. For example, a typical 32-bar AABA tune repeats the eight measures in the A section three times during the head, with possible minor variations in the tune itself and/or the human's rendering of it. When interbreeding these measures with the soloist's measures, then, the repeated measures will likely spawn three children in the soloist's measure population, which has the potential of tiling *GenJam*'s improvization too far in the direction of the tune's head. To correct for this, the selection method for interbreeding the head marks measures as they are interbred. If a human measure would have selected a marked measure as its mate, it will be ignored, under the assumption that a similar measure from the head has already bred with this measure's parent.

7.8. Making *GenJam* Autonomous

By 2000, the author's successful experiences trading fours with *GenJam* sparked a sequence of enhancements that improved *GenJam*'s full-chorus solos, eliminated the fitness bottleneck for training soloists, and ultimately changed the author's view of applying technology in application domains. Along the way, *GenJam* stretched the evolutionary paradigm to what many would consider the breaking point. This section will trace the thinking that led to an autonomous version of *GenJam* and discuss whether that version is still an EC system. The next section will expand on the implications of applying EC in the improvization domain and comment on the mutual interaction between technology and application domains.

When *GenJam* trades fours with a human, it applies its mutation operators in real time without determining fitness, as described in Section 7.7.1. Initially, the author saw this as an unfortunate necessity, both because of failures to come up with an automatic fitness function (Biles et al. 1996) and because when trading fours, *GenJam* has only several milliseconds to mutate the one phrase and four measure chromosomes that resulted from listening to the human's four before it has to perform that phrase as its immediate response. It turned out that *GenJam*'s musically meaningful mutations, which had been developed to facilitate rapid and productive training of a new soloist, were perfect for developing the human's fours in real time because they tended to do nice things to nice phrases. In other words, given a good phrase to start with, the mutations guaranteed a good phrase in response. In actual performance the human's phrases tended to sound good (at least the author thought so!), so *GenJam*'s mutated responses sounded good.

At the same time, the author noticed that the full-chorus solos generated by a well-trained soloist, while competent, were not as compelling as chase choruses where *GenJam* and a human traded fours. Part of that is certainly due to the interactivity and spontaneity inherent in trading fours, but it occurred to the author that the fours he played were better than the phrases *GenJam* evolved interactively under the guidance of a mentor. This, he reasoned, was likely due to the fact that *GenJam*'s initial generation of phrases was random, and that for good phrases to develop, they first had to be generated, heard and rewarded by the mentor. The mutation operators certainly helped, as did the ongoing development of ever more intelligent initializations of the initial generation, from uniform random, to

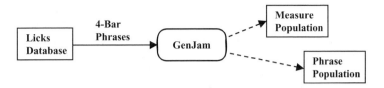

FIGURE 7.16. Autonomous GenJam creating populations from a database of licks.

fractal-based, to Markov-based, as described in Section 7.6.3. Even with the Markov initialization, however, *GenJam*'s generation zero phrases are not as compelling as the author's fours.

But what if *GenJam* started a training session in generation zero with phrases that were as good as human phrases to begin with? In that case the mutations that guaranteed good responses when trading fours might guarantee good soloists with a minimum of training.

At about this time, the author came across a book called *1001 Jazz Licks* (Schneidman, 2000). Upon obtaining a copy, he was delighted to find that it contained 1001 four-bar phrases, categorized in a variety of styles (e.g. bop, post bop, swing, waltz). The author then hand coded about half of the phrases into GJNF to create ten databases of licks in different jazz styles. These lick databases then became the seed material for the measure and phrase populations.

Fig. 7.16 shows schematically how autonomous *GenJam* (Biles 2001b) uses a given licks database to generate the measure and phrase populations for a soloist to be used on a tune. The algorithm to generate the populations is summarized in Fig. 7.17.

Each database must have at least 16 licks to avoid duplicating a lick. The actual databases that the author uses vary in size from 24 to 68 four-bar licks, so even if the same database is used on two different tunes, the specific licks selected should be at least a little different, and two thirds of the phrases will be intelligent crossovers of different pairs of phrases. Finally, many, if not most, of the measures in the measure population will have been crossed over with human measures before *GenJam* takes a full-chorus solo, as described in Section 7.7.3. The result is that on any given tune, the soloist will be unique for that rendition of that song, and *GenJam* will almost never repeat itself verbatim, unlike most humans.

Notice that the mentor from Fig. 7.4 has disappeared in Fig. 7.16. This is because there is no fitness recorded or manipulated in the measure and phrase individuals. Notice also that the measure and phrase populations are not read or written as files,

Select 16 four-measure licks at random from the licks database
Build the measure population from the 64 measures in those licks
Build the first 16 phrase individuals to represents the original 16 licks
Build 32 more phrase individuals by applying intelligent crossover to pairs of the first 16

FIGURE 7.17. Algorithm for generating measure and phrase populations from a licks database.

as they were in Fig. 7.4 because they will not be evolved over the course of several generations. In other words, we've eliminated the fitness bottleneck by eliminating fitness itself.

This is a problem if one wants to continue regarding *GenJam* as an example of EC because fitness is supposed to be a necessary component for EC (Goldberg 1989; Bentley 1999). The argument against the autonomous version of *GenJam* being considered EC runs as follows: Eliminating the mentor clearly means that *GenJam* is no longer an *interactive* genetic algorithm. Since there is no generational search driven by fitness and, in fact, no fitness at all, what remains is simply a sophisticated melodic transducer implemented with the mutation and crossover operators. Therefore, the autonomous version of *GenJam* is not EC.

On the other hand, the autonomous version of *GenJam* uses an abstract genotype (GJNF) and a genotype-to-phenotype mapping (when phrases are performed in real time). It applies crossover and mutation operators, albeit non-traditional ones, to the genotypes. While there is no generational search, there is selection in choosing which measures to crossover with the human measures. That selection is biased toward measures that will integrate well in phrases that use them, which represents an implicit form of fitness. The intelligent crossover is really a form of gene splicing, which while not intentionally done in nature is certainly done in the laboratory. Clearly the autonomous version of *GenJam* is at least EC-inspired.

Another perspective is to consider EC as a generate-and-test strategy. In standard EC the generators (initialization, crossover, mutation) are pretty unintelligent, and the test (fitness) is usually intelligent. The principle is that the intelligent fitness function guides the otherwise random search implemented by the dumb crossover and mutation operators. Schema theory (Goldberg 1989) is built on the assumption that initialization, crossover and mutation are random, and that selection is driven by fitness. The result is that meritorious building blocks are sampled exponentially more often over succeeding generations, which gives EC it's well known leverage in converging on optimal solutions, even in messy solution spaces.

But what if the genetic operators are intelligent? In *GenJam*'s case the mutation operators essentially guarantee that a good human four will always mutate to a good response. Similarly, the crossover operators pick crossover points that almost always guarantee a musically meritorious result. The measure selection/replacement operator intelligently selects individuals to breed such that the children will alter but not disrupt the phrases in which they participate. This selection method uses an implicit fitness in choosing which individuals to crossover with a human measure. Finally, the initialization procedure in Fig. 7.17 seeds the initial population with proven licks from a licks database and safe blends of those licks.

From the generate-and-test perspective, then, autonomous *GenJam*'s generators are so intelligent that they always generate good individuals, so there is no need to test. To quote Garrison Keilor, of *A Prairie Home Companion* fame, 'all the children are above average'. So is the autonomous version of *GenJam* an EC-based system? The author's ultimate answer to that question is, 'I don't care, as long as it plays well'. This rather combative opinion leads us finally to the mutual influence of EC and application domains on one another.

7.9. Technology Versus Domains

Over the last 12 years *GenJam* has evolved from a proof-of-concept experiment to a viable improvization agent that performs regularly in public. That evolution has paralleled the author's thinking about how EC as a technology impacts the musical domain in general and improvization in particular, and more fundamentally, how technology and application domains influence each other.

In Chapter 2, this author tried to drive home the point that many, if not most, applications of EC to music have essentially been solutions in search of problems. In fact, *GenJam* started out very much that way; the author's original goal was to see if a genetic algorithm could generate jazz solos as something of an intellectual exercise. The author assumed that he'd get some papers out of the project and go to some fun conferences, but he didn't expect that the music it produced would actually sound good enough to inflict on an actual audience, other than as a demo of what it produced, much as Lee Spector and Adam Alpern (1994) were coincidentally generating at about that time.

After getting the first version of *GenJam* working in the fall of 1993, the author found that *GenJam*'s solos were not as bad as he thought they would be and ventured to perform a 'low stakes gig' in a lunchtime concert series in the RIT student union in April, 1994. The audience reception was very favourable, and he was asked to return, which led the author to think of *GenJam* not just as a genetic algorithm, but also as a viable musician. In other words, the goal began shifting from finding out whether a genetic algorithm could improvize toward building a viable improviser that happened to use a genetic algorithm. This may seem to be a subtle shift, but it represents a fundamental change in philosophy.

Originally, the author adhered fairly strictly to the standard orthodoxy of genetic algorithms. For example, initialization and crossover were implemented as uniform-random processes. The selection/replacement regimen was a standard tournament technique. Mutation was the only 'cheat' that the author succumbed to, in an effort to make the mentor's task tractable, as described in Section 7.6.1. The author consoled himself in this violation of EC principles by restricting the intelligence to the mutation operators. At least the rest of *GenJam* was still 'pure'.

After adding the interactive feature of trading fours, which leveraged the intelligent mutation operators to develop a human's four in real time without fitness, the author justified this further erosion of EC purity by reasoning that a generational search was impossible in this situation, so fitness was irrelevant. Maybe it wasn't exactly EC, but it sure was fun to play with!

In retrospect, this was something of a tipping point in that the focus clearly had shifted away from EC and toward playing jazz. From this new perspective, then, it was easy to justify embedding intelligence in the initialization and crossover operators and to eliminate fitness entirely to develop the autonomous version of *GenJam*; the result was clearly a better soloist.

When the author then began reviewing the EC-in-music literature in preparation for a tutorial at GECCO on Evolutionary Music (Biles 2004), which formed the starting point for his other chapter in this volume, he noticed that most of the EC-based music systems he encountered definitely came from the EC perspective, not the musical perspective. In other words they were solutions in search of problems that sought to demonstrate that EC in its canonical form could generate music.

This brings to mind the neat versus scruffy 'holy wars' from artificial intelligence. The neats are concerned with theoretical models that attempt to explain human behaviour and seek to be intelligent in the same way that humans are intelligent. The scruffies, on the other hand, are relatively unconcerned with human intelligence, other than its role as an existence proof, and are more concerned with the tangible performance of their systems. Clearly, *GenJam* falls on the scruffy end of this dimension.

In the EC-based improvization arena, one project stands out in contrast to *GenJam* in this regard. George Papadopoulos and Geraint Wiggins (1999) took a decidedly neat perspective in their improvization system. In describing their implementation, they write about

the idea of using an *objective* fitness function, as opposed to the interactive approaches often used elsewhere in the GA music field. The reason for this is that we have a particular interest in understanding the searching behaviour of our GA: we are interested in *simulating human behaviour* and not just in the quality of our results. In order to understand the search patterns produced by our system, it is important to have a fitness function which is consistent, and whose criteria we fully understand. This could not be the case with an interactive GA, because of the subjectivity of the human listener – it would be impossible to determine which choices were made because of emergent behaviour of the system and which were made because of the inconsistencies of the human judge.

This is clearly a 'neat' perspective; they 'are interested in *simulating human behaviour* and not just the quality of [their] results'. They view 'the subjectivity of the human listener' in an IGA as a problem because they can't explain it with their theoretical model. The problem with this perspective is that it elevates theory above experience. If the goal is to test the efficacy of a theoretical model, this is fine. However, if the goal is to create good music, then the theory is useful only to the extent that it facilitates that goal. The author's opinion is that theory should try to explain *why* something sounds good; it should not be used to decide *whether* something sounds good. This is especially true in the improvization domain, where the spontaneity of human improvizers is very difficult to pin down (Berliner 1994).

To generalize further, this tension between the constraints of a given technology and the demands of an application domain is a fundamental issue in applying technology to specific domains. Technologists typically understand the technologies they have studied and/or developed, but they often understand considerably less about problem domains. The author recalls an experience in the mid 1980's where he was brought in as a consultant to build an expert system for a bank. The initial meeting was a series of presentations by department heads who had problems they thought might be suitable for an expert system. The bank's goal, clearly, was to build an expert system, any expert system, rather than to solve a specific problem – a classic solution in search of a problem. While it was remarkable that a bank was motivated to test out a new technology (banks are stereotypically conservative in this regard), it was an odd experience to have a succession of presentations by customers trying to sell the technologist instead of the other way around.

Many applications of technology start this way; a system is built because someone knows how to build it, not because it solves a particular problem. This is not a bad thing, particularly when a technology is new. The literature on early applications of EC is full of notable successes in solving tough problems that defied other approaches (Goldberg 1989). This is important in establishing whether a technology is useful and in what situations it is useful. Sooner or later, however, the focus shifts from research into whether a technology works at all toward research into how to make it more effective. At that point the theoretical work begins to become esoteric, for lack of a less pejorative term, and the emphasis shifts to the needs of the problem domain. This is a difficult shift for technologists because they can no longer rely primarily on their theoretical knowledge of the technology itself. The specific problem being solved takes precedence, and a theoretical solution isn't enough – the solution has to actually work.

When that happens, the demands of the problem domain begin to affect the technology. Technologists are (or should be) used to thinking about how their technology changes problem domains and the ways people perform tasks in those domains. However, the impact of problem domains on technology is not as familiar to many technologists. This is the central goal of the emerging academic discipline of information technology (IT) – to turn out users' advocates who bend technology to fit the needs of people. The emergence of that philosophy is certainly represented in *GenJam*'s evolution. The *GenJam* project began in 1993, one year after the first undergraduate IT program began accepting students, not coincidentally at the author's institution. As IT has become established as an accredited academic discipline (SIGITE 2006), *GenJam* has become very much a system that plays music rather than a system that demonstrates EC. In other words, improvization as a domain has changed the nature of EC as it is deployed in *GenJam*. Most information technologists would agree that 'It's about the users, not about the technology'. The author would apply that to *GenJam* by saying, 'It's about the music, not the EC'.

7.10. *GenJam* as a Musician

So if it's about the music, how good is *GenJam* as a musician? The author hasn't performed a formal study on *GenJam*'s acceptance by an audience, but he has performed a few hundred gigs with *GenJam* and has at least some anecdotal evidence from listeners that *GenJam* is a convincing improvizer. The rest of this section, then, will present anecdotes from playing in public with *GenJam*. To understand these anecdotes, the author finds it useful to cast the experience of an audience member as a 'user interaction' with the performance. This perspective

FIGURE 7.18. Norman model for user interaction (after Norman 88).

basically follows the user interaction model of Donald Norman (1988), shown in Fig. 7.18.

In Norman's model a system designer has a mental model of the system he or she develops. That mental model informs the creation of the System Image, which is the manifestation of the system that is accessed and manipulated by the user. The user forms a mental model of the system by interacting with the system image in the context of whatever task the user is trying to perform using the system.

Fig. 7.19 shows Norman's model applied to a jazz performance, where the designers are the tune's composer and the performing improvizer; the users are the audience; and the system image is the performance itself, including all aspects that are perceivable by the audience. Viewing a performance this way draws attention to the audience's mental model of the performance, which is informed both by the performance itself and by any expectations listeners in the audience might have. For example, a jazz aficionado will have a different set of expectations and will form a different mental model of a jazz performance from that formed by a country music fan who only listens to the lyrics. The listener's mental model of the performance, then, is the basis for his or her impression of the performance. Whether the listener enjoyed the performance or 'got' the performance depends on his or her mental model of the performance.

The anecdotes described below suggest listener mental models that led to interesting interpretations and impressions of *GenJam*. In some cases, the listener under-appreciated what *GenJam* was doing and didn't 'get it', but in other cases, the listener overestimated *GenJam*'s proficiency and gave it too much credit.

7.10.1. Where's the CD?

A common question the author gets when playing at receptions is, 'Where's the CD?' He usually replies with an overly elaborate description of how *GenJam* is listening to the trumpet and mutating what it hears using something called evolutionary computation, and that everything is being generated by the computer and played through the tone generator, and... At about this time, the author is typically interrupted with, 'That's nice, but where's the CD?'

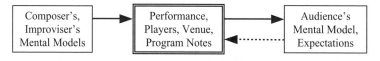

FIGURE 7.19. Donald Norman's model applied to a jazz performance.

This scenario indicates that the listener's musical mental model doesn't accommodate a computer improvizing jazz in real time. The fact that the listener can only explain what he or she hears by looking for a canned CD indicates that *GenJam*'s performance passed the it-must-have-been-recorded test. The listener assumes that the trumpet player is simply doing music minus one. While that conception vastly underestimates what *GenJam* is doing, which used to bother the author, it demonstrates that whatever *GenJam* is doing, it is meeting the listener's expectations of what straight-up jazz is supposed to sound like, which is really the goal after all.

A variation on this theme sometimes comes from listeners who apparently have at least a nodding acquaintance with MIDI. 'So where do you get your sequences with the solos in them?' Again, this implies that *GenJam*'s solos were good enough to be considered 'programmed' by someone. On a few occasions the author has been asked, 'How did you know it was going to play that?' or 'How do you remember what to play on the fours?' This implies that the listener was hip enough to detect that *GenJam* sounded like it was responding to what the author was playing, but the listener assumed that was an illusion. In a situation several years ago, one listener refused to believe that *GenJam* was actually playing off of what the human played until he scat sung into the microphone for a couple of fours. Luckily, *GenJam* 'chose' to mutate his phrases transparently enough to convince him that it really did respond to what he sang.

7.10.2. It Made an Interesting Choice There

Occasionally the author gets the chance to demonstrate *GenJam* for a very knowledgeable musician whose mental model of *GenJam* is fairly accurate, due to the opportunity for the author to play several tunes and explain in some detail what *GenJam* is doing. Often in these situations the listener gives *GenJam* too much credit. For example, one listener, who was a high school music teacher and jazz trumpet player, made very generous attributions of intentionality, for example, 'It made a really interesting choice there'. In probing on the word 'choice', the author found that the listener had interpreted a serendipitously generated phrase as an intentional decision that reflected an improvizational method with which he was familiar.

In another situation, a jazz playing computer science graduate student was impressed at the sophistication of *GenJam*'s knowledge base in putting together its solos because he clearly heard very specific examples of melodic passing tones chosen for specific chord changes, and other improvizational techniques. When told that *GenJam* (and the author, for that matter) knew nothing about the specific techniques he referenced, he was a bit irritated that a simpler system fooled him.

7.10.3. I Thought You Were Playing the Flute

GenJam has, at least twice, passed a 'Turing test' of sorts. The author has occasionally played recordings of tunes for listeners and asked them to identify which instrument was being played by a human. On at least two occasions, a listener thought that the human was the flute player instead of the trumpet player. When asked why they thought so, they indicated that they had keyed in on aspects of the flute's attack, which, with the physical modelling synthesis card the author usually uses for *GenJam*'s voice, generates fairly realistic imperfections when playing fast and loud. One interpretation of this is that *GenJam*'s improvizations were close enough to the human's in overall quality that the listener had to use the instrumental timbre to break the tie. If the listener is musically knowledgeable, this is quite a complement to *GenJam*. If the listener is not, it is less flattering, but still noteworthy. The author tries not to think too much about his performance being perceived as more machine-like than a machine and consoles himself that it doesn't happen often.

7.10.4. Audience-Mediated Performance

The author has played several concerts and demonstrations where the audience acted as a collective mentor to train a new soloist as part of the performance. The author coined the term *audience-mediated performance* to refer to these situations, where the audience exerts some level of control over the content of the performance (Biles 95). As *GenJam* plays three or four training tunes consisting only of solo choruses, audience members signal their opinions using feedback paddles with one red side (for bad) and one green side (for good). The author acts as a collector of this feedback by typing 'g's or 'b's based on his perception of the amount of red or green he sees in the audience. After three or four training tunes, the author then plays a tune with the audience's soloist. Typically during the author's first solo following the training tunes, he sees the feedback paddles again, accompanied by smiles from the audience, indicating that they got the idea of what *GenJam* actually does and were having fun being involved with the technology. Thankfully, the author usually sees more green than red in these situations.

7.11. Conclusions

So what, if anything does *GenJam* mean? At a musical level, the author finds himself preferring to play with *GenJam* over playing with people. While this may have more to say about the people with whom the author plays, he still finds *GenJam* an engaging and stimulating sideman who shows up on time and sober, knows all the obscure tunes the author wants to play, doesn't rush the tempo or mess up the heads, plays competent solos, is a formidable opponent when trading fours, and works for free. What more could you want?

At a technical level, *GenJam* has clearly demonstrated that EC can be applied successfully to the improvization domain and that it is, at least in the author's view, human competitive. Unfortunately, *GenJam* doesn't really fit the criteria for the annual human-competitive awards in genetic and evolutionary computation

(Koza 2004), which focus on science and engineering applications, but the author believes that *GenJam* at least holds its own with competent amateur improvizers.

GenJam's development over the last 12 years has demonstrated not only how technology can influence the way humans perform tasks, but also how human tasks can (and should) fundamentally influence technology. In the case of *GenJam*'s influence on the author's jazz skills, there is no question that the author is now a much stronger musician in general and improvizer in particular than before he began taking *GenJam* seriously as a musical collaborator. This certainly is due in part to the fact the author simply practices a lot more with *GenJam* than he did (or could) without it, but developing and playing with *GenJam* also has forced the author to listen better and be more disciplined as an improvizer.

As for *GenJam*'s influence on EC and the broader issue of how domains influence technology, the *GenJam* project has given the author a valuable perspective that has deeply influenced his view of the emerging academic discipline of information technology as the user-focused computing profession. The user's perspective is often undervalued or ignored when technologists deploy applications, partly because the user's perspective is difficult to grasp, but also because it is messy and makes the application less elegant to build. If *GenJam* has a broader lesson to teach, it might be that the pragmatic needs of the user (in this case, a jazz trumpet player who wants to perform as a single) ultimately take precedence over the theoretical demands of a technology.

References

Apple Computer (2006) GarageBand software, http://www.apple.com/ilife/garageband/.

Bentley P (1999) An Introduction to Evolutionary Design by Computers, in Bentley, PJ (ed) *Evolutionary Design by Computers*. Morgan Kaufmann, San Francisco.

Berliner PF (1994) *Thinking in Jazz: The Infinite Art of Improvization*. University of Chicago Press, Chicago London.

Biles JA (1994) *GenJam*: A Genetic Algorithm for Generating Jazz Solos, in *Proceedings of the 1994 International Computer Music Conference*. ICMA, San Francisco.

Biles JA, Eign W (1995) *GenJam Populi*: Training an IGA *via* Audience-Mediated Performance, in *Proceedings of the 1995 International Computer Music Conference*. ICMA, San Francisco.

Biles JA, Anderson PG, Loggi LW (1996) Neural Network Fitness Functions for a Musical IGA, in *Proceedings of the International ICSC Symposium on Intelligent Industrial Automation (IIA'96) and Soft Computing (SOCO'96)*, March 26–28, Reading, UK, ICSC Academic Press, pp. B39–B44.

Biles JA (1998) Interactive *GenJam*: Integrating Real-time Performance with a Genetic Algorithm, in *Proceedings of the 1998 International Computer Music Conference*, ICMA, San Francisco.

Biles JA (1999) Life with *GenJam*: Interacting with a Musical IGA, in *Proceedings of the 1999 IEEE International Conference on Systems, Man, and Cybernetics*, Tokyo.

Biles JA (2001a) *GenJam*: Evolution of a Jazz Improvizer, in Bentley PJ, Corne DW (eds) *Creative Evolutionary Systems*. Morgan Kaufmann, San Francisco.

Biles JA (2001b) Autonomous *GenJam*: Eliminating the Fitness Bottleneck by Eliminating Fitness, in *Proceedings of the 2001 Genetic and Evolutionary Computation Conference Workshop Program*. GECCO, San Francisco.

Biles JA (2004) Evolutionary Music, *GECCO-2004 Tutorial Program*, Genetic and Evolutionary Computation Conference, Seattle, WA.

Coker J (1964) *Improvizing Jazz*. Prentice-Hall, Englewood Cliffs, NJ.

Dannenberg RB (1993) *The CMU MIDI Toolkit, Version 3*. Carnegie Mellon University, Pittsburgh, PA, 1993, http://www.cs.cmu.edu/~music/music.software.html.

Ellis, D (1967) *Electric Bath*, CK 65522, Columbia Records, NY.

Gannon, P (1991) *Band in a Box*. PG Music Inc., Victoria, BC, 1991–2006, http://pgmusic.com/.

Gardner M (1978) White and brown music, fractal curves and one-over-f fluctuations. *Scientific American*, 238(4):16–27.

Haerle D (1989) *The Jazz Sound*. Hal Leonard, Milwaukee, WI.

Haerle D (1980) *The Jazz Language*. Studio 224, Miami.

Koza J (2004) 2004 Human-Competitive Awards in Genetic and Evolutionary Computation (Web site) http://www.genetic-programming.org/gecco2004hc.html.

Levine M (1995) *The Jazz Theory Book*. Sher Music Company, Petaluma, CA.

Norman DA (1988) *The Design of Everyday Things*. Doubleday, NY.

Papadopoulos G, Wiggins G (1998) A Genetic Algorithm for the Generation of Jazz Melodies, in *Proceedings of STeP 98*, Jyväskylä, Finland, http://www.soi.city.ac.uk/~geraint/papers/STeP98.pdf.

Reti R (1951) *The Thematic Process in Music*. Macmillan, NY.

Russell G (1959) *The Lydian Chromatic Concept of Tonal Organization for Improvization*. Concept Publishing, NY.

Sabatella M (1992) *A Jazz Improvization Primer*. Outside Shore Music, 1992–98, http://www.outsideshore.com/primer/primer/.

Shneidman J (2000) *1001 Jazz Licks*. Cherry Lane Music Company, NY.

Slonimsky N (1998) *Webster's New World Dictionary of Music*, Wiley Publishing, Hoboken, NJ.

Spector L, Alpern A (1994) Criticism, Culture, and the Automatic Generation of Artworks, in *Proceedings of the Twelfth National Conference on Artificial Intelligence*, AAAI-94, AAAI Press/The MIT Press, Menlo Park, CA and Cambridge, MA, http://hampshire.edu/%7ElasCCS/genbebop.html.

8
Cellular Automata Music: From Sound Synthesis to Musical Forms

EDUARDO R. MIRANDA

8.1. Introduction

Cellular automata (CA) are tools for computational modelling widely used to model systems that change some feature with time. They are suitable for modelling dynamic systems in which space and time are discrete, and quantities take on a finite set of discrete values. CA are highly suitable for modelling music: music is fundamentally time-based and it can be thought of as a system in which a finite set of discrete values (e.g. musical notes, rhythms, etc.) evolve in space and time.

CA were originally introduced in the 1960s by John von Neumann and Stanislaw Ulam as a model of a self-reproduction machine (Cood 1968). They wanted to know if it would be possible for an abstract machine to reproduce; that is, to automatically construct a copy of itself. Their model consisted of a two-dimensional grid of cells, each cell of which could assume a number of states, representing the components from which they built the self-reproducing machine. Completely controlled by a set of rules, the machine was able to create several copies of itself by reproducing identical patterns of cells at another location on the grid. Since then, CA have been repeatedly reintroduced and applied to a considerable variety of purposes, from biomedical image processing (Preston and Duff 1984) and ecology (Hogeweg 1988) to biology (Ermentrout and Edelstein-Keshet 1993) and sociology (Epstein and Axtell 1996). Many interesting CA algorithms have been developed during the past 40 years.

Since CA produce large amounts of patterned data and if we assume that music composition can be thought of as being based on pattern propagation and the formal manipulation of its parameters, it comes as no surprise that composers started to suspect that cellular automata could be related to some sort of music representation in order to generate compositional material.

One of the first composers to use CA was Iannis Xenakis, who used them in the mid of the 1980s 'to create complex temporal evolution of orchestral clusters' for his piece *Horos* (Hoffman 2002; p. 122). A number of pioneering experiments on using CA for generating music followed by composers such as Beyls (1989), Millen (1990) and this author (Miranda 1990).

8.2. The Basics of Cellular Automata

CA are dynamic systems in which space and time are discrete. They may have many dimensions, but the most common CA are either one-dimensional or two-dimensional. A cellular automaton consists of an array or matrix of elements, referred to as cells, to which transition rules are applied. The behaviour of a cellular automaton is given by these transition rules, which are applied simultaneously to all cells of the array or matrix. The rules normally take into account the states of the neighbourhood of each cell. All cells are updated simultaneously, so that the state of the automaton as a whole advances in discrete time-steps. The state of each cell is normally associated with a colour, which facilitates the visualization of the behaviour of the automaton, according to the tick of an imaginary clock, like an animated film. The patterns formed by the cells are the result of the automaton's emergent behaviour in the sense that no global trend is explicitly coded beforehand. CA are powerful modelling tools because a cell can represent anything from a simple numerical variable to sophisticated processing units.

This chapter will focus on two-dimensional CA, where each cell may assume values from a finite set of integers. The class of CA studied here is often referred to as the p-state cellular automata because their cells can value a number p of possible integer values $0, 1, 2, \ldots, p - 1$.

By way of an introductory example, Fig. 8.1 illustrates a very simple cellular automaton: it consists of a one-dimensional array of 12 cells where each cell can value either zero or one, represented by the colours white or black, respectively.

From an initial random setting, at each tick of an imaginary clock, the values of all 12 cells change simultaneously from one array to another, according to the transition rules that determine a new value for each cell. These rules normally take into account the values of a cell's nearest neighbours, but they could also consider other distant cells. The cellular automaton shown in Fig. 8.1 is referred to as a binary, nearest-neighbour, one-dimensional automaton, which is the simplest type of CA.

There have been a number of attempts at providing systematic ways to control CA and classify them according to the way in which they behave. Wolfram (1994) is well known for his studies of the properties of one-dimensional CA. There are 256 such automata, each of which is associated with a unique set of transition rules. An illustration of the rules for one of such automaton is shown in Fig. 8.2, together with the pattern produced after 15 steps starting from a single black cell.

Langton (1990) proposed a kind of 'virtual potentiometer', referred to as the λ parameter, to navigate through four types of CA: fixed, cyclic, complex and

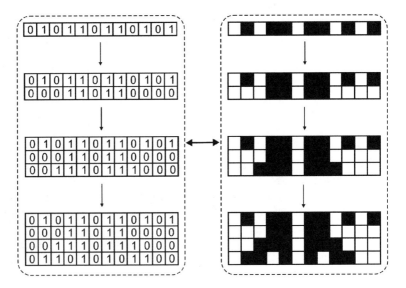

FIGURE 8.1. A simple one-dimensional cellular automaton. One of the transition rules operating in this example reads as follows: if a cell is equal to zero and if both neighbours are equal to one, then this cell continues to equal zero in the next stage.

chaotic (Fig. 8.3). Parameters such as this are very important because they facilitate systematic explorations of the relationship between CA behaviour and the music they produce; an example will be given in the context of the LASy system below.

A number of CA use multi-dimensional arrays of cells that can assume values other than zero and one, which are represented by various different colours. In the case of a two-dimensional array, the evolution rules normally take into account

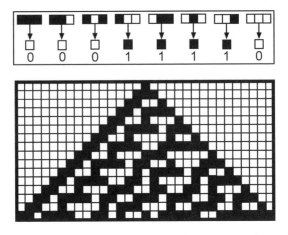

FIGURE 8.2. An example of a one-dimensional cellular automaton. (After Wolfram (1994).)

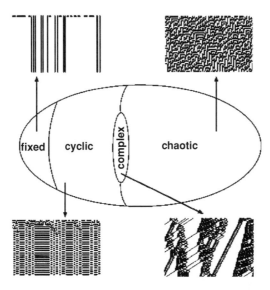

FIGURE 8.3. Langton's λ parameter to navigate through four classes of CA (after Burraston 2005).

the four or eight nearest neighbours, but other neighbourhood schemes may also be devised. Two-dimensional CA normally function in a toroidal space: the right edge of the two-dimensional grid of cells wraps around to join the left edge and the top edge wraps around to join the bottom edge (Fig. 8.4).

The following paragraphs introduce three examples of CA that have been used to synthesize sounds and generate music: Game of Life, Griffeath's Crystalline Growths and ChaOs.

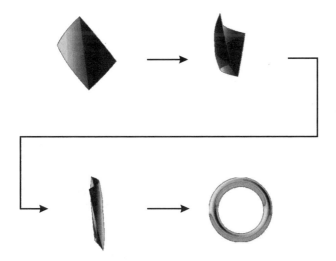

FIGURE 8.4. Two-dimensional CA normally function in a toroidal space.

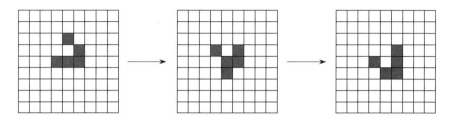

FIGURE 8.5. Game of life is a two-dimensional cellular automaton where each cell can be in one of two possible states: alive or dead.

8.2.1. Game of Life

Game of Life (GL) is a two-dimensional automaton invented by John Conway. 'Conway was fascinated by the way in which a combination of a few simple rules could produce patterns that would expand, change shape or die out unpredictably. He wanted to find the simplest possible set of rules that would give such an interesting behaviour' (Wilson 1988; p. 44).

The automaton consists of a finite $[m \times n]$ matrix of cells, each of which can be in one of two possible states: alive represented by the number one, or dead represented by the number zero; on the computer screen, living cells are coloured black and dead cells are coloured white (Fig. 8.5).

The state of a cell as time progresses is determined by the state of its eight nearest neighbouring cells, as follows:

- Birth: A cell that is dead at time t becomes alive at time $t + 1$ if exactly three of its neighbours are alive at time t
- Death by overcrowding: A cell that is alive at time t will die at time $t + 1$ if four or more of its neighbours are alive at time t
- Death by exposure: A cell that is alive at time t will die at time $t + 1$ if it has one or no live neighbours at time t
- Survival: A cell that is alive at time t will remain alive at time $t + 1$ only if it has either two or three live neighbours at time t

In other words, considering that E represents the number of living neighbours that surround a particular live cell and F defines the number of living neighbours that surround a particular dead cell, the life of a currently living cell is preserved whenever $2 \leq E \leq 3$ and a currently dead cell will be reborn whenever $3 \leq F \leq 3$. A general form for representing transition rules is (E_{min}, E_{max}, F_{min} and F_{max}) where $E_{min} \leq E \leq E_{max}$ and $F_{min} \leq F \leq F_{max}$. The original Game of Life rules are represented as (2, 3, 3, 3). Clearly, a number of alternative rules other than (2, 3, 3, 3) can be set.

The original GL is also characterized by a number of interesting initial cell configurations that have given raise to intriguing emergent behaviour. A few examples of well-known initial configurations are shown in Fig. 8.6.

Cheshire Cat   Cross

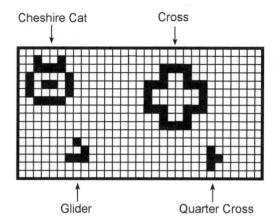

Glider   Quarter Cross

FIGURE 8.6. A few examples of initial GL configurations. Note that the 'glider' configuration was used in the example in Fig. 8.5.

8.2.2. Crystalline Growths

In 1989, Alexander Dewdney's presented in his regular computer recreations column in the *Scientific American* magazine an interesting two-dimensional automaton, invented by David Griffeath (Dewdney 1989). This automaton assumes more than two states. Each of the p possible states is represented by a different colour and they are numbered from 0 to $p-1$. The transition rule is very simple: a cell that happens to be in a certain state k at one tick of the clock dominates any adjacent cells that are in state $k-1$, meaning that these adjacent cells change from $k-1$ to k. This rule resembles a natural chain in which a cell in state two can dominate a cell in state one even if the latter is dominating a cell in state zero. In this case, the chain has no end because the automaton is cyclic: a cell in state zero dominates its neighbouring cells that are in state $p-1$. Initialized with a random distribution of coloured cells, this automaton invariably ends up with stable, patchwork-type patterns, reminiscent of crystalline growths (Fig. 8.7).

8.2.3. Chemical Oscillator (ChaOs)

ChaOs is inspired by an automaton introduced by Gerhardt et al. (1990) to model a chemical reaction known as Belousov–Zhabotinskii. ChaOs is this author's own adaptation of this automaton to generate patterns resembling oscillatory neuronal electrical activity. As the nature of neural communication is essentially electro-chemical, the functioning of communicating neurons generates patterns of oscillatory electrical activity.

Metaphorically, ChaOS can be thought of as a matrix of identical electronic circuits representing neurons. At a given moment, neurons can be in any one of the following states: (a) quiescent, (b) in one of n states of depolarization or (c) fired. A neuron interacts with its neighbours through the flow of electric current between them. There are minimum (V_{min}) and maximum (V_{max}) threshold values, which

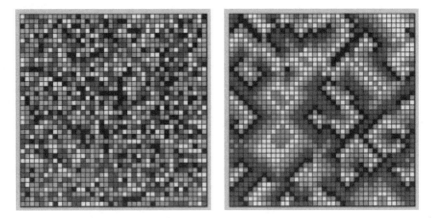

FIGURE 8.7. The behaviour of Griffeath's cellular automaton. Initialization with randomly generated values is shown on the left-hand side and an emergent pattern reminiscent of crystalline growths is shown on the right-hand side.

characterize the state of a neuron. If its internal voltage (V_i) is under V_{min}, then the neuron is quiescent (or polarized). If it is between V_{min} (inclusive) and V_{max} values, then the neuron is being depolarized. The neuron's potential divider is aimed at maintaining V_i below V_{min}. But when it fails (that is, if V_i reaches V_{min}) the neuron becomes depolarized. There is also an electric capacitor, which regulates the rate of depolarization. The tendency, however, is to become increasingly depolarized with time. When V_i reaches V_{max}, the neuron fires. A fired neuron at time t automatically becomes a quiescent neuron at time $t + 1$. The functioning of this automaton is determined by: the number p of possible neural states or colours ($p \geq 3$), the resistors $R1$ and $R2$ for the potential divider; the capacitance k of the electric capacitor.

In practice, the state of a neuron is represented by a number between 0 and $p - 1$, where p is the amount of different states. One of the attractive features of ChaOs is that is allows for a variable number of different neuron states $p + 2$. A cell in state $m[t] = 0$ corresponds to a quiescent state, whilst a cell in state $m[t] = p - 1$ corresponds to a collapsed state. All states in between represent a degree of depolarization, according to their respective values. The closer a neuron's state value gets to $p - 1$, the more depolarized it becomes. All neurons are updated by the application of the following rules to all of them simultaneously:

$$
m_{x,y}[t+1] =
\begin{cases}
\text{int}\left(\dfrac{A}{r_1}\right) + \text{int}\left(\dfrac{B}{r_2}\right) \leftarrow m_{x,y}[t] = 0 \\[2ex]
\text{int}\left(\dfrac{S}{A}\right) + k \leftarrow 0 < m_{x,y}[t] < p - 1 \\[2ex]
0 \leftarrow m_{x,y}[t] = p - 1
\end{cases}
$$

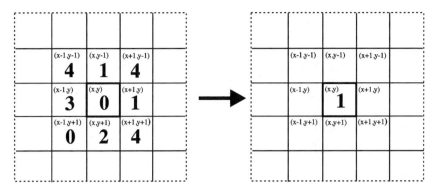

FIGURE 8.8. An example of the application of the transition rules to one neuron. Assume that $P = \{0, 1, 2, 3, 4\}$, $r_1 = 8.5$, $r_2 = 5.2$ and $k = 3$. Considering the eight neighbours of the neuron (x, y), then $A = 3$ (number of fired neurons) and $B = 4$ (number of depolarized neurons). Since the neuron (x, y) is quiescent, then the top rule applies and the value of this neuron at the next tick of the clock will be equal to 1.

where the state of a neuron at a time t is denoted $m_{x,y}[t]$; x and y are the horizontal and vertical coordinates of the a neuron; A and B represent respectively the number of fired and depolarized neurons amongst the eight neighbours, and S stands for the sum of the states of the neighbours. An example of the application of the transition rule to a certain neuron (x, y) is given in Fig. 8.8. In simpler terms, the above rules state that:

- If a neuron is quiescent ($m_{x,y}[x] = 0$), then the neuron may or may not become depolarized at the next tick of the clock ($t + 1$). This depends upon the number of polarized neurons in its neighbourhood, the number of collapsed neurons in its neighbourhood and its resistance to fire.
- If a neuron is depolarized ($0 < m_{x,y}[x] < p - 1$), then the tendency is to become more depolarized as the clock t evolves.
- A fired neuron ($m_{x,y}[t] = p - 1$) at time t becomes quiescent at time $t + 1$.

ChaOs tends to evolve from an initial wide distribution of states in the matrix towards oscillatory cycles of patterns (Fig. 8.9).

8.3. Cellular Automata Sound Synthesis

Before we examine how CA can be used to generate music, this section focuses on synthesizing sounds with CA. There have been a few successful attempts at building CA-based software sound synthesis. For example, the cellular automata workstation, designed by Richard Ortom and colleagues (1991), employed a binary one-dimensional cellular automaton to generate control data for a granular

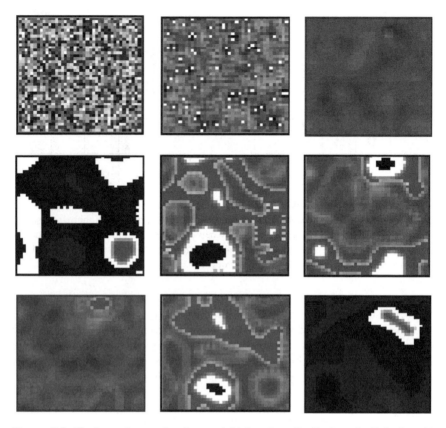

FIGURE 8.9. ChaOs tends to evolve from an initial random distribution of cells in the grid (as shown at the top corner of left-hand side) towards oscillatory cycles of patterns.

synthesizer. (The granular synthesis technique will be introduced below.) Also, we cite the work of Tim Kreger who have used a binary one-dimensional cellular automaton to control the filter coefficients of an analysis and re-synthesis algorithm to modify the spectra of sounds (Kreger 1999); an introduction to the analysis and resynthesis technique can be found in the book *Computer Sound Design: Synthesis Techniques and Programming* (Miranda 2002). Also interesting is the work of Mara Helmut and colleagues who implemented a CA-based real-time sound granulator (Vaidhyanathan et al. 1999). In this case, a sound sample is decomposed into grains, and then these grains are input to a bank of 32 band-pass filters. A binary one-dimensional cellular automaton of 32 cells is used to control their bandwidth and centre frequency values. The behaviour of the automaton therefore transforms the harmonic structure of the grains. In the following paragraphs we examine two examples of CA-based synthesizers in more detail: *LASy* and *Chaosynth*.

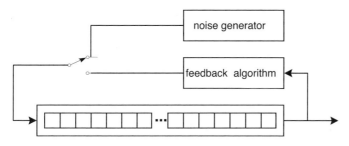

FIGURE 8.10. LASy uses CA to compute the samples of a time-varying look-up table.

8.3.1. LASy: Cellular Automata Lookup Table

LASy (Linear Automata Synthesis), designed by Jacques Chareyron (1990), uses CA to drive a Karplus–Strong type of synthesis algorithm. Karplus–Strong synthesis uses a time-varying lookup table to simulate the behaviour of a vibrating medium. The basic functioning of this method starts with a lookup table (that is, an array of samples) of a fixed length, filled with random values. In this case, the table functions as a queue of sample values, rather than as a fixed array, as it would have been the case of a simple oscillator. As samples are output from the right side of the array they are processed according to a given algorithm, and the result is fed back to the left side (Fig. 8.10). The algorithm for processing the samples defines the nature of the sound or effect. For example, the averaging of the current output sample with the one preceding it in the array functions as a type of low-pass filter. The original Karplus–Strong algorithm (Karplus and Strong 1983), averages the current output sample of a delay line with the preceding one, and feeds the result back to the end of the delay line. In *LASy* the new sample values of the delay line are computed by means of a binary one-dimensional cellular automaton, rather than by the averaging method.

Essentially, *LASy* works by considering the array of cells of the binary one-dimensional cellular automaton as a lookup table; each cell of the array corresponds to a sample. At each playback cycle of the lookup table, the transition rules are applied to the content of the table in order to change the waveform. The intention here is to let the samples of the lookup table be in perpetual mutation. The states of every cell are updated at the rate of the cellular automaton clock and these values are then heard by piping the array into the digital-to-analogue converter (DAC).

LASy is able to synthesize a large variety of sounds with diverse spectral evolutions, particularly sounds with fast transients at the very beginning of the sound. The program is particularly good for producing wind-like and plucked strings-like sounds. Yet, the ingredient that still makes *LASy* unique is its ability to synthesize unusual sounds but with some resemblance to the real acoustic world. Interesting sounds may be achieved using this technique, but the specification of suitable transition rules can be difficult. However, an intuitive framework for the specification of transition rules should naturally emerge after gaining sufficient familiarity with the system; for example, one may find that rules sets that activate more and more cells in time will tend to produce sounds whose spectral complexity increases with time.

According to Chareyron the output of *LASy* can be classified into three main groups, according to the type of transition rules employed:

- Sounds with simple evolution leading to a steady-state ending: transition rules that generate fixed and cyclic behaviour (refer to Fig. 8.3), tend to produce monotonous evolution of the sound spectrum, where the spectral envelope follows either an increasing or decreasing curve, leading to a steady-state ending.
- Sounds with simple evolution but with no ending: transition rules that generate complex behaviour (refer to Fig. 8.3) tend to produce endless successions of similar but not completely identical waveforms.
- Everlasting complex sounds: transition rules that generate chaotic behaviour tend to generate everlasting complex sounds with unpredictable spectra.

This classification is, of course, very general. Nevertheless, as *LASy's* author himself suggests, they are a good starting point for further experimentation. *LASy* was originally implemented in the early 1990s at the University of Milan as part of the Intelligent Music Workstation, which ran under NeXT and Apple MacOS platforms. To the best of this author's knowledge, there has been no further updates. Nevertheless, the technique is well-documented (Chareyron 1990) and a re-implementation of this system would certainly constitue an interesting project for further investigation into CA-based sound synthesis.

8.3.2. Chaosynth: Granular Synthesis with ChaOS

Granular synthesis works by generating a rapid succession of very short sound bursts (e.g. 35 ms long) called grains or granules that together form larger sound events (Fig. 8.11). Granular synthesis sounds tend to exhibit a great sense of movement and sound flow. This synthesis technique can be metaphorically compared with the functioning of a motion picture in which an impression of continuous movement is produced by displaying a sequence of slightly different images at a rate above the scanning capability of the eye (Miranda 1998).

This synthesis technique is inspired by Dennis Gabor's idea of representing a sound using thousands or millions of elementary sound particles (Gabor 1947). The composer Iannis Xenakis is commonly cited as one of the mentors of granular synthesis. In the 1950s, Xenakis developed important theoretical writings where he laid down the principles of the technique (Xenakis 1971). The first fully fledged granular synthesis systems did not appear, however, until Roads (1991), Truax (1998) and a few others began to investigate the potential of the technique systematically. Most of these systems had used stochasticity to generate the parameter values for the production of the individual grains; e.g. one could

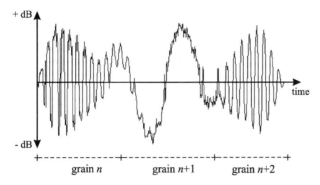

FIGURE 8.11. Granular synthesis works by generating a rapid succession of tiny sounds, referred to as grain or granules.

set up the synthesizer to produce grains of 30 ms duration with 50% probability, 40-ms grains with 20% and 50-ms grains with 30%. *Chaosynth*, however, uses a different method: it employs the ChaOS automaton introduced in Section 8.2.3.

Note that the term 'granular synthesis' has sometimes been associated with a musical signal processing technique whereby a recorded sound is chopped into tiny pieces, shuffled and re-assembled in various ways for playback; an example is the aforementioned granulator system developed by Helmut and colleagues. *Chaosynth* does not use pre-recorded sounds. Rather, it synthesizes all sounds from scratch.

8.3.2.1. Rendering Sounds from ChaOs

Each sound grain produced by *Chaosynth* is composed of several spectral components. Each component is a waveform produced by a digital oscillator which needs two parameters to function: frequency (Hz) and amplitude (dB). In *Chaosynth*, the oscillators can produce various types of waveforms such as sinusoid, square, saw tooth and band-limited noise. ChaOs controls the frequency and amplitude values of each grain. The mechanism works as follows: at each cycle, the automaton produces one sound grain (Fig. 8.12). The standard procedure to visualize the behaviour of CA on the computer is to associate each possible cell state with a colour, but *Chaosynth* also associates these conditions to various frequency and amplitude values. For example: yellow = 110 Hz, red = 220 Hz, blue = 440 Hz and so forth; these are arbitrary associations, which are user-specified. Then the matrix of the automaton is subdivided into smaller uniform sub-matrices of neurons and a digital oscillator is allocated to each sub-matrix (Fig. 8.13). At each cycle of the automaton, the digital oscillators associated with the sub-matrices simultaneously produce signals, which are added in order to compose the spectrum

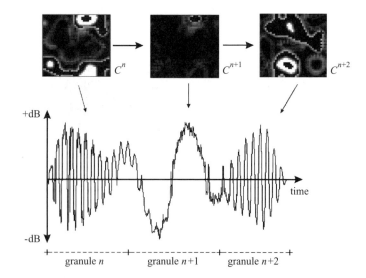

FIGURE 8.12. Each snapshot of the cellular automaton produces a sound grain or granule. (Note that this is only a schematic representation, as the granules displayed here do not actually correspond to these particular snapshots.)

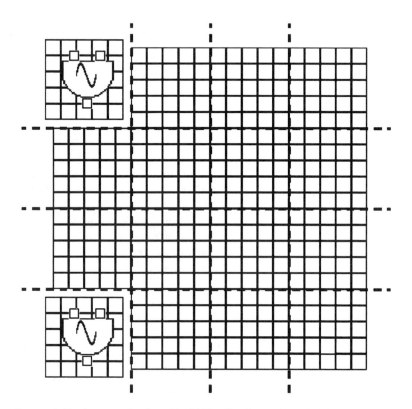

FIGURE 8.13. An example of a grid of 400 cells allocated to 16 digital oscillators.

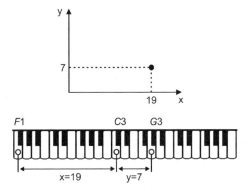

FIGURE 8.14. CAMUS uses a Cartesian coordinate system in two dimensions to represent an ordered set of three notes. In this case C3 is 19 semitones above F1, which is the reference note, and G3 is seven semitones above C3.

ω of the respective grain: $\omega = \sum_{n=1}^{N} S_n$, where S_n stands for the spectrum of the signal produced by oscillator n and N is the total amount of oscillators associated with the matrix. The frequency values F for each oscillator o are determined by the arithmetic mean over the frequency values associated to the states of the neurons of their corresponding sub-grid: $F_o = \frac{\sum_{n=1}^{N} \phi_n}{N}$, where ϕ_n represents the frequency of neuron n and N is the total amount of neurons of the sub-grid. Suppose, for example, that each oscillator is associated with nine neurons and that at a certain cycle t, three neurons correspond to 110 Hz, two to 220 Hz and the other 4 correspond to 880 Hz. In this case, the mean frequency value for this oscillator at time t will be 476.66 Hz. Fig. 8.13 shown as example of a grid of 400 neurons allocated to 16 oscillators of 25 neurons each.

Chaosynth was originally implemented in the early 1990s on a parallel Meiko 1860 supercomputer at the Edinburgh Parallel Computing Centre (EPCC), which enabled experiments with very large matrices of neurons (Miranda 1995). Scaled down versions for desktop personal computers were implemented at a later stage for Unix, Windows and Apple MacOS platforms, including a couple of commercial versions manufactured and distributed by Nyr Sound in the UK.

8.3.2.2. *Chaosynth* and Sound Design

Chaosynth has proved to be a powerful synthesizer, whose abilities to produce unusual sounds are vast. The random initialization of neuron states in the matrix produces an initial wide distribution of frequency and amplitude values, which tend to settle to an oscillatory cycle. This behaviour resembles the way in which the sounds produced by most acoustic instruments evolve during their production: their harmonics converge from a wide distribution (as in the noise attack time of the sound of a bowed string instrument, for example) to oscillatory patterns (the characteristic of a sustained tone). Variations in tone colour are achieved by varying the frequency values, the amplitudes of the oscillators and the number of neurons per oscillator. Different rates of transition, from noise to oscillatory patterns, are obtained by changing the values of $R1$, $R2$ and k.

The main criticism that we have received from *Chaosynth's* users, however, referred to the fact that it was hard to explore its potential. This is probably due to its newness and flexibility. Standard software synthesis systems take for granted a taxonomy for synthesized sounds that is inherited from the acoustic musical instruments tradition; for example, woodwinds, strings, percussion and so on. This scheme clearly does not meet the demands of more innovative software synthesizers. This lack of taxonomy made it difficult for users to establish reference points for exploration of new settings. In order to alleviate this problem, James Correa has attempted to define an alternative taxonomy for *Chaosynth* sounds. His taxonomy is inspired by Pierre Schaeffer's (1966) concept of sound maintenance and to some extent by an article written by Jean-Claude Risset in the book *Le timbre, métaphore pour la composition* (1991).

Undoubtedly, the most important characteristic of the sounds produced by *Chaosynth* is their spectral evolution in time. Some of the classes defined by James Correa include: fixed mass, flow, chaotic and explosive. For instance, the first class, fixed mass, comprises those settings that produce sounds formed by a large amount of very short grains. The overall outcome from these setting is perceived as sustained sounds with a high degree of internal redundancy; hence the label "fixed mass". The notion of fixed mass does not denote a fixed pitch, but rather a stable and steady spectrum where the frequencies of the grains are kept within a fixed band. For more information on this taxonomy, the reader is invited to refer to the paper 'Categorising Complex Dynamic Sounds', published in *Organised Sound* (Miranda et al. 2000).

Such taxonomy serves as a point of departure for exploration of the sonic capabilities of *Chaosynth*. However, as with *LASy*, the classes defined by Correa and colleagues are rather general and their boundaries are vague. Due to the very nature of ChaOs, and CA in general, it is often impossible to fully predict the exact nature of the sound that will be synthesized. Nevertheless, this gives Chaosynth an edge of unpredictability, which may appeal to sound designers and composers.

8.4. Cellular Automata Music: *CAMUS*

8.4.1. Cartesian Representation of Note Sets

CAMUS uses two simultaneous CA to produce music: the GL and Griffeath's Crystalline Growths (GCG). Whilst GL generates musical sequences, GCG designates their instrumentation, or orchestration (Miranda 1993). The cells of the GL automaton are mapped onto a Cartesian plane, where each point represents an ordered set of three notes, which are defined in terms of the intervals between them. Given a reference note, the abscissa represents the interval between the reference and the second note of the set. The ordinate represents the interval between the second note and the third (Figs. 8.14 and 8.15).

Fig. 8.16 illustrates how both CA work together. In this case, the cell in the GL at position (11, 6) is alive and will thus generate a set of three notes. The

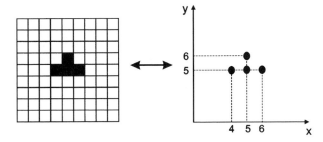

FIGURE 8.15. As the automaton evolves, ordered sets of three notes are produced. These sets are defined in terms of the Cartesian coordinate system shown in Fig. 8.14.

state of the corresponding cell in the GCG is equal to four, which means that the sonic event will be played by the MIDI instrument associated with this state. The co-ordinates (11, 6) describe the intervals separating the notes: given a reference note, the next note will be at 16 semitones above the reference note and the last

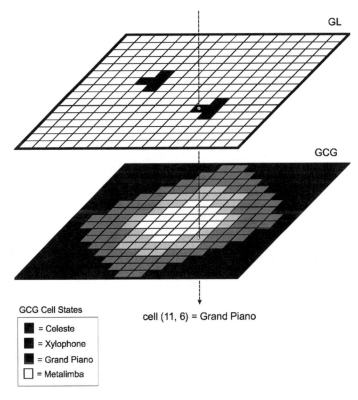

FIGURE 8.16. The cell in the GL at position (11, 6) defines an ordered set of notes played by the instrument associated with the state of the corresponding cell in the GCG at position (11, 6).

note six semitones above the second note (or ten semitones above the reference note).

To begin the composition process, a $[x \times y]$ GL automaton is set up with a given initial configuration of cell states and the associated GCG automaton, of identical size, is initialized with random states. Both are set to run and at each time step, the cells of the GL are analysed column by column, starting with cell $(0, 0)$, continuing through to $(0, x)$, moving on to cell $(1, 0)$ through to cell $(1, y)$ and continuing in this manner until cell (x, y) has been checked. When *CAMUS* arrives at a live cell, its co-ordinates are used to calculate an ordered set of three notes, as shown in Fig. 8.15; a set of reference notes is specified beforehand by the user. Although the cell updates occur at each time step in parallel, *CAMUS* plays the live cells column by column, from top to bottom. Each of these musical cells has its own timing, but the notes within a cell can be of different durations and can be triggered at different times (McAlpine et al. 1999).

8.4.2. Temporal Morphology

The method for staggering the starting and ending times of the notes of a cell (x, y) uses the states of its neighbouring cells in the GL. *CAMUS* constructs a set of values from the states of the neighbouring cells, the value being equal to one if the cell is alive and zero if it is dead, as follows:

$$a = \text{cell } (x, y - 1)$$
$$b = \text{cell } (x, y + 1)$$
$$c = \text{cell } (x + 1, y)$$
$$d = \text{cell } (x - 1, y)$$
$$m = \text{cell } (x - 1, y - 1)$$
$$n = \text{cell } (x + 1, y + 1)$$
$$o = \text{cell } (x + 1, y - 1)$$
$$p = \text{cell } (x - 1, y + 1)$$

Then, the system forms four 4-bit words as follows: *abcd*, *dcba*, *mnop* and *ponm*. Next, it perform the bit-wise inclusive OR operation, '|', to generate two four-bit words: *Tgg* and *Dur*:

$$Tgg = abcd|dcba$$
$$Dur = mnop|ponm$$

CAMUS derives trigger information for the notes from *Tgg*, and duration information from *Dur*. With each relevant four-bit word, *CAMUS* associates a code to represent time-forms where B denotes the bottom reference note, M the middle note, and U the upper one. The square brackets are used to indicate that the note events contained within that bracket occur simultaneously. The codes are as follows:

$$0000 = B[UM]$$
$$0001 = [UMB]$$
$$0010 = BUM$$
$$0011 = UMB$$
$$0101 = BMU$$
$$0110 = UBM$$
$$0111 = MBU$$
$$1001 = U[MB]$$
$$1011 = MUB$$
$$1111 = M[UB]$$

A visual representation of the time-forms assigned to the 4-bit words are shown in Fig. 8.17. Pairs of time-forms define a temporal morphology for the cells. For example, consider the a temporal morphology starting with MBU and ending with B[MU] (Fig. 8.18). Fig. 8.19 shows an instantiation of this morphology in musical notation.

The actual values in milliseconds for the trigger and duration parameters are calculated using a pseudo-random number generator. Finally, the music is written to a MIDI file and/or sent directly to a MIDI sampler or synthesizer to be played. Fig. 8.20 illustrates the main steps of the *CAMUS* algorithm in the form of a flowchart.

8.4.3. CAMUS 3D

Kenny McAlpine and Stuart Hoggar contributed to further develop *CAMUS* by introducing a number of variations to the original program, notably the use of

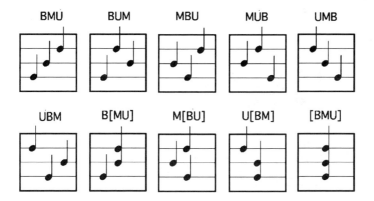

FIGURE 8.17. Ten different time-forms combined in pairs define temporal morphologies for the cells.

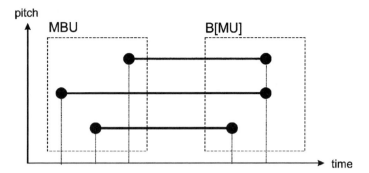

FIGURE 8.18. The temporal morphology starting with MBU and ending with B[MU].

three-dimensional CA. Three-dimensional versions of GL and GPG were configured to behave in much the same way as their two-dimensional counterparts. In order to achieve this, the three-dimensional space was treated as a series of stacked two-dimensional spaces. Therefore, a three-dimensional cellular automaton is defined as a series of two-dimensional CA stacked parallel to the plane $x = 0$. Then each of the stacked planes has the form $x = a$, for some integer value, a. Thus, when it comes to assess the neighbouring cells of an arbitrary cell (a, b, c), the algorithm needs to restrict its attention only to the cells $(a, b + 1, c)$, $(a, b - 1, c)$, $(a, b, c + 1)$, $(a, b, c - 1)$, $(a, b + 1, c + 1)$, $(a, b + 1, c - 1)$, $(a, b - 1, c + 1)$ and $(a, b - 1, c - 1)$, because the focus is on the plane $x = a$. This means that each of the stacked two-dimensional CA evolve independently; that is, none of the neighbouring cells can exert any

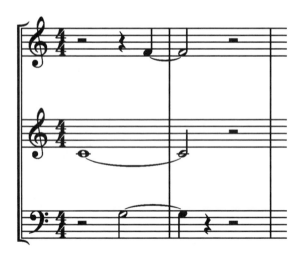

FIGURE 8.19. A musical passage generated by a single cell with the temporal morphology portrayed in Fig. 8.18.

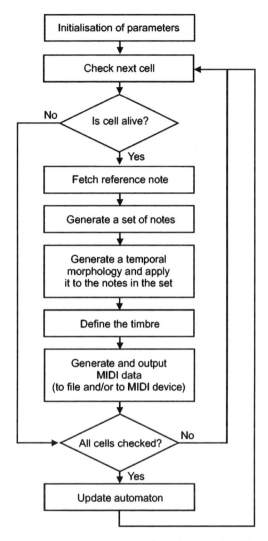

FIGURE 8.20. The main steps of the *CAMUS* algorithm.

influence on the cells in any of the other CA. This configuration is illustrated in Fig. 8.21.

8.4.4. Composing with CAMUS

CAMUS was designed for a rather abstract way of composing. The results tend to sound pointillist due to way in which the notes are generated as sequences of sets of three or fours notes, which are not necessarily played consecutively by the same instrument due to the GCG orchestration scheme.

FIGURE 8.21. A three-dimensional automaton defined as a series of stacked two-dimensional CA. The two-dimensional CA in this case are stacked parallel to the plane $y = 0$. The dark grey cell in the middle layer is currently under examination. Since we treat the y co-ordinate as a constant, only the shaded neighbouring cells in the same plane are also examined. Thus, each two-dimensional game evolves in isolation.

An inevitable problem with *CAMUS* is that the system does not possess knowledge about musical instruments. It often generates musical passages that would be technically impossible to be played on the respective instruments. These pieces often sound unconvincing when played on a MIDI synthesizer or sampler, because the music is not performed idiomatically; the clarinets do not sound 'clarinetistically', the violins do no sound 'violinistically', and so on. Better results can be achieved by amending the score manually in order to render the piece more realistic.

An example of a musical passage composed with *CAMUS* is shown in Fig. 8.22. The passage has been edited manually in order to alleviate the aforementioned problem. Dynamics and articulation were also added manually. Nevertheless, it is still possible to identify the characteristic sequence of patterns of groups of three notes 'evolving' in time.

CAMUS was originally implemented in 1990 on an Atari 1040 computer. In 1997, Kenny McAlpine implemented two new versions for Windows 95, which run seemly in Windows 98: *CAMUS* and *CAMUS 3D*, which are available on the accompanying CD-ROM of the book *Composing Music with Computers* (Miranda 2001). There have been no further updates of *CAMUS*.

8.5. Concluding Discussion

The resulting musical materials produced by the systems discussed in this chapter are very encouraging, as they are good evidence that both musical sounds and abstract musical forms might indeed share similar organizational principles with cellular automata. *LASy* and *Chaosynth* proved to be successful synthesis systems in the sense that they can produce a wide variety of sounds, which have been used in a number of compositions. *Chaosynth* can produce unusual sounds most of which are not found in the real acoustic world, but nonetheless sound pleasing to the ear, possibly due to the dynamic nature of ChaOs. As an example of an electroacoustic piece composed by this author using *Chaosynth* we cite *Olivine Trees*, which was awarded the bronze medal at the International Luigi Russolo Electroacoustic Music Competition in 1998. The core synthesis engine of *Chaosynth* was subsequently adapted to produce vocal-like effects (Miranda 2002).

Despite the arbitrariness of the musical engine of *CAMUS*, we have come to conclude that cellular automata are appropriate for generating musical material. A number of professional pieces were composed using *CAMUS*-generated material, including *Entre o Absurdo e o Mistério*, for chamber orchestra, and the second movement of the string quartet *Wee Batucada Scotica*, both published by Edições Musicais Goldberg, Brazil.

From our experience with these systems, we feel that cellular automata are more suitable for sound synthesis than for musical composition. We reckon that this might be due to the very nature of the phenomena in question. The inner structures of sounds, especially granular synthesis sounds, seem more susceptible to cellular automata modelling than large musical structures. As music is primarily a cultural phenomenon, we suspect that systems such as *CAMUS* would certainly produce improved results if they were programmed to take into account the dynamics of social formation and cultural evolution. This is not, however, a trivial task. Although social scientists have used cellular automata to model social systems (Epstein and Axtell 1996), more research is needed in order to find ways in which cultural and social phenomena could be integrated into generative music systems; refer to Chapter 10 for more discussion on this topic.

FIGURE 8.22. An example of a musical passage composed with *CAMUS*.

References

Beyls, P. (1989). The musical universe of cellular automata. In *Proceedings of the International Computer Music Conference (ICMC 1989)*. Columbus, OH, USA, pp. 34–41.

Burraston, D. (2005). Composition at the edge of chaos. In *Proceedings of the 2005 Australasian Computer Music Conference*. Brisbrane, Australia.

Chareyron, J. (1990). Digital synthesis of self-modifying waveforms by means of linear automata. *Computer Music Journal* 14(4): 25–40.

Cood, E.F. (1968). *Cellular Automata*. Academic Press, London.

Dewdney, A.K. (1989). Computer recreations: A cellular universe if debris, droplets, defects and demons. *Scientific American* August: 88–91.

Epstein, J.M. and Axtell, R.L. (1996). *Growing Artificial Societies: Social Science from the Bottom Up*. The MIT Press, Cambridge, MA.

Ermentrout, G.B. and Edelstein-Keshet, L. (1993). Cellular automata approaches to biological modelling. *Journal of Theoretical Biology* 160: 97–133.

Gabor, D. (1947). Acoustical quanta and the theory of hearing. *Nature* 159(4044): 591–594.

Gerhardt, M., Schuster, H. and Tyson, J. (1990). A cellular automaton model of excitable media. III: Fitting the Belousov–Zhabotinskii reaction. *Physica D* 46(3): 416–426.

Hoffman, P. (2002). Towards and automated art: Algorithmic processes in Xenakis' compositions. *Contemporary Music Review* 21(2/3): 121–131.

Hogeweg, P. (1988). Cellular automata as a paradigm for ecological modelling. *Applied Mathematics and Computation* 27: 81–100.

Karplus, K. and Strong, A. (1983). Digital synthesis of plucked string and drum timbres. *Computer Music Journal* 7(2): 43–55.

Kreger, T. (1999). Real-time cellular automata filters Implemented with Max/MSP. In *Proceedings of the Australasian Computer Music Conference 1999*. Victoria University of Wellington, New Zealand.

Langton, C. (1990). Computation at the edge of chaos: Phase transitions and emergent computation. *Physica D* 42: 12–37.

McAlpine, K., Miranda, E. and Hoggar, S. (1999). "Making music with algorithm: A case study system", *Computer Music Journal* 23(2): 19–30.

Millen, D. (1990). Cellular automata music. In *Proceedings of the International Computer Music Conference (ICMC 1990)*. Glasgow, UK, pp. 314–316.

Miranda, E.R., Correa, J.S. and Wright, J. (2000). Categorising complex dynamic sounds. *Organised Sound* 5(2): 95–102.

Miranda, E.R. (1990). *Cellular Automata Music Investigation*. MSc in Music Technology final project report. University of York, UK.

Miranda, E.R. (1993). Cellular automata music: An interdisciplinary project. *Interface* 22(1): 3–21.

Miranda, E.R. (1995). Chaosynth – Computer music meets high-performance computing. *Supercomputer* 11(1): 16–23.

Miranda, E.R. (2002). Generating source streams for extralinguistic utterances. *Journal of the Audio Engineering Society (AES)* 50(3): 165–172.

Orton, R., Hunt, A. and Kirk, R. (1991). Graphical control of granular synthesis using a cellular automata and the freehand program. In *Proceedings International Computer Music Conference (ICMC 1991)*. McGill University, Montreal, Canada, pp. 416–418.

Preston, K. and Duff, M. (1984). *Modern Cellular Automata: Theory and Applications*. Plenum, New York, NY.

Risset, J.-C. (1991). Timbre et synthèse des sons. In J.-B. Barrière (Ed.), *Le timbre: métaphore pour la composition*. IRCAM/Christian Bourgois Editeur, Paris.

Roads, C. (1991). "synchronous granular synthesis" In G. de Poli et al. (Eds.), *Representations of Music Signals*. The MIT Press, Cambridge, MA.

Schaeffer, P. (1966). *Traité des objets musicaux*. Editions du Seuil, Paris.

Trott, M. (2004). *The Mathematica Guidebook: Programming*. Springer-Verlag, New York.

Truax, B. (1988). "Real time granular synthesis with a DSP computer" *Computer Music Journal* 2(2): 14–26.

Vaidhyanathan, S., Minai, A. and Helmuth, M. (1999). ca: A system for granular processing of sound using cellular automata. In *Proceedings of the 2nd COST G-6 Workshop on Digital Audio (DAFx 1999)*. Norwegian University of Science and Technology (NTNU), Trondheim, Norway.

Wilson, G. (1988). The life and times of cellular automata. *News Scientist* October: 44–47.

Winkler, T. (2001). *Composing Interactive Music: Techniques and Ideas Using Max*. The MIT Press, Cambridge, MA.

Wolfram, S. (1994). Universality and complexity in cellular automata. *Physica D* **10**: 1–35.

Xenakis, I. (1971). *Formalized Music*. Indiana University Press, Bloomington, IN.

9
Swarming and Music

TIM BLACKWELL

9.1. Introduction

Music is a pattern of sounds in time. A swarm is a dynamic pattern of individuals in space. The structure of a musical composition is shaped in advance of the performance, but the organization of a swarm is emergent, without pre-planning. What use, therefore, might swarms have in music?

This chapter considers this question with a particular emphasis on swarms as performers, rather than composers. In *Swarm Music*, human improvizers interact with a music system that can listen, respond and generate new musical material. The novelty arises from the patterning of an artificial swarm. *Swarm Music* is a prototype of an autonomous, silicon-based improvizer that could, without human intervention, participate on equal terms with the musical activity of an improvizing group.

Real-life swarms organize themselves into remarkable, beautiful spatio-temporal structures in a process known as self-organization. This organization is thought to arise from the instantaneous dynamics of the swarming creatures, and not by any central leadership. Swarming animals communicate with each other over long time scales through the modification of the environment in a biological process known as stigmergy. This enables cooperative behaviour such as the construction of termite mounds, despite the absence of a termite architect. Digital swarms are the software equivalent of these remarkable biological systems. A virtual swarm may be visualized, but at a more abstract level, the swarm exists as a set of local rules, or interactions, between digital entities. These rules follow the theoretical models of biological swarms.

At the heart of the answer to the question posed above is a connection between self-organization and structural levels in music, a link that suggests many possibilities for the design of creative systems. This chapter begins therefore with an account of self-organization and swarming, and develops the link to structural levels in music in Section 9.3.

Synthetic swarms, by virtue of the unpredictability of their patterning are ideally suited to improvization, and the remainder of the chapter concentrates on swarms as performing systems. The real-time interaction between people and swarms is enabled with an analogue of stigmergy. A three component model outlines the interactions we might have with a virtual swarm, and by extension with any evolutionary algorithm. An analysis component maps external musical information into objects in the environment of the swarm. A stigmergetic interaction between swarming individuals and these objects takes place. The dynamic interactions within the swarm are described by the second component, the swarming function. The interpretation of swarming patterns into sounds is accomplished by the third component. Section 9.4 outlines the complete framework.

Section 9.5 considers the instantiation of the interactive model in the *Swarm Music* family of improvizers, and discusses the motivation for design. The following section considers live aspects of *Swarm Music*. Other performance systems that use a swarm algorithm are also summarized. Section 9.7 illustrates, by reference to system development in *Swarm Music*, a general scheme for increasing autonomy in music systems. The chapter ends with a look to the future of Swarming and Music.

9.2. Swarm Organization

9.2.1. The Science of Emergence

Self-organization (SO), the science of emergence, can, as yet, only allude to the preconditions for the emergence of large scale forms from local influences. Bonabeau and colleagues (1999) propose that SO relies on multiple interactions between component parts of a system, an ability to amplify fluctuations, and positive and negative feedback between components. Positive feedback forms the basis of morphogenesis, allowing reinforcement of new forms. Negative feedback stabilizes the system and prevents runaway. Random fluctuations play a crucial role in SO, enabling the system to find novel situations, which are exploitable through positive feedback.

The paradigmatic example of SO is the collective behaviour of social insects, for example the organization of army ants in vast foraging patterns (Burton and Franks 1985). The raid patterns of army ants contains hundreds of thousands of virtually blind individuals, a remarkable example of decentralized control (Bonabeau et al. 1999, p. 36). Recruitment to a food source through trail laying and trail reinforcement is an example of positive feedback, with stability arising from the limited numbers of foragers and the exhaustion of the food source. Random fluctuations arise in foragers through error; the occasional wayward ant who has lost a trail might find a new food source. Communication between ants, although it can take place through direct contact, is also mediated indirectly via the environment by the laying of pheromone trails. Individuals are able to exploit this information network, for example by following a trail that leads to a newly discovered food source. Although an individual can interact with its own trail, SO usually requires a minimum density of individuals who are intent on exploiting the network. The indirect and temporally adjusted environment mediated interaction is termed *stigmergy* (Grassé 1959). In a sense, stigmergy happens to humans all the time. A note left on the kitchen table is an indirect interaction between people, influencing our actions several hours later.

Swarms, flocks, herds and shoals are familiar examples of the groupings of social animals. The organization of Atlantic herring into very huge shoals up to seventeen miles long, and with many millions of fish is a stunning example (Shaw 1975). This is particularly remarkable because it is unlikely that an individual herring can, in the murky Atlantic water and tightly packed shoal, see more than a few of its neighbours. The possibility of a leader herring coordinating this shoal is absurd, and besides, how would it orchestrate the shoal movements? It seems likely, therefore, that the shoal is an emergent entity, produced by local, de-centralized interactions.

9.2.2. Artificial Swarms

Evidence that flocks and swarms are self-organising is provided by the 'boid' animations of Reynolds (1987). The centralized approach to animations of particle systems (bees in a swarm, buffalo in a herd) is to formulate the collective behaviour as a script which each entity must obey. Swarming behaviour is not emergent because it is built into the script from the outset. However, Reynold's discovery that convincing animations can result from local, de-centralized rules has done much to support the hypothesis that swarms and flocks are self-organizing. The collective behaviour of the group is emergent because the rules concerning the parts of the swarm do not contain any notion of the whole. Additionally, de-centralization explains the scalability of natural swarms. The variation of swarm sizes over six orders of magnitude suggests that swarms must have linear complexity. Early examples of behavioural animations using the boids algorithm include bat swarms and penguin flocks in the film Batman Returns (Burton 1992) and the wildebeest stamped in The Lion King (Allers and Minkoff 1994).

Contemporary swarm algorithms follow this basic principle and can be split into three groups, although there are overlaps. The grouping is in order of faithfulness to natural swarms:

1. Bio-swarms, the most faithful, are used to develop scientific models of natural systems (for example the refined bio-swarm of Couzin et al. 2005). These swarms may be visualized, but the chief purpose is hypothesis development and testing.
2. Simulation swarms are visualizations for aesthetic and artistic purposes and do not need to accurately represent nature (Reynolds 1987; Burton 1992; Allers and Minkoff 1994). We can include musical swarms such as *Swarm Music* in this category. These swarms move in real time so that the visualisations have a sense of realism.
3. Social swarms use an information network rather than a spatial region to define a neighbourhood for interactions. Social swarms are frequently used to solve mathematical problems, as in ant colony optimization (Bonabeau et al. 1999) and particle swarm optimization (PSO) (Kennedy et al. 2001).

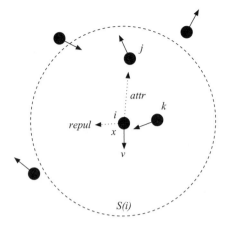

FIGURE 9.1. Swarming rules. Particle i, currently at x and moving with velocity v, is attracted to particle j and repelled from particle k. The other particles are outside i's perception, $S(i)$.

These swarms have the loosest connection to nature: the visualizations take secondary importance to the algorithmic details and in fact they can look quite unrealistic.

Swarms which use a spatial neighbourhood typically assume that the individuals have a finite range of perception in which a given individual feels the influence of neighbours. Typically, individuals repel each other at close range, attract each other at medium range and are oblivious to each other at long range (Fig. 9.1). The attractions provide coherence, maintaining a shared neighbourhood (which may be a sub-swarm or the entire swarm) and the repulsions prevent collisions. Figure 9.1 illustrates the idea. The attractive and repulsive accelerations are the analogues of positive and negative feedback. At its simplest, a swarm algorithm considers the individual swarming participants as purely dynamic entities. These entities are represented as point particles in d-dimensional real space with dynamic state (x, v). The basic rules governing the interactions between neighbouring particles in a swarm or flock are:

1. if apart, move closer (cohesion)
2. if too close move apart (separation)
3. attempt to match velocities (alignment)

The final rule only applies collectives where there the entities move in unison, such as flocks, herds and schools. Swarming entities have more chaotic motions and drop the rule of alignment.

The dynamical update equations of swarm algorithms are discretizations of Isaac Newton's laws. The update of particle i of swarm S is

$$a_i = \frac{1}{m} f(S(i), \alpha) \qquad (9.1)$$

$$v_i(t + 1) = v_i(t) + a_i \qquad (9.2)$$

$$v_i(t + 1) = min(v_i(t), v_{max}) \qquad (9.3)$$

$$x_i(t + 1) = x_i(t) + v_i(t + 1) \qquad (9.4)$$

where the time increment $dt = 1$ and $S(i)$ is the sub-swarm comprised of i and its neighbours. The rules 1–3 above are embodied in the particle accelerations a_i. These accelerations are computed by a force law f, which is a function of dynamic variables, neighbourhood $S(i)$, and parameters α. The mass m of the particle is usually set to unity, and the physics terms 'force' and 'acceleration' are synonymous in this context. The acceleration parameters characterise the strength of the intra-particle forces and the construction of $S(i)$, for example by specifying a radius of perception (bio and simulation swarms), or a network topology (social swarms).

Equation (9.3) is an optional speed clamp that can be used to limit particle velocity in the case of high accelerations. Some swarm implementations, especially bio and simulation swarms, use a swarming function, Eq. (9.1), that produces accelerations of fixed magnitude and clamping is never necessary. These 'steering' accelerations cause the velocity vector to rotate, and do not cause changes in speed. For example, the attraction of a particle at x_i towards a neighbouring particle at x_j might be a steering acceleration,

$$a_i = \frac{x_j - x_i}{|x_j - x_i|} \tag{9.5}$$

The calculation of a_i in Eq. (9.1) consists of a sum of attractive and repulsive terms. Particles perceive each other and other attractors with a region of perception. At long distances, particles attract, but at shorter distances repulsion will dominate. Bio-swarms use three concentric zones; the rule of cohesion applies in the outer zone, alignment applies in a middle zone and at short distances the rule of separation dominates (Couzin et al. 2002). Individuals in simulation and bio-swarms may also have a 'blind volume' in which neighbours are undetectable.

Social swarms employ an information network that is topological rather than spatial. Additionally, the particles possess a memory and so are more than merely dynamic entities. The accelerations in PSO are not constant magnitude steering vectors but are spring-like,

$$a_i = C(p_i - x_i) \tag{9.6}$$

where C is a spring constant and p_i is a good location previously visited by particle i, or by any other particle in i's topological neighbourhood. Convergence, and the stabilization of the swarm within a search space, occur through energy loss and the particle displacements become progressively smaller and the search intensifies. This energy loss is invoked by a frictional drag force. The attraction of a particle to a previous best position can be viewed as a stigmergetic interaction. Particles leave behind markers p_i at promising locations, and the markers are available to any other particle in the social network, irrespective of distance.

The music swarms that will be discussed in this chapter, employ elements of simulation and social swarms. *Swarm Music* and *Swarm Granulator* use spatial neighbourhoods and spring or steering accelerations. The particles in *Swarm Techtiles* communicate stigmergetically by depositing markers at a highly textured region of an image. The neighbourhood is again spatial although the rule for interpretation of each particle in terms of musical parameters is social in origin.

In summary, simulation swarms and visualisations of social and bio-swarms reveal self-organizational properties: the swarm as a whole has a spatial identity with globally connected neighbourhoods, the swarm can act as a single entity (spontaneous movement of every particle in an arbitrary direction defined, for example, by a breakaway particle) and the formation of spatially separate subswarms that may later merge. The swarm rules are simple to implement—considerably simpler than trying to write top–down rules—and the behaviour does not depend on fine tuning of the acceleration parameters. The emergent organisation at the swarm level fits with the premises of SO since the algorithm incorporates positive feedback (coherence), negative feedback (separation) and complexity (many particles, stigmergetic effects, blind volumes, etc.).

9.3. Swarming and Descriptions of Music

This section establishes the link between swarming, SO and *descriptions* of music. We distinguish here the formal, music–theoretic description of music as notes, metre, dynamics, harmony, etc. and the performance itself, which is an inter-musician exchange of sonic events. The following section considers the relationship between swarming, stigmergy and the *performance* of music.

9.3.1. Levels of Description

From a music–theoretic perspective, music is commonly analysed hierarchically. For example, a work of (classical) Western art music is usually thought of as the organization of melodies, which themselves are built from phrases. The phrases are comprised of individual notes, and the whole structure is bound together by rhythm and metre. A classification loosely based on perceptual time-scales can be summarized, with suggested time-scales, (Xenakis 1989; Roads 2001);

1. Micro. This scale extends from the limit of timbre perception (tenths of a millisecond, Gabor 1947) up to the duration of notes or other sound objects.
2. Mini (note). This level includes notes and any other sound from a known or even unidentifiable source (sound objects, Schaeffer 1959) of duration tenths of a second to several seconds.
3. Meso (phrase). This level corresponds to phrases or groups of mini-events and occupies several to dozens of seconds. Melodic, contrapuntal and rhythmic relationships between objects are noticeable at this level.
4. Macro. This longer lasting duration of time encompasses form and lasts several minutes or more. Corresponding to the architecture of a composition or improvization, this level is perceived either through recollection or by knowledge of a particular macro-structure (for example, knowledge that a piece is written in sonata form).

Digital music also includes an imperceivable sample level of sound, ranging from a single digital sample at hundredths of a millisecond, up to the shortest timbred-sound. Clearly such schemes are not unambiguous, and arguably over-confine music to a rigid structure that is subservient to notation (Wishart 1966). However the analysis by levels is useful for our purpose here, which is to establish how swarming might relate to music.

9.3.2. Swarming

Imagine, rather whimsically, an abstract note-to-be as some kind of autonomous individual, able to wander at will in a 'music parameter space'. This space might be a score, or some other abstract space of musical dimensions. As it moves through this space, its characteristics—pitch, loudness, duration and onset time—will change. The note-to-be does not wander aimlessly, however; it is attracted to other note individuals, and soon groupings of notes form. Notes avoid collisions and sometimes dart away from the group. Other groupings are formed in distant regions of music space; sometimes groups collide and unite.

These swarms of melody are composed of notes that *do not know they are part of a tune*. The notes have not been placed by a higher level imperative; rather, melody is an emergent property of the note-swarm, related to the self-organized pattern of the swarming individuals (Blackwell 2001). Collision avoidance between notes mitigates against too much repetition, which is balanced by an inter-note attraction which prevents too much variation. Observation of composed melodies shows that they occupy constrained regions of music parameter space, frequently moving step wise, suggesting a strong tensile force between notes, and with leaps for excitement, as produced, in our analogy, by random fluctuations. Examples of melodic movement are to be found in many books on composition, for example Sturman (1983).

Swarming can be also be inferred from the harmonic principles of consonance and dissonance (Piston 1978), endemic in the common practise of Western art music, and in contemporary popular music. Harmony can be simplistically viewed as an attraction towards the consonant musical intervals. Dissonance can occur, but the result of such a collision is a relaxation back to consonance.

Rhythmically too, we can discover the same forces; an attraction of note onsets to the subdivisions of the beat, and a repulsion away from non-metricity (unless the music is deliberately rubato, in which case the opposite rule applies).

An analogy has been suggested between musical organization at the note level, but similar principles can be construed at the meso level where a phrase may be considered as a 'unit of musical thought, like a sentence or a clause' (Piston 1978, p. 93), or at the macro level where groups of phrases produce sectional structuring, as in the exposition, development, recapitulation and coda sections of the classical sonata form, or the AABA structure of popular songs. These principles might also be applied at the micro or sample levels (Blackwell and Young 2004a, b; Blackwell and Jefferies 2005).

At each level we notice a tension between repetition and variation, a force for similarity (positive feedback) that is balanced by a repulsion (negative feedback) away from sameness. Too much similarity is boring for the listener, and too much variation can imbue the music with a feeling of disorganization (Coker 1986, p. 15). The idea from emergence is that structure at level n can arise from local interactions at level $n - 1$ and need not be enforced by top–down pressure. SO provides an appealing picture for the creation of novelty through random exploration and reinforcement, and the relationship between positive and negative feedback is compatible with our psychological expectations of music. These arguments suggest a different view of musical organization, complimenting the traditional syntactical, top-down description.

As we have seen, swarming particles move in a d-dimensional real space with a swarming algorithm f that moves the particles forward in time. Swarming patterns can be *interpreted* musically as a succession of musical/sonic events. In this picture, music is regarded as a temporal structure of meaningless level-dependent entities, since the rules governing the interactions do not derive from musical concerns. Meaning itself can only emerge, and is only apparent at, the next highest level.

9.4. Performing Swarms

9.4.1. Interactive Model

This section considers the performative, rather than the descriptive, aspects of music and self-organization. Music performance, in contradistinction to the structural analysis of music, is highly interactive and uncertain. Whether rehearsed or extemporized, unknowable features of performance enter through the unpredictability of individual interpretation, audience involvement, acoustics and other external factors. This section describes a model of performance that encompasses current computer music practise and is well suited for the development of new evolutionary and swarm-based music systems.

Improvised music is highly interactive and is the best exemplar of the parallels between performance and SO. A performance of freely improvized music is distinguished from jazz (which includes improvization within a pre-defined structure) and other compositional genres by the lack of advance planning. There is no leader, no rehearsal, no score and no written instructions. Musicians simply assemble on stage and begin playing their instruments. All musical directions, cues, initiatives and roles are therefore communicated by musical utterances, and by body language. Surprisingly, this de-centralized, potentially lawless, style of music making can produce remarkably well formed improvizations. In other words, spontaneous improvizations are capable of structuring at the macro level; the emergence of form is a consequence of the temporally local interactions between performers.

An examination of group dynamics in the light of the ingredients of self-organization—positive and negative feedback, amplification of fluctuations and complex interactions—is revealing. There is a human tendency to conform. If the direction of an improvization is towards increasing excitement (for example by playing louder, faster and with more dissonance), there is a strong compulsion to join in and reinforce this flow. In dynamical terms, this can be regarded as an attraction towards a gestural, emotional target. This positive feedback is counter-balanced by a personal desire to innovate. In the language of dynamic systems, the musical target or attractor has a repulsive force that deflects away from exact repetition. Improvisations can include sudden changes in mood and musical direction, as if orchestrated. Dynamically, a small fluctuation caused by a random exploration can precipitate a movement by the whole group and the proto-idea is amplified. The unique constitution of the performing group and the non-linearity of the abstract performance space provides uncertain, complex, non-linear interactions. It seems therefore that a group performance has the potential to be self-organizing.

Swarms are, as we have seen, self-organizing, and might therefore implement these ideas. However, for the analogy between SO and improvization to be practically useful, the relationship between the performing group, and a computer music system running a virtual swarm, must be fleshed out. One approach is to model each individual as a particle. However particles in a swarm move in a shared space, and it is very hard to see how to define this space without giving the musicians (and the computer) precise instructions about how to interact and move. Although there is some precedent for this approach in dance (Turner 2006), this scheme is in conflict with a musicians' own perspective on what it is to improvize. Rule specification, after all, is a compositional rather than an improvizational device.

Instead, each individual carries with her/him a unique representation of music and of sound events. This representation is a product of aesthetics, experience, training, temperament and many other factors. He/she might 'hear' a sound event in a different way: as a C#, as a squeal, as the fourth note in a sequence, as angry, etc., or indeed in many of these at the same time. Ideas, as expressed in this space, evolve until an intention is formed, and new sound output produced. The representations are personal, hidden even; fellow musicians can only access external sound events, and possibly infer intention from visual cues.

The solution adopted in *Swarm Music* (Blackwell 2001) mirrors this informal account. Each individual is regarded as a sub-swarm rather than a particle. The sub-swarms move in secret, hidden spaces; external sound events are parameterized as objects in the environment of each sub-swarm. Interaction between sub-swarms is now possible through a stigmergetic mechanism. Events at micro, mini and meso levels are parameterized according to the internal representations available to any individual. These parameterizations constitute 'sound objects' which populate the internal spaces of each individual, whether human or machine. To the participant, these objects act rather like messages, influencing stigmergetically the flow of one's own internal states. Collaboration and self-organization between the sub-swarms can still happen, but unlike natural systems, each subswarm/individual moves in a distinct space, Figure 9.2.

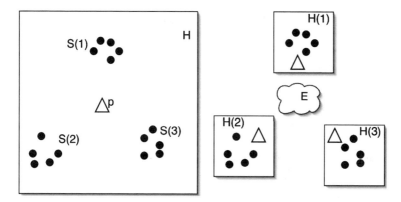

FIGURE 9.2. In this diagram, particles are blobs and attractors are triangles. The left diagram shows three sub-swarms $S(1-3)$ swarming in a space H around an attractor p. The right hand diagram depicts the interactive model. Here the sub-swarms move in separate spaces $H(1-3)$. Each space is replete with an image of the sound object, E.

9.4.2. Live Algorithms

The model of performance as a self-organizing system suggests ways that machines might interact autonomously, rather merely automatically or manually, with people. Autonomy implies that an interacting system can support group activity, as well as introduce novel elements, and all without the presence of an operator. The model sketched in the preceding section suggests that internal state flow, as generated by a swarm simulation, can act as an 'ideas generator'. Interaction with the real world is effected by forming an image, as an attractor for example, of external events in the state space of the system. This image informs, but does not govern, state flow. State flow, and hence output, is not contingent on input: the system is capable of making contributions in periods when the group is silent and is capable of silence when the group is active. Self-organization around attractors is a supportive activity and the amplification of spontaneous fluctuations away from an attractor gives rise to novelty.

The idea that interaction involves state change rather than parameter selection is an important aspect in the design of 'live algorithms' (Blackwell and Young 2005). A live algorithm is an autonomous music system capable of human-compatible performance. Several live algorithms have been developed; the Voyager system of Lewis (2000), Al Biles' GenJam (2006) and Francois Pachet's Continuator (Pachet 2004) are notable examples. Many issues surrounding machine interaction are covered in Rowe (2004). The proposed architecture for live algorithms builds on the interactive model of Section 9.4.1. A major advantage of the interactive model is that knowledge of collaborators' internal states are not necessary. This circumvents the difficulty of modelling, in a live algorithm, human intentionality and lessens the problems humans might have in interacting with an algorithm whose logical process depart greatly from human experience.

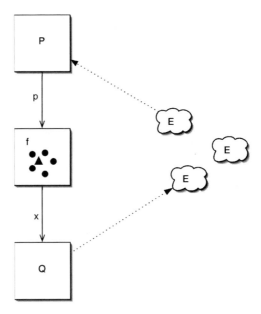

FIGURE 9.3. Modular structure of a live algorithm showing analysis (P), synthesis (Q) and patterning (f) modules. In this figure, a swarm provides spatio-temporal patterns as it self-organizes around an attractor (triangle). Q converts swarming configurations into musical patterns E.

A modular structure for live algorithms has been proposed by this author and Young (2004b, 2005). This architecture is shown is shown in Figure 9.3. External sound objects E are parameterized as internal images p by an interpretative, analytical module P. P corresponds to our ability to interpret incoming sound in terms of internal representations. A patterning, ideas engine f transforms internal states x in an internal space H. This module represents the restless flow of ideas that an improviser might have, ideas that are guided, but not determined by, inputs p. Many possible choices of patterners f exist, including neural networks, evolutionary algorithms and swarm simulations. A third module, Q, re-interprets internal x as external sound. This involves a mapping onto synthesizer controls q. Q is a synthesis module, for example a MIDI sythnesizer or a granular synthesizer, and represents the conversion of volition into action. This architecture is general enough to subsume contemporary computer music practices such as (manual) live electronics and live coding and the automated process of algorithmic/generative music (Blackwell and Young 2005).

Since interaction with internal states can only occur if the state space contains an image of the environment, and participation with the environment can only happen if system state is mapped to sound, the live algorithm architecture is minimal. Systems of arbitrary complexity can be built by layering and cross-wiring between modules. However, all interactive systems (where interaction is defined as state change) must reduce to this PQf architecture. Since analysis (P), synthesis (Q) and generative (f) algorithms are individually the subject of much current research, it is hoped that much progress in live algorithm research can be made by connecting pre-existing units.

9.4.3. Autonomy

The swarming function f can be written as

$$x(t + 1) = f(x(t), v(t), p(t), \alpha) \tag{9.7}$$

where $\{x, v\}$ are dynamic variables, $p = P(E)$ is the image of the environment and α is a list of undetermined parameters, for example maximum velocity, spring constants and radius of perception. The α's can be thought of as controls, presets or algorithmic constants. They can be adjusted in real time by an operator as in the practices of live electronics and live coding. Potentially the α's, along with the choice of representation, will have a huge affect on the musicality of the system, governing many features of the output. It is important to distinguish system characteristics from autonomy. Live algorithms, just like humans, may be quite idiosyncratic, and this would be an advantage in an improvized context, but this need not affect their ability to interact. The α's might be interdependent, $\alpha_1 = \alpha_1(\alpha_2, \alpha_3, \ldots)$ and/or contextual $\alpha = \alpha(x, v, p)$ and often the α's are descriptions at the next higher musical level. The challenge for the designer of an autonomous system is to find a self-regulating, contextual condition for each undetermined parameter α_j so that the system is flexible, adaptable to the musical context and does not require any tuning by hand. One solution for determining an α and increasing system autonomy in *Swarm Music* is presented in Section 9.7.

9.4.4. Visualizing the Algorithm

Figure 9.3 does not depict a feed-through system. The arrows show direction of parameter flow, not ordering, and each module is intended to operate concurrently. The state flow $x(t) \rightarrow x(t + 1)$ can be run as a simulation, i.e. a visualization shows entities moving at realistic speeds. A visualization serves as an embodiment of the algorithm, and gives clues on system behaviour to participating musicians (and to the audience). This visualization will only be useful to us if it proceeds at a comprehensible pace, and does not include too much information. In a sense, the visualization aids overall transparency of the system; visual cues are important for person–person interaction, and their value cannot be underestimated in machine–human interaction too.

The requirement that the algorithm is running a simulation of a real, or an imagined, natural system means that the update loop must contain a sleep function that links the iterative time t to real time τ. For example, the desired velocity of the particle across the screen is a function of the clamping velocity, v_{max}, and the nominal update time interval $\Delta\tau$. A sleep function can halt the update loop at each iteration in order to preserve $\Delta\tau$ and ensure that states move at a fixed speed. Without such a consideration, the algorithm will run as fast as a CPU will allow, tying the algorithm to a particular machine, and making behaviour inconsistent.

9.5. Swarm Music

9.5.1. Overview of Live Algorithms Based on Swarming

The interactive model of Section 9.4.1 and the live algorithms architecture of Section 9.4.2 has been implemented in three systems, *Swarm Music* (Blackwell and Bentley 2002), *Swarm Granulator* (Blackwell and Young 2004a) and *Swarm Techtiles* (Blackwell and Jefferies 2005). In each case, the internal states x are particle positions in a swarm and f is the swarming function, Eq. (9.7). The systems differ, however, in representational levels and on the interpretation of the internal space H.

The space in *Swarm Music* is spanned by parameters salient at mini (note) and meso (phrase) levels. *Swarm Granulator* has an internal representation at the micro (granular) and *Swarm Techtiles* operates at the sample and micro level. In both *Swarm Music* and *Swarm Granulator*, attractors p are parameterizations of the input stream and are placed directly in an otherwise featureless H. Swarm particles are drawn towards any attractors in their zone of perception, and particle positions are interpreted one by one as synthesizer parameters. The flow of the swarm through H therefore corresponds to a melody (*Swarm Music*), or a stream of texture (*Swarm Granulator*).

Swarm Techtiles uses elements from social and simulation swarms and operates between sample and micro-levels. Particles fly over a landscape of 'woven sound' (a warp-weft mapping of incoming samples onto pixels), searching for optimum regions of local texture. Particles communicate stigmergetically by leaving markers at regions of high image texture, and produce sonic improvizations by unweaving small image tiles into sound. Swarm Granulator and Swarm Techtiles are described in detail in a review of swarm granulation (Blackwell, forthcoming).

9.5.2. Interpretation

Swarm Music has developed from a four to a seven dimensional system. Four dimensions are occupied by mini (note) level parameters and the other three dimensions correspond to phrase level parameterizations. A screen shot from *Swarm Music*, Fig. 9.4, shows the first three dimensions of an N-particle swarm.

The listening module, P can receive either audio or MIDI. Digital audio is converted into MIDI messages by an inbuilt event and pitch detector which relates average event energy in decibels to MIDI 'velocity', and the dominant frequency of a fast Fourier spectrum to MIDI note number (middle C $= 60$, C# $= 61$ etc.). Otherwise, a MIDI source is plugged directly into P.

P extracts note loudness a and pitch f from the MIDI message. Additionally, P keeps track of five other features. All seven axes are specified in Table 9.1. Axis seven has only recently been incorporated in *Swarm Music* and is reported here for the first time. These features become the seven components of the attractor p. There are as many attractors as there are particles, and attractors are replaced in turn, so the system only as a memory of the last N events (this constitutes a

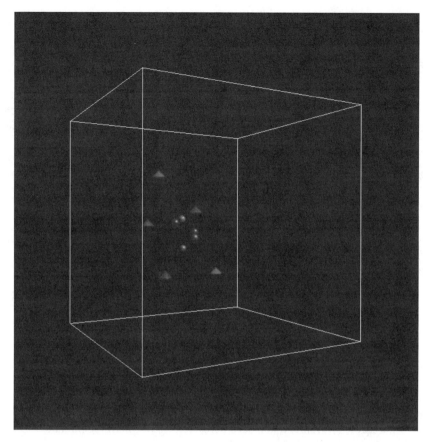

FIGURE 9.4. A five particle swarm. Particles are depicted as spheres and attractors as cones. The mappings into the three dimensions of this visualization are: loudness → out-of-page; onset time interval → left–right and pitch→ up–down

single phrase in *Swarm Music*) that it has heard. The attractors, which act like pheromones to the swarm, rapidly evaporate.

Apart from the four note-level axes, 1–4, *Swarm Music* incorporates three phrase-level dimensions, allowing for swarming in a subspace of phrase param-

TABLE 9.1. The seven dimensions of *Swarm Music*

Axis	Description	Symbol
1	Event energy/note loudness	a
2	Time interval between events	Δt
3	Event pitch	f
4	Time duration of events	Δt_{event}
5	Number of simultaneous events in a phrase	n_{chord}
6	Number of ascending or descending pitches in a phrase	n_{seq}
7	Similarity between successive phrases	s

eterizations. The fifth axis is chord number. Each incoming phrase is examined for the number of coincident, or near coincident, events and this number becomes the fifth component, p_5 of the new attractor. The sixth dimension is the number of consecutive ascending note-numbers (ranging from $-N$ to $+N$, with negative values indicating descending sequences) over the phrase. The seventh dimension represents the similarity of two adjacent phrases with a similarity measure. The similarity s is a value in the unit interval with $s = 1$ for a perfect N note match (by note number only) between the last two phrases. A similarity of zero means that there were no matches.

The swarm has N particles and these are interpreted, by the synthesis module Q, as a set S_N of N notes. Each note is described by four parameter 1–4, $\{a, \Delta t, f, \Delta t_{event}\}$. The loudness a of each note in S_N is determined by the first component, x_1 of each particle's position. Onset time interval (in the absence of chords) between notes, pitch and note duration correspond to components x_{2-4}.

Phrase descriptions are the properties of a group of notes and not of an individual. Similarly, the phrase descriptions for S_N must be a property of the swarm as a whole. The swarm centre of mass,

$$\bar{x} = \sum_{all\ particles} x \qquad (9.8)$$

is a convenient measure of swarm configuration. Q uses components $\bar{x}_{5-7}$ of the centre of mass to modify the phrase S_N. If the chord number, $n_{chord} = \bar{x}_5$ is larger than 1, then the Δt's of the first n_{chord} notes of S_N are set to zero. This will ensure that they will sound simultaneously. The first $n_{seq} = \bar{x}_6$ notes of S_N are sorted by pitch. (The system also allows sorting by any of the other three note level parameters $\{a, \Delta t, \Delta t_{event}\}$.) The final phrase parameter, $\bar{x}_7$, is unusual because it does not affect S_N; rather it adjusts a parameter in the swarming module f. This is discussed in detail below.

9.5.3. Design

The design of a swarming system for music requires two major decisions, namely representation and dynamics. Representational issues govern the interpretations of particle state and the design of P and Q. The choice of dynamics (the swarming function f) is seemingly independent of representation, but ultimately they must be related because different particle dynamics might be more or less appropriate for a given representation. The appropriateness of a dynamics to a representation is the personal choice of the algorithm designer; there is no prima facie guide to representation and dynamics, since the design of a creative system is not logically determined.

Interpretation of the swarming patterns must be accomplished by a mapping of the state of each particle onto a musical/sonic parameter, which in turn is rendered by a synthesizer. This general scheme allows for mappings of any complexity (or simplicity). Since the mappings are essentially arbitrary, some guiding principle is needed, at least to get started. The principle of transparency has been suggested (Blackwell and Young 2004b): the interpretative mapping should be comprehensible to the audience, and to collaborating musicians, so that the relationship between the particle movements and the output is clear. The swarm itself may be visualized in order to negotiate the digital divide between the workings of the algorithm and the output.

The principle of transparency urges the design to be as simple as possible, even to the extent of a literal interpretation of music descriptions. *Swarm Music* was originally intended as a note-level improvizer, and notes have loudness, pitch and timing corresponding to dimensions 1 to 4. The interpretation of these dimensions is very transparent. If a particle were to find itself at an attractor at p, it would output the same MIDI-parameterized notes that the system captured. In fact, due to the finite kinetic energy and the erratic particle movements, the swarm arranges itself *around* the attracting group, and outputs a melody that has a resemblance in rhythm, pitch sequence and loudness to the captured phrase.

In terms of the visualisation, a literal interpretation might be a map of pitch to height (x_3-axis, towards the top of the screen) and loudness to closeness to the viewer (x_1-axis, 'out' of screen). The mapping in each case is linear. The temporal parameters of note onset time and note duration are harder to map. One idea is to use the velocity of the particles as an indicator of rhythm, but this is problematic for two reasons. Firstly, particles in swarm simulations usually fly at a set speed, as determined by a velocity clamping which occurs immediately after velocity update, Eq. (9.3). *Swarm Music*, and optimisation swarms, use spring like forces,

$$a_i^{\text{attr}} = C \sum_{\text{all perceived attractors}} (p - x_i) \qquad (9.9)$$

but *Swarm Music* uses a stiff spring constant C so that clamping is nearly always employed, and only steering occurs. The second problem with possible interpretations of velocity is that self-organization would have to take place in the $2Nd$-dimensional phase space of position and velocity. However, there is little, if any organization in velocity for a swarm, rather the organization is revealed in the sequence of spatial patterns. Whilst velocity organization does occur in flocks, it arises by virtue of the velocity aligning term in the dynamics and is not emergent.

Swarm Music, *Granulator* and *Techtiles* therefore derive their temporal interpretations from the spatial configuration of the particles. In *Swarm Music*, the x_2-axis is calibrated in beats per minute ($\sim \frac{1}{\Delta t}$); each particle's position along this axis is interpreted as the time interval between the onset of this particle's note and the immediately proceeding one. Spatially coherent swarms, where each particle has a similar x_2, will yield regular rhythms, and widely scattered particles or sub-swarms will produce a high diversity of onset times. A similar scheme is used for the x_4 component, note durations.

9.6. Experience

9.6.1. Performance

An important aspect of *Swarm Music* is the use of performance variables as part of the generative framework. Human performers will invariably 'interpret' a score, since a complete set of performance characteristics cannot be specified. For example, a musician can, in performance, vary tempo and rhythm, as well as dynamics (changes in loudness). Variations can happen at any structural level. *Swarm Music* could be used as a score generator by saving output MIDI events to file. However, *Swarm Music* is better exploited as an improviser in partnership with a human(s). The system is able to quickly respond to incoming musical gestures with swarming melodies and rhythms. There is no notion of fixed tempo; rather, rhythms and dynamics are constantly changing due to the swarming motion of the particles, yet there is always a connection to the external sonic environment because of the mapping from incoming sounds to attractors. The system moves freely with the improvization, appearing to interact responsively with a partner (Fig. 9.5).

Another reason for the perceived musicality of *Swarm Music* is the use of spring forces to determine particle accelerations. Typically, spring forces produce oscillatory motion, with the period of oscillation governed by the strength of the spring. The update rule, Eq. (9.1), is a sum of attracting spring forces, Eq. (9.9), and Coulomb repulsions between neighbouring particles,

$$a_i^{\text{repul}} = K \sum_{\text{all perceived particles}} \frac{(x_i - x_j)}{(x_i - x_j)^3} \tag{9.10}$$

where K is a constant. Although particle motion is subject to irregular fluctuations due to the disturbances caused by the positioning of new attractors, the finite step size of the update, and the Coulomb repulsions, a remnant of oscillatory motion remains. This motion produces swings to loudness, pitch, note duration and rhythm and are a characteristic of the system. It is expected that live algorithms, just like human improvizers, should be idiosyncratic (Blackwell and Young 2005).

9.6.2. Other Examples of Swarming in Music

This summary reviews three other examples of music systems employing swarms and flocks. These systems represent alternative approaches to swarm simulations: visualizations, sonifications and non-sonic interaction. Each system is viewed from the perspective of the PQf architecture.

Visualizations of music in terms of swarms and flocks has been explored by various workers. An early example is Rowe and Singer (1997); the behaviour of a boid animation is controlled by acoustical information supplied by musicians. The flocks do not themselves produce sounds however; in the language of PQf, the system consists of analysis module P and swarming function f.

Sonifications of swarms have also been attempted. Spector and Klein (2002) were inspired by *Swarm Music* to add musical events to their swarm and flock

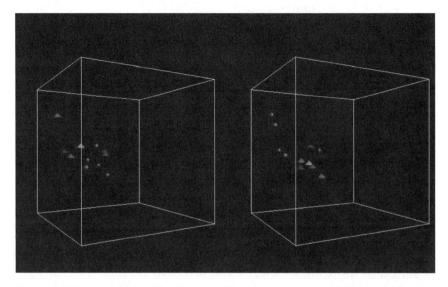

FIGURE 9.5. Improvisation with a 2-swarm. The left swarm (swarm A) has spontaneously began to move along the x_1 and x_3 axis (towards the bottom right-hand corner of H). The image of this movement in the right swarm (swarm B) can be seen in the distribution of attractors which mirror the positions of particles of swarm A. It is impossible to say if the swarm B will follow swarm A's initiative; attractors may be placed in the top right-hand corner of H_A, reflecting the positions of swarm B, and this may draw swarm A back

simulations, implemented in the BREVE simulation system. Notes are associated with certain events within the system, for example, feeding. Different instrument timbres are associated with each of the three species, and gradual musical transitions occur as each species enjoys a period of feeding. This is an example of sonification of a flock of agents, although the interpretation module Q depends on agent behaviour and not directly on flock spatial patterning. The authors report that in an extension of their system, spectrum and dynamics information from recorded music was used to alter constants in the swarm update formula although few details are given. The shift to live music would presumably be easy to make so that this system would comprise a full PQf architecture, although it is not apparent how transparent it would be.

Non-sonic interactions with swarms may proceed through physical gestures, rather than by music. Unemi and Bisig (2005) have developed an interactive boid simulation that acts as a virtual instrument. The boids move in a 3D space, with boid coordinates interpreted as pan, pitch and loudness. Users interact with the flocks by making physical movements which are captured by a camera. The user can change the instrumentation, melodic and rhythmic patterns of the flock in a process not dissimilar to conduction. The synthesis Q and f modules of this system bear much in common with *Swarm Music*, but since their P only accepts visual information, the system would not serve as a live algorithm.

9.7. Autonomy

Swarm Music has a user interface enabling direct access to many system parameters. The parameters α of the swarming function, Eq. (9.1), for example spring constants and maximum speeds along each dimension, can be controlled in real time. Interpretative parameters in Q such as the size of each axis can also be manipulated; pitch interpretation of particle position might be placed in the range MIDI 60 to 95, note onset times between $\frac{1}{120\,BPM}$ and $\frac{1}{60\,BPM}$, loudness between MIDI 64 and 127 etc. These real-time adjustments enable swarm 'conduction', a term that refers to Morris's conducted improvizations of groups and orchestras through a vocabulary of signs and gestures (Morris 2006). In a sense, conduction regards an entire orchestra as an instrument. This centralized control, of course, departs markedly from emergence through local interactions. A user may directly influence the swarm and its interpretation manually, and this has a considerable affect on the output, but the system is not operating as a live algorithm.

Swarm Music began as a four dimensional system operating solely at the note (mini) level. Live experience with the system showed that hand-tuning of f and Q often occurred during improvizations. Intervention at the interpretative stage is equivalent to adjusting phrase-level characteristics of the system. However, in the interests of autonomy, meso and macro level characteristics should be emergent rather than controlled. Luckily, a mechanism to transform (controllable) parameters into variables is suggested by the PQf architecture.

Any interpretative action can become autonomous by extending the dimensionality of the system. A P_{new} must be written that listens for the required characteristic in E (Figure 9.2). P_{new} parametrises this feature of E and maps to an attractor in H. Swarm interpretation must also be extended so that particle position components in the new dimension are correctly interpreted by Q_{new}, ideally for transparency with $Q_{new} = P_{new}^{-1}$. The first conduction controls to be automated in this way were chord number and pitch sort number, n_{chord} and n_{seq}. The conceptual mapping between the environment and the internal spaces is shown in Figure 9.6

Further live experience with the six dimensional system revealed that the particle speed control had a big impact on system performance and was frequently adjusted by the operator. The speed control is v_{max} in Eq. (9.3). Small v_{max} means small particle displacements leading to small changes in the output phrase. This sounds like a variation of a theme or an idea. At $v_{max} = 0$, the swarm is stationary and

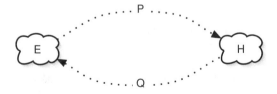

FIGURE 9.6. Interpretative functions P and Q map from the external environment, E to the internal space H of the live algorithm

the output riffs; large v_{max} increases the energy of the particles so they fly further from the attractors and the musical output is more diverse.

In a big advance towards autonomy, the speed control has recently become automated. P listens for similarity between incoming phrases, and sets the v_{max} attractor component along axis 7 according to a similarity measure. A simple matching algorithm is currently used. P hears a sequence of notes $\{\ldots, e_i, \ldots, e_j\}$, ending on the current (most recently received) note e_j. Denote an N note phrase $\{e_i, \ldots, e_j\}$, $j = i + N - 1$ by $\{i \rightarrow j\}$. The similarity $s(\{i \rightarrow j\}, \{k \rightarrow l\})$ between a sequence $\{i \rightarrow j\}$ and an earlier N note sequence $\{k \rightarrow l\}$, can be defined as

$$s(\{i \rightarrow j\}, \{k \rightarrow l\}) = \frac{1}{N} \sum_{n=0}^{N-1} c(e_{i+n}, e_{k+n}) \qquad (9.11)$$

where the correlation between notes, $c(e_i, e_j)$, can be defined to lie in the interval $[0, 1]$. A simple measure of note similarity is the absolute value of the number of steps between e_i and e_j, normalized to unity. Another measure might set $c(e_i, e_j)$ to one if $e_i = e_j$, and to zero otherwise. In order to look for the re-occurrence of an n note sequence, $n \leq N$, in the last two N note phrases (the repeated pattern may have intervening notes), it is necessary to compute $s(\{i \rightarrow j\}, \{k \rightarrow l\})$ for $k = i - 1, i - 2, \ldots, i - N$. The maximum of the N comparisons will then certainly reveal a match if there is one. This defines the overall similarity

$$s = \max_k s(\{i \rightarrow j\}, \{k \rightarrow l\}))$$

(Note that identical computations arising from earlier phrase comparisons in Eq. (9.11) do not need to be performed so the computation of s has linear complexity.)

Suppose for the sake of argument that P has heard a high similarity over the last few phrases; perhaps the human partner is playing riffs. P sets the seventh component of p to $p_7 = (1 - s) X$ where X is the linear box size, $H = [0, X]^7$. The swarm will be consequently be attracted to a region of H where particle positions x_7 are high. Q calculates a speed limit from the swarm centre of mass according to

$$v_{max} = \bar{x}_7 \frac{V}{X} \qquad (9.12)$$

where V is a maximum speed limit, and modifies Eq. (9.3) accordingly. This will ensure that particle motion is small or zero even, and the output is also riffing, or slowly evolving. The problem with this scenario is that, should $\bar{x} = 0$, the swarm becomes frozen and incapable of movement, even if later attractors have small s values! If $\bar{x}$ is finite but small, it may take the swarm a very long time to move across H towards the new attractor. The solution implemented in *Swarm Music* is to ensure that Q clamps all v_{max} components *except* the seventh (similarity) component. $v_{max\,7}$ itself remains fixed and finite, allowing movement in this dimension. Particles can now move towards p_7, shifting the swarm centre of mass, and increasing particle speed and diversity.

9.8. Outlook

What use do swarms have in music? This chapter has answered this question by arguing that

1. Theoretic descriptions of music use a hierarchy of levels n, where each level corresponds to a perceptual time-scale
2. Composing music is a centralized, top-down process: $n \rightarrow n - 1 \rightarrow n - 2$
3. Self-organization (SO) is an emergent process, observed in natural systems, producing high level structure from low level interactions: $n \rightarrow n + 1 \rightarrow n + 2$
4. By analogy with SO, the interaction of musical objects at any level might produce, without implicit composition, new structure at higher levels
5. Improvised music is a de-centralized activity exhibiting an emergence of form through the low-level interactions of performers
6. Swarms are an exemplary, paradigmatic model of SO
7. Swarms might be used in music to self-organize musical objects at any level (sound granules, notes, phrases) into structures at a higher level
8. A model of interaction based on stigmergy has led to the design and implementation of swarm music systems that can interact with people in an improvized setting *as if they were musicians*

At the heart of the *Swarm Music* family of systems is a swarming module f. The function of f is to provide an almost limitless stream of spatial patterns. Analysis modules map the external sonic environment into the internal space of the system where interaction between system state and the external image can take place. A synthesis module interprets system state as sound.

This three component architecture can be readily adapted to include other patterning algorithms by substitution for f. Natural computation provides many examples of possible patterners, for example, evolutionary algorithms and neural networks. Other examples of possible f's include chaotic and non-linear systems from the field of dynamical system, multi-agent systems from artificial intelligence and many models from artificial life.

One aim of this research effort is to develop autonomous music systems (live algorithms). A swarm inspired interactive model based on stigmergy is proposed here, although of course other approaches may also be profitable. The goal of live algorithms research is not to replace human music making with an automatic machine; rather it is to augment human experience through the development of new, algorithmic ways of playing music. The desire is to find artificial music that is different from human expression, yet comprehensible. This overarching principle of transparency should be foremost in the design of algorithmic systems. The virtue of swarm systems is that a visualisation of internal process is already in a form that is understandable to us.

It is impossible to predict how live algorithms research might proceed, but a few observations are pertinent. To start, the description of music into separate levels is an activity of classification much loved by computer scientists and music theoreticians. Human performers, whilst acknowledging this system, perhaps see granularities[1] rather than levels. Granularities do not exist in a hierarchy, but co-exist in a network of relationships. Features at any granularity may inform choices at any other granularity; no granularity is uppermost. Furthermore, performers always have the option of merging, deleting, re-configuring and even spontaneously inventing new granularities during the course of a performance. Granularity can be incorporated within the PQf architecture by remarking that state variables x in the state machine $f(x, \alpha)$ at one granularity can be mapped to parameters α of another granularity. In this way, emergence can propagate through the network. Section 9.7 outlines the general scheme.

Artificial Intelligence might also have much to offer. AI provides reasoning, a top-down activity, and learning, an activity based on memory. Advances may be made by combing a swarm-like system with a deductive mechanism that develops a degree of top-down structuring; the self organizer becomes an organizing self. The individuals in swarm systems do not possess any memory and so cannot learn. However, some type of memory is present in the system as a whole (swarm plus environment). Future swarm music systems might exploit this by including long-lived pheromone trails.

Machine consciousness is another fertile are for exploration (Holland 2003). The defining feature of a 'conscious algorithm' is the ability to self-model. An artificial improvizer, if endowed with such a facility, would be able to compare its own contributions with those of other participants. Such comparisons might involve an aesthetic function, as well as reference to past experience. The research issue is not plagued by questions of whether or not artificial improvizers are actually conscious; the idea is to see what other algorithms can be useful to the overall aim.

Potentially, a biologically inspired system might be able to negotiate the criticism that computer music cannot produce 'interesting' music without human intervention. This is due to its perceived inability to break rules (Miranda 2001, p. 206). Rules are a feature of top-down organization. A self-organizing system might produce appealing music, not so much by breaking rules, but by allowing new rules to spontaneously emerge. Swarm simulations are simple to implement and provide a complete model of self-organization. They are therefore a natural choice for exploring the potential of performing machines.

References

Allers, R. and Minkoff, R (Dirs.) (1994). The Lion King (USA).

Biles, A. (2006). In A. Biles and E. Miranda (Eds.), *Evolutionary Improvisation. Evolutionary Computer Music.*, Springer-Verlag, Berlin.

Blackwell, T.M. (2001). Making Music with Swarms. MSc thesis, University College London.

---

[1] I am grateful to Professor Mark d'Inverno for suggesting this term.

Blackwell, T.M. (2003). Swarm music: Improvised music with multi-swarms. In *Proc. the 2003 AISB Symposium on Artificial Intelligence and Creativity in Arts and Science*. pp. 41–49.

Blackwell, T. (Forthcoming). Swarm Granulation. In Machado, P. and Romero, J. (Eds.), *The Art of Artificial Evolution: A Handbook*. Springer-Verlag, Berlin.

Blackwell, T.M. and Bentley P.J. (2002). Improvised music with swarms. In *the 2002 World Congress on Evolutionary Computation*. pp. 1462–1467.

Blackwell, T.M. and Jefferies, J. (2005). Swarm techtiles. R. Rothlauf et al. (Eds.), *Evo Workshops 2005, LNCS 3449*. Springer-Verlag, Berlin. pp. 468–477.

Blackwell, T.M. and Young M.W. (2004a). Swarm Granulator. Raidl, G. R. et al. (Eds.), *EvoWorkshops 2004, LNCS 3005*. Springer-Verlag, Berlin. pp. 399–408.

Blackwell, T.M. and Young M.W. (2004b). Self-organised music. *Organised Sound 9*(2): 123–136

Blackwell, T.M. and Young M. (2005). Live algorithms. *Society for the Study of Artificial Intelligence and Simulation of Behaviour Quarterly* **122**: 7.

Bonabeau, E., Dorigo, M. and Therualaz, T. (1999). *From Natural to Artificial Swarm Intelligence*. Oxford University Press: New York.

Burton, T. (1992). (Dir.) Batman Returns USA/UK 1992.

Burton, J.L. and Franks, N.R. (1985). The foraging ecology of the army ant. *Ecol. entomol* **10**: 131–141

Coker, J. 1986. Improvising jazz. New York: Simon and Schuster

Couzin, I., Krause K., Ruxton G. and Franks N. (2002). Collective memory and spatial sorting in animal groups. *J. theor. Biol.* **218**: 1–11

Gabor, D. (1947). Acoustical quanta and the theory of hearing. *Nature* **159** (4,044): 591–4.

Grassé, P. (1959). La reconstruction du nid et les coordinations inter-individuelles chez Bellicosi-termes natalensis et Cubitermes sp. La theorie de la stigmergie: essai d'interpretation des termites constructeurs. *Insect Societies* **6**:41–83

Holland, O. (2003). *Journal of Consciousness Studies* **10**: 4–5.

Kennedy, J., Eberhart, R.C. and Shi, Y. (2001). *Swarm Intelligence*. Morgan Kaufmann, San Francisco.

Lewis, G. (2000). Too many notes: Computers, complexity and culture in voyager. *Leonardo Music Journal* **10**:33–39.

Miranda, E. (2001). *Composing Music with Computers*. Focal Press, Oxford.

Morris, L. (2006). Available online at http://www.conduction.us (accessed 18 March 2006).

Pachet, F. (2004). Beyond the cybernetic jam fantasy: *The continuator. IEEE Computers Graphics and Applications*, January/February 2004.

Piston, W. (1978). *Harmony, 5th ed.* Norton, New York.

Reynolds, C. (1987). Flocks herds and schools: A distributed behaviour model. *SIGGRAPH' 87* **21**(4):25–34.

Roads, C. (2001). *Microsound*. MIT Press, Cambridge, MA.

Rowe, R. (2004). *Machine Musicianship*. MIT Press, Cambridge, MA.

Rowe, R. and Singer, E. (1997). Two highly-related real-time music and graphics performance systems. *Proc. Int'l Computer Music Conference*, pp. 133–140.

Schaeffer, P. (1959). The interplay between music and acoustics. *Gravensaner Blatter* **14**: 61–69.

Spector, L. and Klein, J. (2002). Complex adaptive music systems in the BREVE simulation environment. In Bilotta et al. (Eds.), *Workshop Proceedings of the 8th Int'l Conf. on the Simulation and Synthesis of Living Systems*. University of New South Wales, Sydney, pp. 167–23.

Shaw, E. (1975). Fish in schools. *Natural History* **84**(8): 4046.

Sturman, P. (1983). Harmony, melody and composition. Longman, Singapore.

Turner, J. (2006). http://www.janeturner.net/current.php (accessed March 14th 2006).

Unemi, T. and Bisig, D. (2005). Playing by interaction among two flocking species and a human. In *Proceedings of the Third Int'l Conf. on Generative Systems in Electronic Arts,* Melbourne, Australia, pp. 171–179.

Wishart, T. (1996). *On Sonic Art* (revised ed.). Harwood, Amsterdam. Academic.

Xenakis, I. (1989). Concerning time. *Perspectives of New Music* **27**(1): 84–92.

10
Computational Evolutionary Musicology

EDUARDO R. MIRANDA AND PETER M. TODD

10.1. Introduction

The beginning of Chapter 2 offered a sensible definition of music as *temporally organized sound*. In the broader sense of this definition, one could arguably state that music is not uniquely human. A number of other animals also seem to have music of some sort. Complex vocalizations can be found in many birds (Marler and Slabbekoorn 2004), as well as in mammals such as whales (Payne and McVay 1971) and bats (Behr and von Helversen 2004). In a chapter suggestively entitled 'Zoomusicologie' in the book *Musique, Mythe, Nature ou Les Dauphins d'Arion*, Mâche (1991) presents an interesting discussion on the formal sophistication of various birdcalls. Recently Holy and Guo (2005) demonstrated that the ultrasonic vocalizations that male mice produce when they encounter female mice or their pheromones have the characteristics of song. What is intriguing is that primates who are close related to humans are not as 'musical' as those mammals that are far more distantly related to us. This intriguing fact suggests that music might have evolved independently among various types of animals, at various degrees of sophistication. In this context, it would be perfectly plausible to suggest the notion that robots might also be able to evolve music.

In order to build systems for the emergence of music one needs to establish the factors that may shape the course of musical evolution, such as physiological and cognitive factors, including models of interaction.

The physiological factors comprise the sensors and actuators of interacting individuals. These involve models of the hearing system, body, limbs and so on. It may also involve models of the sensory-motor cortex and associated neural mechanisms involved in sensory-motor tasks. A discussion on the expertise for building these models is beyond the scope of this chapter; it includes fields such as Biomechanics (Zinkovsky, Sholuha and Ivanov 1996) and Biophysics (Glaser 2001). Readers are invited to consult the literature in these fields.

As for the cognitive factors, the brain certainly uses different mental modules to process music and these modules have varying degrees of independence from each other. Parsons (2003) has conducted a number of brain-imaging experiments, which indicate that the neural system for processing music is widely distributed throughout our brain. This finding is confirmed by studies of patients with brain lesions (Peretz et al. 1994). Peretz and Coltheart (2003) proposed a functional architecture of the brain for music processing that captures the typical properties of such distributed modular organization. Basically, they have identified two main processing modules: One concerned with processing pitch and the other with rhythm. Both modules process incoming musical signals backed by a musical lexicon; a kind of memory bank of musical segments. Surely, this basic architecture can be refined into smaller and perhaps more specialized components, depending on the level of detail at which one wishes to study its functionality. This is likely to become increasingly complex as research in the emerging field of Cognitive Neuroscience of Music progresses. What is important, however, is that this modularity of the brain for music processing suggests a plausible methodology for building computational models of music processing. By focusing on relatively simpler cognitive tasks, one can adopt a bottom up approach to tackle the problem of modelling cognitive factors. In most cases it may be more effective to address the individual pieces of the jigsaw first, rather than the whole picture at once.

Following the development of fields such as Artificial Life (Levy 1993) and Memetics (Brodie 1996), we propose a computational modelling approach to Evolutionary Musicology: *Computational Evolutionary Musicology*. Evolutionary Musicology is the branch of Biomusicology (Wallin 1991) that studies the origins and evolution of music (Wallin, Merker and Brown 2000). For example, it studies the question of animal song and selection pressures underlying the evolution of music in humans and possibly in other species.

In gross terms, whereas Artificial Life attempts to understand evolutionary processes via the computer simulation of life forms Memetics studies the replication, spread and evolution of information patterns called memes. A fundamental notion of Memetics is that cultural evolution can be modelled through the same basic principles of variation and selection that underly biological evolution. This implies a shift from genes as units of biological information to a new type of units of cultural information, which are the *memes*. Computational Evolutionary Musicology therefore involves the use of computer modelling and simulations to study the circumstances and mechanisms whereby music systems might originate and evolve in artificially created worlds inhabited by communities of interacting autonomous agents (e.g. software agents or robots).

Scholars throughout the ages have attempted to trace the origins of music. The book *Music and the Origins of Language*, by Thomas (1995) presents a review of the theories purported by philosophers of the French Enlightenment. For example, in his *Essai sur l'origine des langues* (*Essay on the origins of language*) the philosopher Rousseau (1990) described the earliest spoken languages as being composed of vocal inflexions such as warnings, cries for help and hunting-related shouts. In the beginning, he proposed, gestures were preferred to communicate rational ideas, whereas vocal utterances were primarily used to express feelings and passions. As human society grew in complexity, these vocal utterances needed to become more precise and less passionate. And as language followed the path of logical argumentation, the intonation of these primordial utterances evolved into music. Music, according to Rousseau, thus evolved from the sounds of passionate speech.

More recently, *The Singing Neanderthals: The Origins of Music, Language, Mind and Body*, by Mithen (2005), discusses this subject from an evolutionary perspective supported by archaeological evidence. Also, *The Origins of Music*, edited by Wallin and colleagues (Wallin, Merker and Brown 2000), collates a series of chapters expressing a diversity of theories and viewpoints.

Computational Evolutionary Musicology is in many ways akin to the computational modelling approach of Evolutionary Linguistics to study of the origins and evolution of language (Cangelosi and Parisi 2001; Christiansen and Kirby 2003), but its goals are more pragmatic, in the sense that they can readily inform the development of new technologies for music making. For instance, a better understanding of basic mechanisms of musical origins and evolution is of great importance for musicians looking for hitherto unexplored ways to create new music works with computers. Broadly speaking, current techniques for implementing generative music systems can be classified as *abstract algorithmic* or *music knowledge-based*. Abstract algorithmic techniques are suitable for generating music from the behaviour of algorithms that were not necessarily designed for music in the first instance, but embody pattern generation features that are suitable for producing musical materials. Such algorithms include fractals (Milicevic 1996) and chaotic systems (Bidlack 1992) to cite but two examples. Music knowledge-based techniques generate music using algorithms derived from or inspired by well-established music theory. Most of these systems can learn compositional procedures from given examples, adopting either a symbolic approach (Steedman 1984; Cope 1996; Papadopoulos and Wiggins 1998) or a connectionist (neural networks) approach (Todd and Loy 1991; Mozer 1994), depending on the way they store information about music. Hybrid systems also exist (Burton and Vladimirova 1997).

Both classes of techniques have their merits and pitfalls. Abstract algorithmic techniques tend to produce rather complex music, most of which may sound too remote from what the majority of people, including expert listeners, would consider musical. This is possibly so because abstract algorithmic music tends to lack the cultural references that people normally rely upon when listening to music. Conversely, knowledge-based techniques tend to produce pastiches of existing musical pieces, which often are of little interest for composers aiming to create new music; that is, music that is not based on mimicking existing pieces or well-known musical styles. Computational Evolutionary Musicology brings the merits of both approaches closer to each other by offering the possibility of evolving new musical systems informed by the same principles that might have helped to shape existing musical styles. Inspired by Casti's (1997) use of the term 'would-be worlds', Artificial Life's goal of looking at 'life as it could be,' we refer to these emerging new musical systems as 'would-be music' or 'music as it could be'.

In this chapter, we explore some examples of Computational Evolutionary Musicology that employ a range of Artificial Life-inspired computational approaches. We begin by describing a model for studying the role of mating-selective pressure in the evolution of musical taste. Next, we introduce a mimetic model for studying the evolution of musical lexicons in a community of autonomous robots furnished with a vocal synthesizer, a hearing apparatus and a memory device. Finally, we present the application of neural networks to evolving simple generative sequencing rules in a community of rhythm players and imitators.

10.2. Mating Selective Pressure and Surprise

Todd and Werner (1999) proposed a model for studying the role of sexual selection, specifically the selective pressure that comes from the processes of choosing mates, in the evolution of music. The model employs mating selective pressure to foster the evolution of fit composers of courting tunes. The model co-evolves 'male' composers who play simple musical tunes along with 'female' critics who judge these tunes and decide with whom to mate in order to produce the next generation of composers and critics.

Todd and Werner's model is largely inspired by Charles Darwin's theory of sexual selection as outlined in the book *The Descent of Man and Selection in Relation to Sex*, where he argued that male birdsong had evolved via a mechanism of female choice (Darwin 1992). Miller (2000) attempted to take this notion even further by arguing that the evolution of human music was shaped by sexual selection to function as a courtship display.

Each male composer holds a tune of 32 musical pitches from a set of 24 different pitches spanning two octaves. The female critics encode a transition-table that rates the transitions from one note to another in a heard tune. The table is a 24-by-24 matrix, where each entry represents the female's expectation of the probability of one pitch following another in a song. Given these expectations, a critic can decide how well she likes a particular tune. When she listens to a composer, she considers the transition from the previous pitch to the current pitch for each note of the tune, gives each transition a score based on her transition table and adds those scores to come up with her final evaluation of the tune. Each critic listens to the tunes of a certain number of composers who are randomly selected; all critics hear the same number of composers. After listening to all the composers in her courting-choir, the critic selects as her mate the composer who produces the tune to which she gives the highest score. In this selective process, all critics will have exactly one mate, but a composer may have a range of mates from none to many, depending on whether his tune is unpopular with everyone or if he has a song that is universally liked by the critics. Each critic has one child per generation created via crossover and mutation with her chosen mate. This child will have a mix of the musical traits and preferences encoded in its mother and father. The sex of the child is randomly determined and a third of the population is removed at random after a mating session in order not to reach a population overflow.

From the many different scoring methods proposed to judge the tunes, the one that seems to produce the most interesting results is the method whereby critics enjoy being surprised. Here the critic listens to each transition in the tune individually, computes how much she expected the transition and subtracts this value from the probability that she attached to the transition she most expected to hear. For example, if a critic has a value 0.8 stored in her transition table for the A–E transition, whenever she hears a note A in a tune, she would expect a note E to follow it 80% of the time. If she hears an A–C transition, then this transition will be taken as a surprise because it violates the A–E expectation. A score is calculated for all the transitions in the tune (e.g. the expected probability of the heard A–C transition, which might be 0.1, is subtracted from the expected A–E transition probability of 0.8 to yield a surprise rating of 0.7) and the final sum registers how much surprise the critic experienced; that is, how much she likes the tune. What is interesting here is that this does not result in the composers generating random tunes all over the place. It turns out that in order to get a high surprise score, a tune must first build up expectations, by making transitions to notes that have highly anticipated notes following them and then violate these expectations, by not using the highly anticipated note. Thus there is constant tension between doing what is expected and what is unexpected in each tune, but only highly surprising tunes are rewarded.

Overall, this model has shown that the selection of co-evolving male composers who generate surprising tunes and female critics who assess these tunes according to their preferences, can lead to the evolution of structured melodies and the maintenance and continual turnover of tune diversity over time.

In addition to mating selective pressure, this model embodies an important cognitive trait for survival: The ability to identify an unexpected element in a sequence of sound events. The preference for surprising tunes reflects this ability, which is very sophisticated in humans, even to the extent that our brain does not require our attention to perform this task. Neuroscientists have reported a component of the auditory event-relation potential (ERP), called mismatch negativity (MMN), which is elicited by a deviant stimulus in a repetitive auditory event, even in the absence of attention. ERP is a stereotyped electrophysiological response to a stimulus detected with the electroencephalogram (EEG). MMN is normally detected between 100 and 200 ms after the odd stimulus is heard. Näätänen and colleagues (2001) suggested that different sounds develop their representation in the neurophysiological substrate of the auditory memory and the MMN indicates an attention-independent change detection mechanism.

In Todd and Werner's model, the composers are initiated with random tunes and the critics with transition tables set with probabilities calculated from given folk-tune melodies. There is, however, a puzzling fundamental question that has not been addressed in this model: Where could the expectations of the female critics come from if they are not to be built in by hand? Would it be possible to evolve such expectations from scratch? A model that may provide support for addressing this question is introduced next.

10.3. Social Bonding and Imitation: Evolution of Intonation

Miranda (2002b) proposed a mimetic model where a small community of interactive robots programmed with appropriate motor, auditory and cognitive skills can evolve a shared lexicon of sonic intonation patterns from scratch, after a period of spontaneous creation, adjustment and memory reinforcement. In this case, expectation is defined as a sensory-motor mechanism whereby the robots evolve vectors of motor control parameters to produce imitations of heard intonation patterns. The robots thus expect to hear pitch sequences that correspond to their evolved motor vectors.

Intonation is generally defined as the melody of speech; it is characterized by the variations in the pitch of a speaker's voice. The rationale for attempting to model the evolution of intonation patterns comes from the fact that intonation is fundamental for the development of vocal communication. There have been a number of research reports giving evidence that babies are born with an acute sensitivity to intonation (Locke 1993; Nazzi et al. 1998). This ability probably evolved due to the need for enhanced mother-infant interactions. Baby talk or infant-directed-speech, sounds like music due its exaggerated intonation, which helps babies and very young children to develop their linguistic ability. Mothers use baby talk to influence the behaviour and elicit emotions in pre-linguistic infants. Ultimately, those mothers whose intonation abilities made them more able to provide infant care and those infants who were receptive to such care, have gained a reproductive advantage.

Following this idea, Miranda's robots are programmed with two fundamental instincts:

a) To imitate what they hear
b) To foster social bonding

Imitation is defined here as the task of hearing an intonation pattern and activating the motor system to reproduce it. Sociability is assessed in terms of the similarity of the robots' repertoires. In other words, in order to be sociable a robot must form a repertoire that is similar to the repertoire of its peers. The intonations thus create a social identity for the robots.

The importance of imitation for evolution has gained much attention after the discovery of mirror neurons in the frontal lobes of macaque monkeys. Mirror neurons are neurons which fire both when an animal performs an action and when the animal observes the same action performed by another animal, especially of the same species. Thus, the neurons mirror the behaviour of another animal, as though the observers were themselves performing the action. These neurons have subsequently been observed in some birds and in other primates including humans (Rizzolatti and Craighero 2004). The mirror system is sometimes considered to represent a primitive version of a simulation heuristic that might underlie a theory of mind (Gallese and Goldman 1998); the notion of theory of mind will re-appear in our discussion later. Interestingly, while mirror neurons are present in macaque monkeys, these monkeys have not been observed to imitate each other's behaviour. It is questionable whether mirror neurons evolved for learning by imitation. Instead, their function might rather be to allow an individual to understand what another individual is doing or to recognize the other individual's action.

The rationale for programming the robots with a drive for social bonding is supported by research by neurobiologists such as Freeman (1995), who brings his knowledge of brain chemistry to support the notion that music plays an important role in social bonding. According to Freeman, the brain releases oxytocin in the basal forebrain during group music making and dancing. The theory goes that by loosening synaptic links associated with prior knowledge, this hormone clears the path for the acquisition of new knowledge by sharing and imitating behaviour in a group.

Mithen (2005) also supports the notion that joint music making forges a group identity with high emotional content. 'Hominids would have frequently and meticulously examined the likely intentions, beliefs, desires and feelings of other members of a group before deciding whether to cooperate with them. But on other occasions simply trusting them would have been more effective, especially if quick decisions were necessary.' Those individuals who suppressed their own self-identity and instead forged a group identity by joint music making had better chances to thrive than those individuals who tended to act selfishly.

10.3.1. The Robots

The robots are equipped with a voice synthesizer, a hearing apparatus and a memory device. The model was initially implemented with software agents and the original interaction algorithms were largely inspired by the work of Luc Steels (1997) on evolutionary language games. Drouet subsequently helped to implement the robotic version described below, with refinements to the interaction algorithms (Fig. 10.1) (Miranda and Drouet 2006).

The voice synthesizer is essentially implemented as a physical model of the human vocal mechanism (Boersma 1993; Miranda 2002a). The robots need to compute three vectors of parameters in order to produce intonations: Lung pressure, the width of the glottis and the length and tension of the vocal chords, represented here as $lung\_pressure(n)$, $interarytenoid(n)$ and $cricothyroid(n)$, respectively. As for the hearing apparatus, it employs short-term autocorrelation-based analysis to extract the pitch contour of a vocal sound (Miranda 2001). The algorithm features a parameter that defines the sensitivity of the auditory perception of the robots. In essence, this parameter regulates the resolution of the hearing apparatus by controlling the precision of the short-term autocorrelation analysis.

Essentially, a robot's memory stores its repertoire of intonations, but it also stores other information such as probabilities, thresholds and reinforcement parameters. They have two distinct modules to store intonations in their memories: A motor map and a perceptual map. The motor map stores information in terms of three vectors of motor (vocal) parameters and the perceptual map stores information in terms of pitch contour.

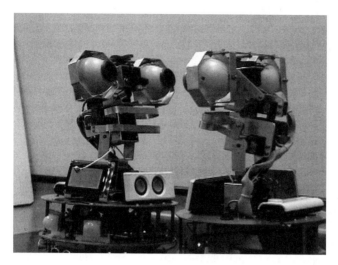

FIGURE 10.1. The robotic implementation uses DRK8000 robots, manufactured by Dr. Robot®.

An intonation is represented as a graph whose vertices stand for initial (or relative) pitch points and pitch movements and the edges represent a directional path. Whilst the first vertex must have one outbound edge, the last one must have only one incoming edge. All vertices in between must have one incoming and one outbound edge each. Vertices can be of two types, initial pitch points (referred to as *p-ini*) and pitch movements (referred to as *p-mov*) as follows (Fig. 10.2):

$p\text{-}ini = \{\text{SM, SL, SH}\}$

$p\text{-}mov = \{\text{VLSU, LSU, MSU, SSU, RSB, SSD, MSD, LSD, VLSD}\}$

where:

SM = start the intonation in the middle register
SL = start the intonation in the lower register
SH = start the intonation in the higher register

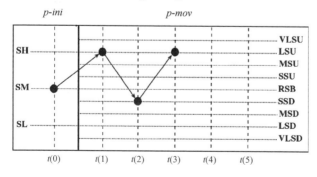

FIGURE 10.2. The representation of an intonation, where $t(n)$ indicates an ordered sequence of n pitches.

and

VLSU = very large step up
LSU = large step up
MSU = medium step up
SSU = small step up
RSB = remain at the same band
SSD = small step down
MSD = medium step down
LSD = large step down
VLSD = very large step down

An intonation will invariably start with a *p-ini*, followed by one or more *p-movs*. It is assumed that an intonation can start at three different voice registers: Low (SL), middle (SM) and high (SH). Then, from this initial point $\{t(n), n = 0\}$ the next pitch at $t(n + 1)$ might jump or step up or down and so forth.

It is important to note that labels or absolute pitch values are not relevant here because this scheme is intended to represent abstract melodic contours rather than a sequence of musical notes drawn from a specific tuning system. The tuning should emerge during the interactions.

10.3.2. The Algorithms

The main algorithms for the robotic interactions are given as follows:

Algorithm 1: Robot-player produces an intonation
1. Motor_control[α] $\Leftarrow$ pick-any-motor-control in **Motor-Repertoire**(robot-player)
2. synthesize-sound(motor_control[α])

Algorithm 2: Robot-imitator produces an imitation
3. Pitch_vector[β] $\Leftarrow$ perceive-intonation
4. Intonation[β] $\Leftarrow$ perceptual-representation(pitch_vector[β])
5. Intonation[Δ] $\Leftarrow$ search-similar(intonation[β]) in **Perceptual-Repertoire** (robot-imitator)
6. Motor_control[Δ] $\Leftarrow$ retrieve_motor_control(motor-control[intonation[Δ]])
7. synthesize-sound(motor_control[Δ])

Algorithm 3: Robot-player hears the imitation and gives a feedback
8. Pitch_vector[ψ] $\Leftarrow$ perceive-imitation
9. Imitation[ψ] $\Leftarrow$ perceptual-representation(picth_vector[ψ])
10. Intonation[ϕ] $\Leftarrow$ search-similar(imitation[ψ]) in **Perceptual-Repertoire** (robot-imitator)
11. Intonation[α] = perceptual-representation(motor_control[α])
12. IF intonation[α] = intonation[ϕ]
13.   THEN { feeback $\Leftarrow$ *positive*
14.   reinforce(motor_control[α]) in **Motor-Repertoire**(robot-player)
15.   reinforce(intonation[α]) in **Perceptual-Repertoire**(robot-player)}
16.   ELSE { feeback $\Leftarrow$ *negative* }
17. output-signal(feedback)

Algorithm 4: Robot-imitator reacts to robot-player's feedback
18. IF feedback = *positive*
19.   THEN { approximate(intonation[Δ] → intonation[β])
                 in **Perceptual-Repertoire**(robot-imitator)
20.   reconfigure_motor_control(intonation[Δ])
                 in **Motor-Repertoire**(robot-imitator)
21.   reinforce intonation[Δ] in **Perceptual-Repertoire**(robot-imitator)
22.   reinforce motor_control(Δ) in **Motor-Repertoire**(robot-imitator) }
23.   ELSE IF feedback = *negative*
24.   THEN IF success-history(intonation[Δ]) > success-threshold
25.   THEN { motor_control[λ] ⟸ produce-new-motor-control
26.   Intonation[λ] ⟸ perceptual-representation
                              (motor_control[λ])
27.   save-new(intonation[λ])
                              to **Motor-Repertoire**(robot-imitator)
28.   save-new(motor_control[λ])
                              to **Perceptual-Repertoire**(robot-imitator) }
29.   ELSE { distantiate(intonation[Δ] ↔ intonation[β])
                              in **Perceptual-Repertoire**(robot-imitator)
30.   reconfigure_motor_control(intonation[Δ])
                              in **Motor-Repertoire**(robot-imitator) }

Algorithm 5: End of interaction updates
31. interaction-updates(robot-player)
32. interaction-updates(robot-imitator)

Figs. 10.3, 10.4 and 10.5 give a glimpse at the functioning of these algorithms. For didactic purposes, these are reduced two-dimensional representations of the motor and perceptual repertoires; the co-ordinates do not fully correspond to the actual motor and perceptual representations. The numbers in the figures indicate actions corresponding to the line numbers of the algorithms.

All robots have identical synthesis and listening apparatuses. At each round, each of the robots in a pair plays one of two different roles: The *robot-player* and the *robot-imitator*. The robot-player starts the interaction by producing an intonation α, randomly chosen from its repertoire. The robot-imitator then analyses the intonation α, searches for a similar intonation Δ in its repertoire and produces it. The robot-player in turn hears and analyses the intonation Δ and checks if its perceptual repertoire holds no other intonation φ that is more perceptibly close to Δ than α is. If it finds another intonation φ that is closer to Δ than α is, then the imitation is unsatisfactory, otherwise it is satisfactory. Fig. 10.3 shows an example where the robot-player and the robot-imitator hold in their memories two intonations each. The robot-player picks the intonation α from its motor-repertoire and produces it (1). The robot-imitator hears the intonation α and builds a perceptual representation β of it (4). Then it picks from its own perceptual repertoire the intonation Δ that is most perceptually similar to the heard intonation β (5) and produces it as an imitation (6). Next, the robot-player hears the imitation Δ and builds a perceptual representation ψ of it (9). Then it picks from its own perceptual

Robot-player

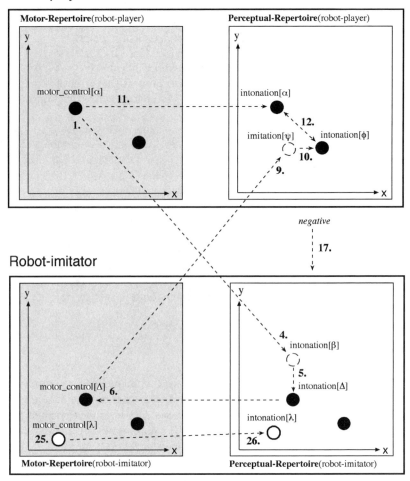

FIGURE 10.3. Example of an unsuccessful imitation.

repertoire the intonation ϕ that is most perceptually similar to the imitation ψ (10). The robot-player babbles the original intonation α to itself (11) and it concludes that α and ϕ are different (12). In this case the robot-player sends a negative feedback to the robot-imitator (17), indicating that the imitation is unsatisfactory.

When an imitation is unsatisfactory the robot-imitator has to choose between two potential courses of action. If it finds out that Δ is a weak intonation in its memory (because it has not received enough reinforcement in the past) then it will move it away from α slightly, as a measure to avoid repeating this mistake again. But if Δ is a strong intonation (due to a good past success rate), then the robot will leave Δ untouched (because it has been successfully used in previous imitations and a

Robot-imitator

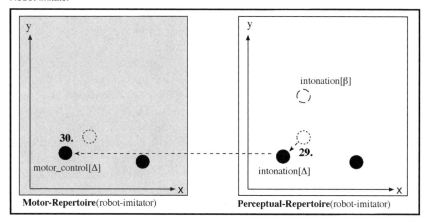

FIGURE 10.4. An example where the unsuccessful imitation involved an intonation that has a poor past success rate.

few other robots in the community also probably consider this intonation as being strong) and will create a new intonation λ similar to Δ to include it in its repertoire; that is, the robot produces a number of random imitations and then it picks the one that is perceptually most similar to Δ. Let us assume that the intonation Δ in Fig. 10.3 has a good past success rate. In this case, the robot-imitator leaves it untouched and creates a new intonation λ to include in its repertoire (25, 26).

Fig. 10.4 shows what would have happened if the intonation Δ did not have a good past success rate: In this case the robot-imitator would have moved Δ away from β slightly (29 and 30). Finally, Fig. 10.5 shows what would have happened

Robot-imitator

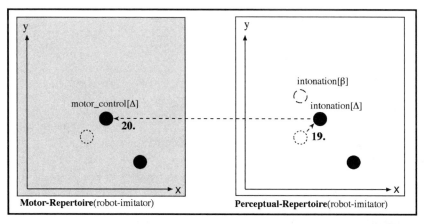

FIGURE 10.5. An example of a successful imitation.

if the robot-player had concluded that α and ϕ were the same, meaning that the imitation was successful. In this case, the robot-imitator would have reinforced the existence of the intonation Δ in its memory and would have moved it slightly towards the representation of the heard intonation β.

Before terminating the round, both robots perform final updates. Firstly they scan their repertoire and merge those intonations that are considered to be perceptibly close to each other; the merge function removes two intonations and creates a new one by averaging their values. Also, at the end of each round, both robots have a certain probability P_b of undertaking a spring-cleaning to get rid of weak intonations; those intonations that have not been sufficiently reinforced are forgotten. Finally, at the end of each round, the robot-imitator has a certain probability P_a of adding a new randomly created intonation to its repertoire; we refer to this coefficient as the 'creativity coefficient'.

10.3.3. A Typical Simulation Example

The graph in Fig. 10.6 shows a typical example of the evolution of the average repertoire of a group of five interacting robots, with snapshots taken after every 100 interactions over a total of 5000 interactions. The robots evolved repertoires averaging 12 intonations each. (Note that some may have developed more or less than 12 intonations.) After a drastic increase of the repertoire at about 800 interactions, the robots settled to an average of seven intonations each until about 2200 interactions, when another slight increase took place. Then they settled to an

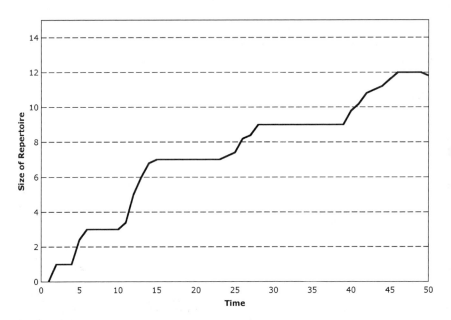

FIGURE 10.6. The evolution of the average size of the repertoire of intonations of the whole group of robots. In this case the group developed an average repertoire of 12 intonations.

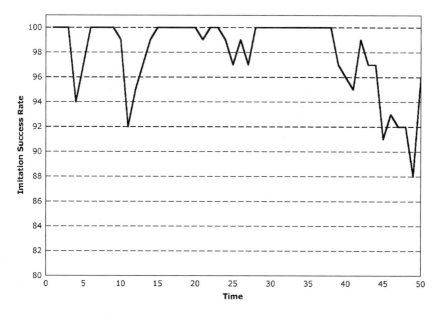

FIGURE 10.7. The imitation success rate over time.

average of nine intonations until about 3800 interactions. From 3800 interactions onwards the robots steadily increased their repertoires. The pressure to increase the repertoire is mostly due to the probability P_a of creating a new random intonation, combined with the rate of new inclusions due to unsatisfactory imitations. The size of the repertoire tends to stabilize with time because the more the robots use strongly settled intonations, the more these intonations are reinforced in their repertoires and therefore the more difficult for new intonations to settle in.

The graph in Fig. 10.7 plots the imitation success rate of the community, measured at every 100 interactions. Note the decrease of imitation success rate during those phases when the robots were increasing the size of their repertoires. Although the repertoire size tends to increase with time, the success rate tends to stay consistently high. However, this is highly dependent upon the number of robots in the group. The higher the number of robots, the deeper the fall of the success rate and the longer it takes to re-gain the 100% success rate stability.

Fig. 10.8(a) portrays the perceptual memory of a robot randomly selected from the group after 5000 interactions. In this case the length of the intonations varied from three to six pitches. (The minimum and maximum length of the intonation to be evolved is fixed beforehand.) This particular robot evolved 11 intonations; one below the average. Fig. 10.8(b) shows only those intonations that are three pitches long.

An interesting feature of this model is that the lexicon of intonations emerged from the interactions of the robots. The actions of each robot are based solely upon their own evolving expectations. Also, the robots do not necessarily have to evolve the same motor representations for what is considered to be perceptibly identical.

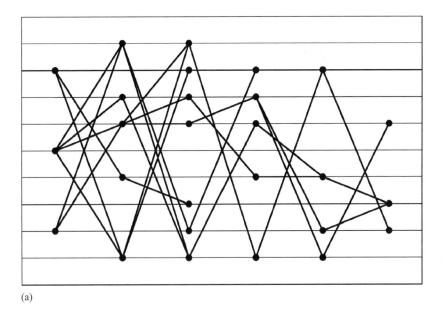

(a)

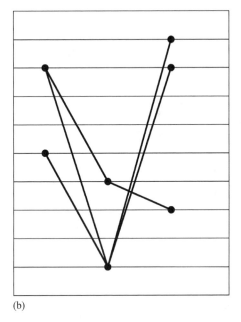

(b)

FIGURE 10.8. (a) The perceptual memory of one robot. (b) Only those intonations that are three pitches long. For the sake of clarity, the background metrics and labels of the graphs are not shown.

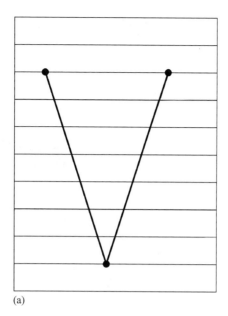

(a)

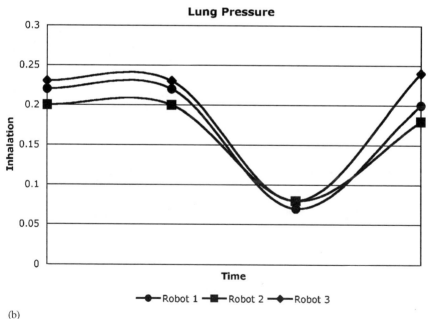

(b)

FIGURE 10.9. (a) One of the perceptual patterns from Fig. 10.8(b) and its corresponding motor control vectors developed by three different robots, (b) the *lung_pressure* vector, (c) the *cricothyroid* vector and (d) the *interarytenoid* vector.

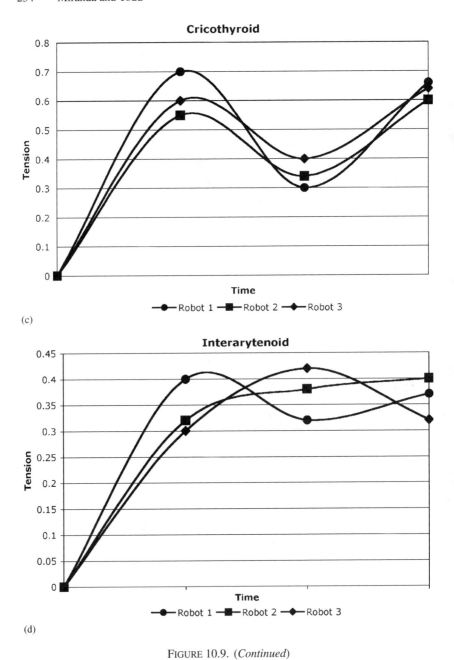

(c)

(d)

FIGURE 10.9. (*Continued*)

Fig. 10.9 shows the motor functions evolved by three different robots to represent what is essentially the same intonation.

The imitation of an intonation pattern requires the activation of the right motor parameters in order to reproduce it. The robot-imitators assume that they always can recognize everything they hear because in order to produce an imitation a robot will use the motor vectors that best match its perception of the sound in question. It is the robot-player who will assess the imitation based on its own expectations. Expectation here is a social convention but it is grounded on the nature of their sensory-motor apparatus. This mechanism provides a robot with the rudiments of the ability to appreciate the knowledge of another robot from its own perspective. Intuitively, this ability might relate to what is referred to as theory of mind. The notion of theory of mind is central to social life: The ability to understand that others have beliefs, desires and intentions that are different from one's own. The theory of mind probably emerged from the challenge of surviving in a complex social environment, in which decisions about cooperation were of vital importance. It is possible that possessing a theory of mind gave early hominids an evolutionary advantage over its ancestors, which was the ability to predict the behaviour of others and hence attain greater cooperation.

Both models discussed in this chapter so far deal with short intonations. But how about dealing with longer pitch sequences or proper musical compositions? Although the symbolic sensory-motor-like memory mechanism proposed for storing intonations served well the objectives of the model presented above, we must admit that it is not efficient for storing longer pitch sequences, let alone fully fledged pieces of music. In order to increase the complexity of the model, it is necessary to improve the memory mechanism, which would probably be more efficient by storing information about generating the sequences rather than the sequences themselves. Martins and Miranda (2006) are currently developing a connectionist approach to address this problem. Connectionism is an approach to modelling systems resembling biological neural networks whereby neurons are represented by nodes and connections between neurons are represented by links. The definition of the nature of the nodes and links determines the ability of the neural network to execute certain operations in a way that reproduces observed behaviours of the simulated biological system (Salu 2001).

10.4. Toward a Connectionist Memory for Evolving Sequencing Rules

João Martins developed a tentative connectionist memory for the aforementioned interacting robots consisting of two neural-network modules: A perceptual module and a categorization module. The former implements a Sardnet (for self-organizing activation, retention and decay network) neural network and the latter uses a feedforward neural network.

The input for the perceptual module is a sequence of sounds, which produces a pattern of activations on the Sardnet, representing the types of sounds and their position in the sequence. The pattern of activations then becomes the input for the categorization module, which, as its name suggests, categorizes this information.

Each sound in the sequence presented to the Sardnet is represented as a vector of three variables. The first variable indicates its timbre, the second its loudness and the third the inter-onset interval (IOI) in milliseconds; pitch is not taken into account here. An inter-onset interval is the time between the beginnings or attack-points of successive sounds, not including their durations. For example, two 16th notes separated by a dotted eighth rest would have the same inter-onset interval as between a quarter note and a 16th note. As we are not so concerned with a detailed representation of timbre at this stage of the research, the value of the first variable is merely a label identifying the percussion instrument that played the sound; e.g. 1 = snare drum, 2 = bass drum, 3 = tom-tom, etc.

10.4.1. The Perceptual Module

The Sardnet is a self-organizing neural network for the classification of sequences (James and Miikkulainen 1995). The Sardnet is an extension of the self-organizing map (Som), which is a neural network used for unsupervised learning developed by Kohonen (1997). Fig. 10.10 shows a Som with 16 output nodes and one input vector $\mathbf{V}_t$, where t is the index of the sound event in the sequence. The dimension of $\mathbf{V}_t$ determines the dimension of the weights vector $\mathbf{W}_{jk}$ for each node. The Euclidean distance measure d_2 determines the distance from the input vector $\mathbf{V}_t$ to the weight vector $\mathbf{W}_{jk}$:

$$d_2(\mathbf{V}_t, \mathbf{W}_{jk}) = \sqrt{\sum_{i=1}^{n} \left| v_{t,i} - w_{jk,i} \right|^2}$$

where $\mathbf{V}_t$ is the input vector, with index t in the sequence, $\mathbf{W}_{jk}$ is the weight vector of the corresponding node jk and n is the dimension of both $\mathbf{V}_t$ and $\mathbf{W}_{jk}$.

The Som (Fig. 10.10) is also referred to as a competitive network or 'winner-takes-all net', because only the node whose weight vector is the closest to the input vector wins the activation. The weight vector of the winning node is subsequently updated in order to render its values even closer to the values of the input vector. The neighbouring nodes of the winning node are also similarly updated to a lesser degree according to a neighbourhood function that organizes representations of similar stimuli on the network topographically.

The Sardnet carries forward most of the essential features of the Som, but adds two important features, which enables it to deal with sequences of events:

a) The neuron that wins the competition for being closest to the input at one point in time is removed from subsequent competitions
b) All previous neuron activations decay at each time step

The dynamics of the Sardnet is illustrated in Fig. 10.11. Here a stream of events t at the input activated three nodes sequentially: $\mathbf{W}_{4,2}$, $\mathbf{W}_{2,3}$ and $\mathbf{W}_{1,2}$, respectively. The training algorithm for the Sardnet is as follows:

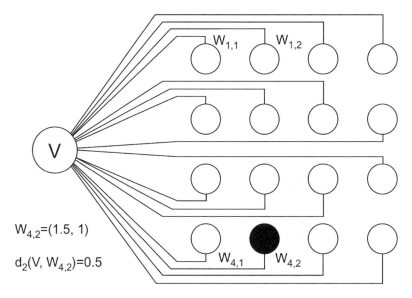

FIGURE 10.10. Kohonen's self-organizing map (Som). $\mathbf{V}_t$ is the input vector and the $\mathbf{W}_{j,k}$ are the weight vectors, which define the distance d_2 between the input vector and the various nodes of the network. In this example, the winner is node $\mathbf{W}_{4,2}$ with $d_2 = 0.5$.

INITIALIZATION:
  Reset the network
MAIN LOOP:
  While not end of sequence do:

1. Find inactive neuron that best matches the input
2. Assign activation $= 1.0$ to the found unit
3. Adjust weight vectors of the neurons in the neighbourhood
4. Exclude the winning neuron from subsequent competitions
5. Decrement the activation values for all other active neurons

RESULT:
  Activated nodes ordered by activation values.

As with the Som network, the Sardnet uses the same distance $d_2(\mathbf{V}_t,\mathbf{W}_{jk})$ to estimate which node's weight vector best matches the input vector. In step 3 of the main loop of the training algorithm shown above, the weights of the winning neuron and of the neighbourhood neurons are changed according to the following adaptation rule:

$$\Delta w_{jk} = \alpha(w_{jk,i} - v_i)$$

where j and k are the spatial coordinates of the network, i is the index of the

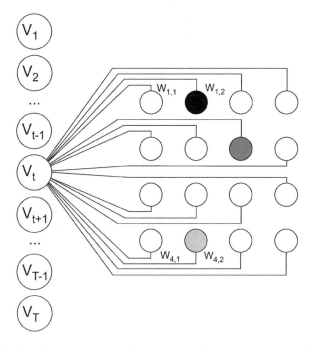

FIGURE 10.11. The Sardnet, with variable activation of three nodes sequentially, indicated by different colours: from black (node $\mathbf{W}_{1,2}$, the last in the sequence) to light grey (node $\mathbf{W}_{4,2}$, the first in the sequence).

individual components of the vectors and α denotes the learning rate of the Sardnet.

All active neurons are decayed proportionally to the decay parameter d as follows (step 5 of the main loop):

$$\eta_{jk}(t+1) = d\eta_{jk}(t), \qquad 0 < d < 1$$

where η is the value for the activation of the network in the element (j, k).

10.4.2. Categorization Module

The categorization module is a feedforward neural network (also called Multi-layer Perceptron) for learning patterns of activity with layers of nodes interconnected in a feed-forward way. Each input node is fully connected to the middle layer (referred to as the hidden layer) of nodes and each node of the hidden layer is subsequently connected to every output node (Fig. 10.12). The outputs of the network are explicit functions of activations in the hidden layer, which are themselves functions of the input nodes.

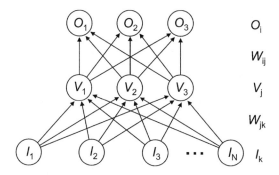

FIGURE 10.12. A generic feedforward neural network. I_n are the input nodes, V_n are the hidden nodes and O_n the output nodes. W_{jk} corresponds to the strengths (or weights) of the connections between the nodes j and k.

The network uses the backpropagation algorithm to adjust its weights in order to best match the values of the input nodes to a desired set of values at the output nodes.

The number of inputs to the categorization network must be the same as the number of units in the Sardnet, because each Sardnet unit becomes an input to the feedforward network. The number of output neurons is arbitrarily set to three because it facilitates the visualization of the resulting categorization in a tri-dimensional plotting.

10.4.3. Assessing the Behaviour of the Networks

As an example, let us consider an agent with a Sardnet of 50 nodes (10×5) with a learning rate $\alpha = 0.1$. The network is initialized with random values for weight vectors in the range of -1 to 1. Assume that five rhythmic sequences played on one or two percussion instruments each (Fig. 10.13) are fed into the network a number of times.

After a few iterations, an organization pattern begins to emerge. The graphs in Fig. 10.14 show the evolution of the input weights corresponding to the inter-onset intervals (IOI) (the third component of the input vectors). Fig. 10.14(a) shows the initial value of the weights, as explained above and Fig. 10.14(b) shows the pattern of IOI weight values that emerged after 20 iterations. Then graph 14(c) shows the values of IOI weights that emerged after 80 iterations and 14(d) shows the difference between the sums of the weights on consecutive iterations.

Now, let us consider that the agent has a categorization network with 50 input units, whose values are given by the activations patterns of the Sardnet. These input nodes are fully connected to three nodes forming the hidden layer, which in turn are fully connected to three output nodes. This allows for straightforward visualization of the categorization of the rhythms in a tri-dimensional space. The first three activation layers of 50 Sardnet nodes corresponding to three rhythms were used to train the feedforward network to match them with three different

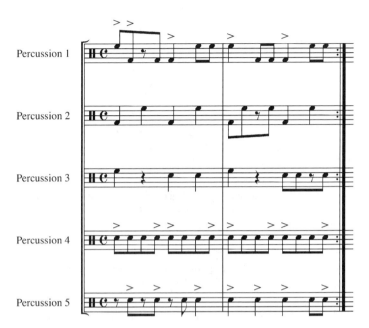

FIGURE 10.13. The five training rhythmic sequences.

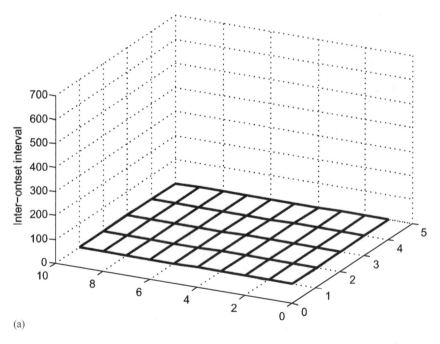

(a)

FIGURE 10.14. The evolution of the weights corresponding to IOI without change of neighbourhood: (a) Random initialization of weight values; (b) After 20 iterations; (c) After 80 iterations; (d) Difference between the sum of the weights for consecutive iterations.

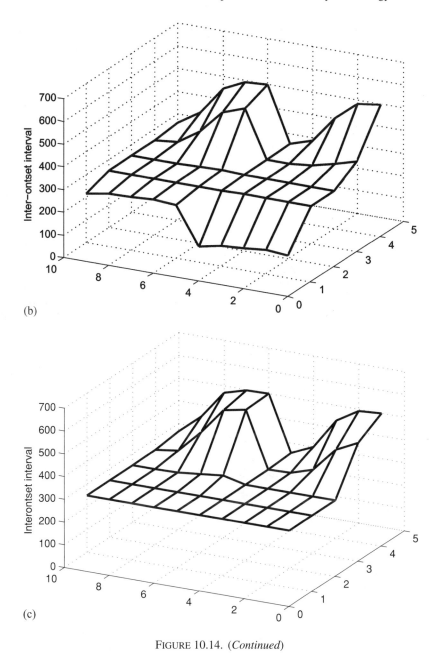

(b)

(c)

FIGURE 10.14. (*Continued*)

output targets: [0, 0, 1], [1, 0, 0] and [0, 1, 0]. The three learned rhythms are
marked with an 'o' in the categorization space (Fig. 10.15). Next, the Sarnet
nodes corresponding to the remaining two rhythms were fed into the feedforward
network. These are marked with an 'x' in the categorization space. Clearly, the

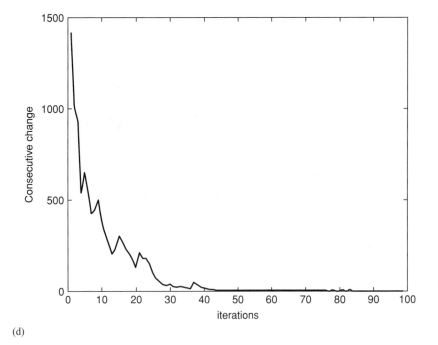

(d)

FIGURE 10.14. (*Continued*)

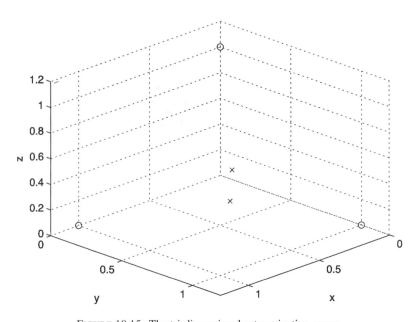

FIGURE 10.15. The tri-dimensional categorization space.

agent is able to distinguish the latter two rhythms from the previous three. This example shows the meaning of the categorization space: For this case the extreme points are the ones acknowledged by the agent as being part of its own repertoire.

As an initial step to test if this architecture would be suitable to be used as a memory mechanism to evolve and store information about sound sequences, two robots were programmed with a Sardnet with 400 (20 × 20) nodes coupled with a feedforward network with 400 input nodes, three nodes in the hidden layer and three output nodes. The choice for number of input nodes is a trade-off between scale and computational weight. The size of the network determines the number of different events that can be encoded, but the larger the network, the slower the computation. The Sardnet was programmed with an initial value for the learning rate $\alpha = 0.08$ and $\sigma = 10$; the latter denotes the scope of the neighbourhood, which is a Gaussian function centered on the winning neuron that multiplies all the elements in the network.

The Sardnet of one of the robots (the robot-player) was trained with eight rhythms (the five ones shown in Fig. 10.13 plus additional three) for 100 iterations. Then its feedforward network was trained with the backpropagation algorithm to respond to these rhythms in the extreme positions of the categorization space. Fig. 10.16(a) depicts the robot-player's pattern of IOI weights, which emerged after the 100 iterations. Fig. 10.17(a) shows the categorization of the rhythms in the tridimensional categorization space.

The other robot (the robot-imitator) was not trained. Its task was to evolve its own rhythmic categorization by imitating the rhythms produced by the robot-player.

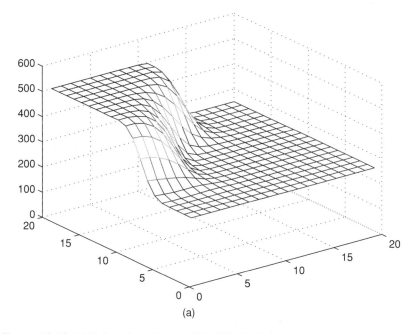

(a)

FIGURE 10.16. (a) Robot-player's map of the IOIs; (b) Robot-imitator's map of the IOIs.

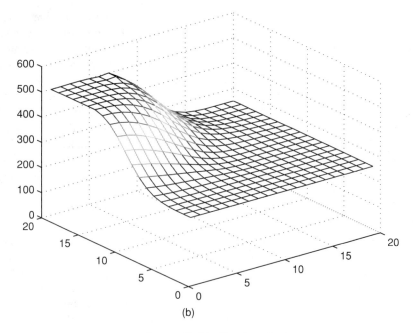

(b)

FIGURE 10.16. (*Continued*)

The interaction is as follows: The robot-player plays rhythms randomly picked from its memory and the robot-imitator tries to imitate them. The robot-imitator's learning takes place during this process of imitation. The robot-imitator's neural networks are programmed with the same parameters as the robot-player. Each time the robot-imitator hears a rhythm, it calculates its respective position in its categorization space. Then it 'babbles' a few rhythms (i.e. it generates random rhythms and categorises them) until it finds one that is close enough to the one it that it is trying to imitate. This rhythm is then played as an imitation to the robot-player, who evaluates the imitation in its categorization space. Depending on the distance between the imitation and the original rhythm, the robot-player sends a feedback to the robot-imitator, which indicates two possible outcomes:

a) Satisfactory: The imitation is closer to the original rhythm than to any other rhythm in its categorization space.
b) Unsatisfactory: The imitation is closer to a rhythm other than the original rhythm in its categorization space.

If the imitation is satisfactory, then the feedforward network of the robot-imitator is trained with one iteration of the backpropagation algorithm to respond to the desired category. Conversely, if the imitation is unsatisfactory, then the robot-imitator will benefit only from the adaptation of the Sardnet weights according to its self-organizing behaviour.

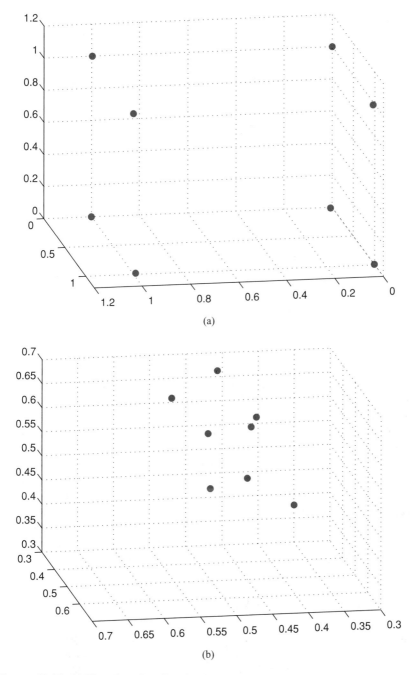

FIGURE 10.17. (a) The robot-player's trained categories; (b) The categorization map of the robot-imitator at very early stages of the learning process; (c) The categorization map of the robot-imitator at a very late stage of the learning process.

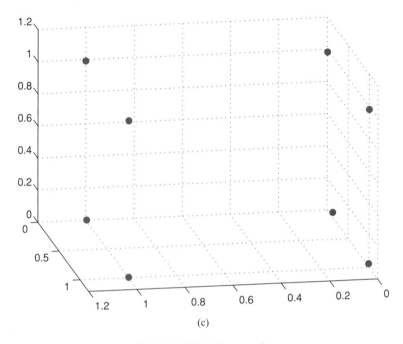

(c)

FIGURE 10.17. (*Continued*)

Fig. 10.16(b) portrays the Sardnet of the robot-imitator after 80 interactions, which is slightly different from the Sardnet of the robot-player, although they seem to be representing the same rhythms.

Fig. 10.17 shows the categorization maps for both robots. Notice that initial categories of the robot-imitator in Fig. 10.17(b) do not match the categories of the robot-player in Fig. 10.17(a), but as the learning process progressed, the categories converged to the extreme points of the tri-dimensional space in Fig. 10.17(c).

A preliminary test of the connectionist memory demonstrated that it is possible to combine the learning capabilities of neural networks with the dynamics of the mimetic model introduced in Section 3. At the time of writing, the connectionist memory is being further improved (e.g. to include information about pitch and timbre) and embedded in the mimetic robotic model.

10.5. Concluding Remarks

This chapter provided a glimpse of the exciting new field of Computational Evolutionary Musicology by demonstrating how music can be studied as an adaptive complex dynamic system. In this context, the origins and evolution of music can be studied using computer models and robotic simulations.

One interesting hypothesis that is emerging from the research of a number of scholars is that there might have been a single precursor for both music and language: A communication system that had the characteristics that are now shared by music and language, but split into two systems at some date in our evolutionary history. For instance, Steven Brown (2000) refers to this single precursor as *musilanguage*, whereas Alison Wray (1998) proposed the notion *holistic protolanguage*, which essentially is the same thing.

In the introduction we suggested that it would be perfectly plausible to suggest that robots might be able to evolve music. Then we demonstrated how this can be done. However, we acknowledge that the examples introduced here cannot evolve proper music yet, but rather the rudiments of what one might refer to as *proto-music*.

Much work is still needed in order to embed the robots with the minimum necessary physiological and cognitive abilities to evolve music. Nevertheless, the models discussed in this chapter are encouraging in the sense that they provide strong indications that music might indeed emerge in a society of interacting autonomous robots.

References

Behr, O. and von Helversen, O. (2004). Bat serenades—Complex courtship songs of the sac-winged bat *Saccopteryx bilineatta"*. *Behavioral Ecology and Sociobiology,* **56**: 106–115.

Bidlack, R. (1992). Chaotic systems as simple (but complex) compositional algorithms. *Computer Music Journal,* **16**(3): 33–47.

Boersma, P. (1993). Articulatory Synthesizers for the Simulations of Consonants. *Proceedings of Eurospeech'93*, Berlin, Germany, pp. 1907–1910.

Brodie, R. (1996). *Virus of the Mind: The New Science of the Meme*. Integral Press, Walnut Creek, CA.

Brown, S. (2000). The "Musilanguage" model of music evolution. In N.B. Merker and S. Brown (Eds.), *The Origins of Music*. The MIT Press, Cambridge, USA.

Burton, A.R. and Vladimirova, T. (1997). A Genetic Algorithm Utilising Neural Network Fitness Evaluation for Musical Composition, In G.D. Smith, N.C. Steele and R.F. Albrecht (Eds.), *Proceedings of the 1997 International Conference on Artificial Neural Networks and Genetic Algorithms*, Springer-Verlag, Vienna, pp. 220–224.

Cangelosi, A. and Parisi, D. (Eds.) (2001). *Simulating the Evolution of Language*. Springer Verlag, London, UK.

Casti, J.L. (1997). *Would-be Worlds: How Simulation of Changing the Frontiers of Science*. John Wiley & Sons, NY.

Christiansen, M.H. and Kirby, S. (Eds.) (2003). *Language Evolution: The States of the Art.* Oxford University Press, Oxford, UK.

Cope, D. (1996). *Experiments in Musical Intelligence*. Madison, A-R Editions Inc., WI.

Darwin, C. (1992) (1st published in 1871). *The Descent of Man and Selection in Relation to Sex*. Princeton University Press, Princeton, NJ.

Freeman, W. (1995). *Societies of Brains: A Study in the Neuroscience of Love and Hate*. Lawrence Erlbaum Associates, Mahwah, NJ.

Gallese, V. and Goldman, A. (1998). Mirror-neurons and the simulation theory of mind-reading. *Trends in Cognitive Sciences,* **12**: 493–501.

Glaser, R. (2001). *Biophysics*. Springer, Heidelberg.

Holy, T.E. and Guo, Z. (2005). Ultrasonic Songs of Male Mice. *PLoS Biology,* **3**(12): e386.

James, D.L. and Miikkulainen, R. (1995). SARDNET: a self-organizing feature map for sequences. In G. Tesauro, D. Touretzky and T. Leen (Eds), *Advances in Neural Information Processing Systems 7.* MIT Press, Cambridge, MA.

Kohonen, T. (1997). *Self-Organizing Maps.* Springer Series in Information Sciences. Springer-Verlag, Heidelberg.

Levy, S. (1993). *Artificial Life: A Report from the Frontier where Computers meets Biology.* Vintage, London, UK.

Locke, J.L. (1993). *The Child's Path to Spoken Language.* Harvard University Press, Cambridge, MA.

Mâche, F.-B. (1991). *Musique, Mythe, Nature ou les Dauphins d'Arion.* Méridiens Klincksieck, Paris.

Marler, P. and Slabbekoorn, H. (Eds.) (2004). *Nature's music: The science of birdsong.* Elsevier, Boston, MA.

Martins, J. and Miranda, E. R. (2006). A Connectionist architecture for the evolution of rhythms. *Proceedings of EvoWorkshops 2006,* LNCS 3970. Springer, New York, pp. 696–706.

Milicevic, M. (1996). The Impact of Fractals, Chaos and Complexity on Computer Music Composition. *Proceedings of International Computer Music Conference (ICMC 96).* Hong Kong, International Computer Music Association, San Francisco, pp. 473–476.

Miller, G. (2000). Evolution of human music through sexual selection. In N. Wallin, B. Merker and S. Brown (Eds.), *The Origins of Music.* The MIT Press, Cambridge, MA, pp. 329–360.

Miranda, E. R. and Drouet, E. (2006). Evolution of musical lexicons by babbling robots. *Proceedings of Towards Autonomous and Robotic Systems 2006,* University of Surrey, Gilford, UK. On-line proceedings: http://taros.mech.surrey.ac.uk/schedule.php (Accessed 17 Nov 2006).

Miranda, E.R. (2002b). Mimetic model of intonation. In C. Anagnostopoulou, M. Ferrand and A. Smaill (Eds.), *Music and Artificial Intelligence—Second International Conference ICMAI 2002.* Lecture Notes on Artificial Intelligence 2445, Springer-Verlag, Berlin, Germany, pp. 107–118.

Miranda, E.R. (2002a). *Computer Sound Design: Synthesis Techniques and Programming.* Focal Press, Oxford, UK.

Miranda, E.R. (2001). Synthesising prosody with variable resolution. *AES Convention Paper 5332.* Audio Engineering Society, Inc., NY, USA.

Mithen, S. (2005). *The Singing Neanderthal: The Origins of Music, Language, Mind and Body.* Weidenfeld & Nicolson, London.

Mozer, M. (1994). Neural network music composition by prediction: Exploring the benefits of psychophysical constraints and multiscale processing. *Connection Science,* **6**: 247–280.

Näätänen, R., Tervaniemi, M., Sussman, E., Paavilainen, P. and Winkler, I. (2001). Primitive intelligence in the auditory cortex, *Trends in Neurosciences,* 24: 283–288.

Nazzi, T., Floccia, C. and Bertoncini, J., (1998). Discrimination of pitch contours by neonates. *Infant Behaviour,* **12**: 543–554.

Papadopoulos, G. and Wiggins, G. (1998). A Genetic Algorithm for the Generation of Jazz Melodies. *Proceedings of 8th Finnish Conference on Artificial Intelligence,* Jyväskylä, Finland.

Payne, R.S. and McVay, S. (1971). Songs of humpback whales, *Science,* **173**: 585–597.

Parsons, L.M. (2003). Exploring the Functional Neuroanatomy of Music Performance, Perception and Comprehension, In I. Peretz and R. Zatorre (Eds.), *The Cognitive Neuroscience of Music*. Oxford University Press, Oxford, UK, pp. 247–268.

Peretz, I. and Coltheart, M. (2003). Modularity of music processing. *Nature Neuroscience*, **6**: 688–691.

Peretz, I., Kolinsky, R., Tramo, M., Labrecque, L., Hublet, C. and Demeurisse, G. (1994). Functional dissociations following bilateral lesions of auditory cortex. *Brain*, **117**: 1283–1301.

Rousseau, J.-J. (1990) (1st published in 1765). *Essay sur l'origine des langues*. Gallimard, Paris.

Rizzolatti, G. and Craighero, L. (2004). The mirror-neuron system. *Annual Review of Neuroscience*, **27**: 169–192.

Salu, Y. (2001). *Understanding Brain and Mind: A Connectionist Perspective*. World Scientific, Singapore.

Steedman, M. (1984). A generative grammar for jazz chord sequences. *Music Perception*, **2**: 52–77.

Steels, L. (1997). The Origins of Syntax in Visually Grounded Robotic Agents. *Proceedings of International Joint Conference on Artificial Intelligence (IJCAI'97)*. Nagoya, Aichi, Japan.

Thomas, D.A. (1995). *Music and the Origins of Language*. Cambridge University Press, Cambridge, UK.

Todd, P.M. and Loy, D.G. (Eds.) (1991). *Music and Connectionism*. The MIT Press, Cambridge, MA.

Todd, P.M. and Werner, G.M. (1999). Frankensteinian Methods for Evolutionary Music Composition. In N. Griffith and P.M. Todd (Eds.), *Musical Networks: Parallel Distributed Perception and Performance*. The MIT Press/Bradford Books, Cambridge, USA, pp. 313–339.

Wallin, N.J., Merker, B. and Brown, S. (Eds.) (2000). *The Origins of Music*. The MIT Press, Cambridge, USA.

Wray, A. (1998). Protolanguage as a holistic system for social interaction. *Language and Communication*, **18**: 46–667.

Zinkovsky, A.V., Sholuha, V.A. and Ivanov, A.A. (1996). *Mathematical Modelling and Computing Simulation of Biomechanical Systems*. World Scientific, Singapore.

Appendix: The Accompanying Music CD

Most of the authors in this book are accomplished composers and performers, using evolutionary computer music in their professional activities in one way or another. The accompanying music CD features a selection of pieces by these authors in a variety of styles, ranging from electroacoustic and contemporary music to jazz improvisation, which all serve to illustrate that theory can be put into practice rather successfully.

Track: 1
Title: *Olivine Trees*
Year: 1994
Duration: 09:02 minutes
Composer: Eduardo Reck Miranda

Olivine Trees is perhaps the first piece of electroacoustic music composed using a parallel computer. The piece was composed using sounds synthesised almost entirely by *Chaosynth* (refer to Chapter 8), a granular synthesis system that the composer created at the Edinburgh Parallel Computing Centre in the early 1990s. It works by generating a rapid succession of very short sound bursts called sound grains that together form larger sound events. *Chaosynth* uses cellular automata to control the production of the sound grains. *Olivine Trees* is inspired by Vincent van Gogh's painting 'Olive Trees.' As with impressionist painting, where small touches of unmixed colour mingle in the spectator's eyes, *Olivine Trees* is composed of short sounds segments that mingle in the spectator's ears. In addition to *Chaosynth*, a number of audio processing tools were used to mould the synthesised sounds.

Tracks: 2, 3, 4
Title: *Swarmpieces I–III*
Year: 2006
Durations: 04:22, 03:01, 05:51 minutes
Composers: Tim Blackwell and Michael Young
Piano: Michael Young

Swarmpieces I–III were performed on a single MIDI-enabled grand piano by the *Swarm Music* system (refer to Chapter 9). *Swarm Music* is heard here as two

5-particle swarms, one for each 'hand' of the live algorithm. The system was extended by two dimensions for this piece: phrase duration and phrase interval were added to the seven dimensions described in the chapter. The effect is to allow the swarms to rest between bursts of flight. The improvisations are tonally free and texturally dense and feature Young's highly responsive and energetic playing.

Track: 5
Title: *Lovey*
Year: 2006
Duration: 05:32 minutes
Composer: Al Biles
Trumpet: Al Biles

Lovey is a 5/4 Bossa Nova written by Al Biles to commemorate the passing of a family cat. This arrangement of the tune was set up to demonstrate *GenJam's* interactivity (refer to Chapter 7) and features a chorus of fours between Al and *GenJam* followed by a chorus of collective improvisation in which *GenJam* tries to intelligently echo what Al played a measure earlier. The IGA version of *GenJam* was used for this tune, with a soloist trained for seven generations in about 2 hours on various 5/4 tunes. This recording was essentially a first take and was the first time Al had attempted an echo chorus on this particular tune. Many thanks to Jay Alan Jackson, who engineered and produced this recording.

Tracks: 6, 7, 8
Title: *Three Pieces*
Year: 2006
Durations: 03:18, 01:57, 02:30 minutes
Subtitle of movements:

  I. *It didn't happen at Lan Franchis*
 II. *The ant's ear view*
III. *The larvae's ear view*

Composer: Alice Eldridge
Cello and voice: Alice Eldridge

These pieces are recordings of live improvisations on stage between cello and voice and a simulated Ashbian homeostat. The original homeostat was an electro-mechanical device built by Cybernetician Ross Ashby to demonstrate his theory of ultra-stability. The behaviour of the system illustrates the use of 'life-time' adaptive mechanisms as opposed to generational evolutionary search and are used here to parameterise a granular synthesis engine operating on samples taken live during the performance. All material is created in real time by the system splicing and re-composing the performer's improvisations.

Track: 9
Title: *Singing in Traffic*
Year: 1997

Duration: 08:21 minutes
Composer: Rodney Waschka II
Saxophone: Steve Duke

Singing in Traffic uses a single short recording of one car driving on a suburban road in North Carolina, USA, together with synthesised bell-like sounds to create the recorded part. A computer program, written by the composer, uses a Markov process and a kind of 'mosaic' technique to manipulate the sampled sound and control the synthesised sound. The instrumental part was composed with the help of an evolutionary computation computer program created by the composer (refer to Chapter 6). The piece was composed for and premiered by Jonathan Kramer.

Track: 10
Title: *Change Tranes*
Year: 2006
Duration: 02:05 minutes
Composer: Al Biles

Change Tranes features the autonomous version of *GenJam* improvising over four choruses of 'Coltrane Changes', as described in the coffeehouse vignette at the beginning of Chapter 7. *GenJam* always acquits itself much better on this tune than its creator, Al Biles, who mercifully lays out on this performance. Recorded and produced by Jay Alan Jackson.

Tracks: 11, 12, 13, 14, 15, 16, 17, 18, 19, 20, 21, 22, 23, 24
Title: *Ossia Suite*
Year: 2002
Durations: 00:45, 01:04, 00:38, 01:09, 00:45, 01:06, 01:06, 00:40, 01:08, 01:30, 01:11, 00:43, 01:26, 01:43 minutes
Composer: Palle Dahlstedt

These 14 short pieces are excerpts from a larger suite derived from the interactive installation *Ossia*, premiered at the Gaudeamus Music Week in Amsterdam, 2002. The pieces were composed and performed on a MIDI-enabled grand piano by a computer, with no human intervention, except when people visiting the installation interacted with the system by playing something on the piano. The computer continuously composed and performed new pieces, either from scratch or based on what the visitors have played on the piano. The pieces are generated with autonomous evolutionary algorithms, that is, the software breeds a population of pieces through a number of generations and selects which candidates 'sound good', based on programmed 'quasi-aesthetic' criteria (refer to Chapter 4). The expressive performance quality is a direct result of how the music is generated and mirrors the underlying structure of the piece.

Index